MALTA: THE LAST GREAT SIEGE

MALTA:
The Last
Great Siege

The George Cross Island's
Battle for Survival
1940-43

by

DAVID WRAGG

LEO COOPER

First published in Great Britain 2003 by
LEO COOPER
an imprint of Pen & Sword Books Ltd
47 Church Street
Barnsley,
South Yorkshire,
S70 2AS

Copyright © David Wragg 2003

ISBN 0 85052 990 5

A CIP record for this book is available from The British Library

Typeset in Meridien by
Phoenix Typesetting, Burley-in-Wharfedale, West Yorkshire.

Printed by
CPI UK

CONTENTS

	Acknowledgements	vi
	Introduction	vii
	Glossary	xii
I	A SUNNY MORNING IN JUNE	1
II	THE RUMBLE OF DISTANT WARS	6
III	ISLANDS IN HISTORY	19
IV	POWER IN THE MED	30
V	AN OUTPOST AGAIN	47
VI	ONSLAUGHT FROM THE SKIES	65
VII	GRIM REALITY	81
VII	INVASION THREATENS	104
IX	OFFENSIVE AND DEFENSIVE IN THE SKIES	116
X	THE WAR AT SEA	139
XI	LIVING AMONGST THE MALTESE	150
XII	THE HUNGRY SPRING	154
XIII	RATIONING FOR VICTORY	186
XIV	SALVATION – OR A FALSE DAWN?	201
XV	THE TIDE TURNS	218
XVI	WHAT MIGHT HAVE BEEN	222
	Chronology	227
	Bibliography	235
	Index	236

ACKNOWLEDGEMENTS

In researching and writing any book like this, the author is always grateful to those who have helped to ease his way. Acknowledgements for quotations are given at the end of each chapter and in the captions to the photographs. Nevertheless, I would also like to thank Ian Carter and his colleagues in the Imperial War Museum Photograph Archive and John Stopford-Pickering in the Imperial War Museum Sound Archive for their excellent help and efficiency, all of which is given with such good grace.

INTRODUCTION

There is something old fashioned about the concept of siege. This is an aspect of warfare that seems more appropriate to the Middle Ages, or even earlier, perhaps to Biblical times, than the twentieth century. Nothing could be further from the truth. The Second World War is regarded by many historians as having introduced so much of the strategy, tactics and technology that features in modern warfare, including the primacy of the aircraft carrier and the submarine and the use of missiles, but siege was once again an important feature of the conflict. Possibly those at Berlin and Singapore can be dismissed as simply being prolonged battles, but Moscow and Stalingrad were worthy of the term siege, particularly the latter after the besieging German Army itself became besieged. More significant was the great siege at Leningrad, lasting almost 900 days. These were all sieges by encircling armies. A completely different kind of siege was endured by those in Malta, not a single island but a small group of islands situated in the Mediterranean, 'in the middle of the Middle Sea', almost halfway between Gibraltar and Suez, and conveniently between Europe and North Africa. Malta truly sits at the cross roads of the Mediterranean. For Malta and her people, this was a siege by sea and enforced mainly by air power.

One could argue that Malta was besieged by the Axis Powers from Italy's entry into the war in June, 1940, to the invasion of Sicily in July, 1943. In fact, it was not until the beginning of 1941 that the siege really began to bite hard, while the beginning of the end came with the successful convoy, known to the Allies as Operation Pedestal, to the Maltese as the Santa Marija Convoy, in August, 1942. By November, 1942, a convoy managed to reach Malta without loss.

Before the war, anticipating Italian involvement, the Air Ministry and the War Office had decided that Malta, just sixty miles south of Sicily, could not be defended, but the Admiralty insisted that it should be, so that it could remain as a base for light forces and for submarines. Malta was seen as being a thorn in the side of the Axis, and so it proved to be. Had Malta been surrendered, perhaps in much the same way as the Channel Islands were, the Italian and, later, the German operations in North Africa would have been so much easier, and Rommel would have been spared the shortages of fuel and water that so hindered his plans to advance to the Suez Canal. In short, defending Malta must have shortened the war in Europe.

The concept of siege was not new to the Maltese, for it bore heavily on their history. They had endured the 'Great Siege' by the Ottoman Empire in 1565. The scourge of the Turks was only brought to a standstill by Christendom's victory in the great naval battle at Lepanto six years later. The Maltese were also used to their country changing hands, having been occupied by the Phoenicians, Romans, Arabs and the French, and then by the British after they had invited them to remove the French in 1799, whereupon the French themselves became besieged in the island's capital, Valletta, by Maltese insurgents.

During wartime, they were to prove that their association with the British was the more enduring for both nations. No convoys were fought harder, no convoys lost a greater proportion of their ships, than those to Malta. At the height of the conflict, the central Mediterranean became so dangerous that Allied convoys to Egypt had to be re-routed via the Cape of Good Hope and the Suez Canal. The Royal Navy was reduced to using fast minelaying cruisers, such as HMS *Welshman* and her sister *Manxman*, and minelaying submarines to enable Malta to survive, but to survive themselves, the submarines had to lie submerged in harbour during the day. The desperate need for fighter aircraft saw two supply trips by the USS *Wasp*. The need to guard the convoys resulted in the loss of the elderly aircraft carrier HMS *Eagle*.

Even when ships did reach the Grand Harbour with supplies, the small islands and their small population lacked the facilities to discharge several large ships quickly – a weakness of any convoy system – and ships were sunk before their supplies could be discharged.

That greatest of warships, the fast armoured aircraft carrier HMS *Illustrious*, which had lived up to her name in the successful attack on the Italian fleet at Taranto, herself came under heavy aerial attack by the Luftwaffe off Malta early in 1941, seeking refuge and emergency repairs in Malta during which time her presence provoked the 'Illustrious Blitz'.

Despite this, the island did become a base for attacks against the enemy. Most notable was the submarine campaign, including the epic part played by HMS *Upholder* and her CO, Lieutenant Commander Malcolm Wanklyn, VC, against Italian naval and merchant vessels. Malta-based warships and aircraft soon turned the tables on the Axis, and played their part in the eventual defeat of Rommel's *Afrika Korps*. The major blunder by the Axis was the failure to invade, although forces were assembled and plans laid. Instead, the Germans chose to invade Crete, where they suffered such appalling losses, nearly failing in their objective, that Hitler forbade the use of paratroop assaults for at least a year or so. These would have been essential to take Malta given the paucity of good landing beaches and the difficult road access from most of them. In an island of small fields with dry stone walls, there were few locations for glider-landed troops to be set down.

This, then, is the story of Malta's stand against the Axis powers during the Second World War that led to the award of the George Cross to the island by King George VI.

David Wragg
Edinburgh
January 2003

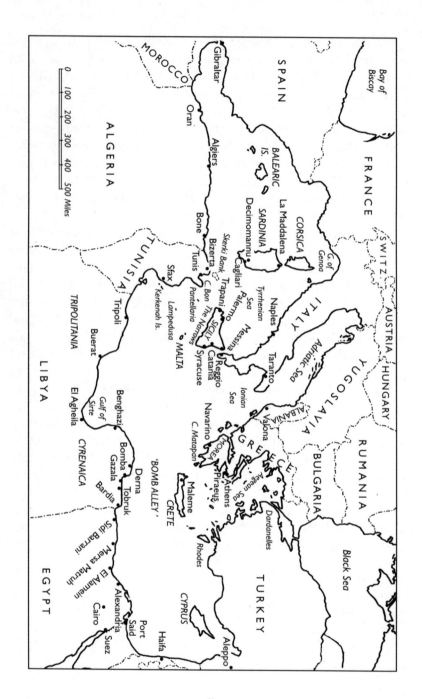

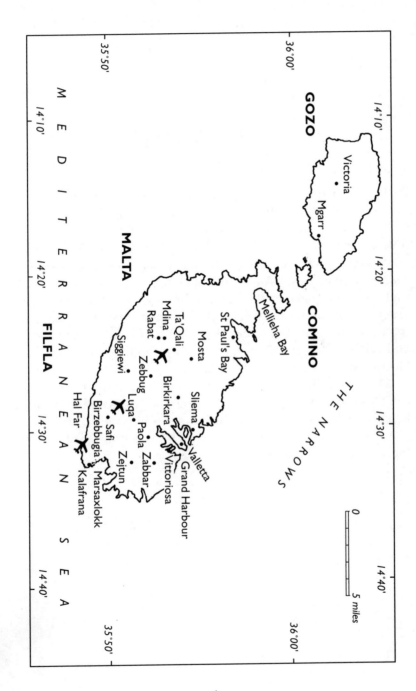

MEDITERRANEAN

GOZO

Victoria
Mgarr

COMINO

THE NARROWS

MALTA

Mellieha Bay

St Paul's Bay

Mosta
Ta'Qali
Mdina
Rabat
Siggiewi
Zebbug
Birkirkara
Sliema
Luqa
Paola
Zabbar
Valletta
Grand Harbour
Vittoriosa
FILFLA
Hal Far
Birzebbugia
Safi
Zejtun
Kalafrana
Marsaxlokk

SEA

0

5 miles

xi

GLOSSARY

Rather than confuse the reader with copious footnotes or an extensive glossary at the outset of the book, descriptions of items of food, for example, are given in the text whenever these might not be obvious. One question that will arise, however, is over place names, where there is sometimes a difference between Maltese spelling and Anglicized spelling. For the record, while Valletta can be spelt as Valetta, I have chosen to stick with what seems to be the more widely used former version, and again I have favoured Ta'Qali rather than Ta'Kali for the same reasons, and Paola rather than Pawla, and having lived in the latter place, I know that it is never spelt as Paula!

Place names have been spelt in full even in those cases where the Maltese will often abbreviate them, as in Birzebbugia, more usually spelt as B'Bugia, and Birkirkara, often seen as B'Kara.

As for the rest, I have used the Maltese 'Santa Marija' rather than the Italian Santa Maria.

I

A SUNNY MORNING IN JUNE

The early Mass was interrupted as what must have been a personal prayer was taken up and spread like wildfire as a chant through the frightened congregation, '*Gesu, Guzeppi, Marija, Itfghu l-bombi fil-hamrija*', 'Jesus, Joseph and Mary, make the bombs drop in soil'.

Not far away from the parish church in ancient Birgu, in the dockyard a group of British women were taking shelter in an old boathouse.

'In June, 1940, when Italy first came into the war, no one quite knew what to expect,' recalled Queenie Lee, some years later.

> Our first raid was six hours after war was declared – at dawn on June 11th. There was what seemed like a terrific amount of noise. I didn't know the difference between guns and bombs, as I sat in an old boathouse under some fortifications with other women on war work. We felt comparatively safe as we'd been told that it was an air raid shelter and we could sleep there. We were later to learn what safety is – that it's perhaps to be had under sixty feet of rock, but not in an old boathouse . . .[1]

Queenie Lee and her companions wouldn't have been so relaxed had they realized that in the months to come, her boathouse would be buried under rubble!

Outside, in the now deserted streets, the headlines of the newspapers on the newsstands told the story. The front pages of the

[1] Imperial War Museum Sound Archive, Accession No.1172.

four daily newspapers offered no comfort to the reader. 'Mussolini Cowardly Act' proclaimed the front page headline of *The Times of Malta*, while a glance at the front page of the other English language newspaper, *The Malta Chronicle*, showed 'Rash and Foolhardy Decision – Italy Plunges into Horrors of War'. The Maltese-language newspapers told the same story. *Il-Berqa*, the Maltese stablemate of *The Times of Malta*, had a front page headline reading 'L-Italja Tiddikkjara Gwerra', 'Italy declares war', while its rival *Lehen is-Sewwa*'s front page ran 'Mussolini jixhet l-Italja fil-Gwerra', 'Mussolini throws Italy into war'.

Italy had entered the Second World War the previous day, Monday, 10 June, 1940, as France reeled under the overwhelming might of the Wehrmacht and the Luftwaffe. An ultimatum to surrender by midnight had been issued to Malta. The terror and anxiety of those on the receiving end of this first air raid was intensified by the fear that the Italians would not simply use high explosive, but would also use gas, just as they had in Abyssinia, present-day Ethiopia, when they had invaded that country just five years earlier.

Many had spent a sleepless night, expecting an air raid as soon as the ultimatum had expired. Even those who had heard the engines of the aircraft had been caught by surprise, most had assumed that the aircraft were British so their first warning had been when the anti-aircraft defences surrounding the dockyard had opened up. 'I thought they were ours . . .' as one Maltese put it. At 06.00, a population not yet used to the horrors of war were shaken first by the heavy roar of the barrage from the anti-aircraft defences ringing the Grand Harbour, described by one observer as 'terrific and frightening – never heard before', and then the scream of bombs falling, followed by the crump of exploding bombs and collapsing buildings, the ground shaking under the feet, and the screams and prayers of those caught in the open in the streets and alleyways below. Those who could hid under stairs, under tables or in alcoves, as the bombs rained down. One man, worried about being hit by shrapnel in the street, or being buried alive if his house receive a direct hit, tried to compromise by seeking shelter under the arch of a window.

The raid had not been a complete surprise. Some distance away from the crowded cities surrounding the Grand Harbour on the empty cliff top of Dingli, the highest point on Malta, the duty operator at the RAF radar station installed only the previous year had noticed the small formation of aircraft gathering over Sicily before heading in the direction of Malta. He realized that they could only be Italian bombers. The warning had been quickly passed on. In the dockyard, an air raid siren began its dismal wail, but elsewhere across Malta, the warning of attack was given by the Rediffusion cable radio service. The more affluent amongst those living in Valletta and some of the towns close to the capital had the luxury of a Rediffusion receiver in their homes, but away from the capital, the warning was given by public speakers placed in the main squares of the towns and villages. Many didn't hear these warnings. A number of special constables had arrived in the streets of the capital and of the other towns and cities bordering the Grand Harbour, hastily directing people to whatever shelter was available.

Those living in Gozo and Comino, the two sister islands to the north of the island of Malta itself, saw the enemy aircraft first, the Savoia-Marchetti SM79 trimotor bombers' engines throbbing as they passed high overhead on their way to Valletta and the Grand Harbour. These were large aircraft by the standards of the day, but there were just ten of them in two waves, seven in the first and three in the second. Above them flew an escort of nine Macchi C200 fighters.

The air raid was over within minutes. It ended even as a terrified crowd in Valletta headed for the largest shelter readily available, the disused railway tunnel running from the old railway station in Valletta and through Floriana to the Porte des Bombes. The tunnel had been part of the one-time Malta railway that had operated a single line out across the Maltese plain to Rabat. The attacking aircraft continued on their way, turning north and heading for home, safe in the knowledge that Malta had no fighter aircraft with which to strike back.

As that morning passed, other raids followed, none of them heavy, but with few places to hide, a huge exodus of people started away from the worst affected areas, the lower part of Valletta, Floriana and Pieta, where the marina had been hit.

This was a day with a difference. Generations of naval personnel, used to seeing Grand Harbour, for so long the main base for the Royal Navy's Mediterranean Fleet, crowded with grey warships, would have hardly recognized it on this morning. It was empty. The previous day, just three smaller warships had been in port, the elderly monitor HMS *Terror*, and two gunboats, *Aphis* and *Ladybird*, remnants of the Royal Navy's second largest fleet. They too were now gone.

This was war.

Mussolini's Ultimatum

Mussolini's declaration of war had come over the radio during the previous evening. It was greeted with shock and anger by the Maltese, and in Valletta there was almost a breakdown in public order as the police attempted to stop large groups of angry men from attacking the offices and houses of people suspected of having sympathy with Fascism.

Crowds, many of them consisting of young men who had come from the surrounding villages, gathered on many street corners that first evening. The largest crowd was opposite the Police Station in Valletta's Kingsway, watching as Italians resident in Malta arrived having been rounded up, ready to be sent to an internment camp. The more thoughtful sought refuge against whatever the night might bring in some recently re-opened tunnels in the walls of Valletta and the three cities across the Grand Harbour, or in the old railway tunnel running from Valletta under most of Floriana.

Before the outbreak of hostilities, Italian propaganda had attempted to arouse the sympathies of the Maltese. A small number of Maltese did support Italy, but the numbers have been estimated at being around eighty of those actually on the island. As with the Japanese in Asia, Italian propaganda played on nationalist feelings amongst the Maltese. In the hours follow-ing the declaration of war, a wall plaque to Fortunato Mizzi, a

4

nationalist who had been known in his lifetime for his pro-Italian sympathies, was defaced. Some time before, many Maltese had been offended when Mussolini had unveiled a bust of Mizzi in the so-called 'garden of heroes' in Rome.

Members of the Special Constabulary were summoned to police stations across Malta and Gozo for briefings. Many were expecting a gas raid, possibly after midnight. This reflected official advice; gas, rather than high explosive, was expected to be the weapon of choice. Their fears were shared by the air raid wardens, and by those who left the harbour districts and moved to shelter with families in less crowded parts of the island. Most just stayed put and waited.

The authorities knew as little about what fate had in store for Malta as did any of the Maltese. All that was certain was that Italy had now joined Germany, which had so recently thrust northwards into Denmark and Norway, and then westwards through the Netherlands and Belgium and across northern France, and that Malta was now part of this war.

II

THE RUMBLE OF
DISTANT WARS

The outbreak of war in September, 1939, following the Anglo-French ultimatum to Germany over its invasion of Poland, immediately set the alarm bells ringing in Malta. The connection between Hitler and Mussolini was well known and well understood by everyone in Malta, Maltese and British alike. Already, in April, Mussolini had invaded Albania. War had loomed over the islands much earlier than elsewhere in Europe when Italy had invaded Abyssinia in 1935 and it looked at one time as if the democracies would do something about it through the League of Nations, which could have meant only one thing: war.

At first, Mussolini sat on the fence. After holding a meeting of his Council of Ministers on 3 September, he announced that he was not taking any military initiatives. He maintained this position not only throughout the long months of what the British described as the 'phoney war' (to the Germans it was the 'sitting war'), but he also remained officially neutral once the German advances began. These effortless victories over ill-equipped and poorly coordinated forces finally tempted Mussolini to declare war on the United Kingdom and France on 10 June, 1940, just seven days before the new French President, Marshal Petain offered Germany an armistice.

Adolf Hitler had also been surprised when his Italian allies did not join him when war broke out on 3 September, 1939. The expectation was not unreasonable. Mussolini's son-in-law, Italy's Foreign Minister, Count Galeazzo Ciano, had negotiated the Axis Treaty, signed in June, 1936, that had allied Italy and

Germany. In 1939, the two countries had signed the Pact of Steel, although neither Ciano nor Mussolini realized that Germany was prepared to make war whether or not Italy was ready. To some extent, Italian hesitation was understandable. The country was not really ready for war. Even many senior German officers had not expected war with the United Kingdom until much later, in some cases 1945 was seen as the most likely date.

Since coming to power in 1922, Mussolini had made it clear that he saw Malta as belonging to Italy, and that the Mediterranean was *Mare Nostrum*, 'Our Sea', to the Italians. Broadcasts claimed that the Maltese were part of the Italian race and that the islands belonged to Italy. There was some historical basis for this, since at one time Malta had been part of the kingdom of Sicily, but that had been a long time ago, and there was little Italian blood in the Maltese, and little that was Italian about their language.

In London, the role of Malta in wartime had been a matter of considerable controversy among those charged with planning.

In 1935, with the Abyssinian crisis at its height, the Grand Harbour had AA defences of around twelve guns, with some searchlights. This inadequate level of defence for such a major port was hastily increased to twenty-four guns with additional searchlights, but most of the guns were obsolete 3-in. weapons. The RAF took the attitude that Malta could not be defended against heavy aerial attack from bases in Sicily, and the Army accepted this view. Both services would have abandoned Malta, but the Admiralty insisted that it could be used as a base for offensive operations. The Admiralty was probably the only service ministry to appreciate that in the wrong hands, Malta also posed a threat to shipping across the Mediterranean.

The problems of Abyssinia were soon replaced by the horrors of the Spanish Civil War, in which the two sides were more evenly matched. This conflict did not affect either the United Kingdom or Malta directly. Either way, the outcome posed a threat to Europe's peace of mind, with the Soviet Union supporting the Republicans. Nevertheless, the victory of Franco's Nationalists, with German and Italian assistance, alarmed those who had already noted Germany's growing military might and had seen war in Europe as inevitable. A grand alliance of Germany, Italy and Spain would have made the Mediterranean untenable. It was indeed a godsend that later Franco wisely declined to involve Spain in the Second World War.

War seemed even closer with the Munich Crisis of September, 1938. The commander-in-chief of naval forces in the Mediterranean was by this time Admiral Sir Dudley Pound. Pound was in no doubt that the balance of naval power in the Mediterranean was in Italy's favour, and would remain so unless the Mediterranean Fleet was substantially augmented by units from the Home Fleet and the Far East Fleet. Reinforcements from the Home Fleet were something that Pound should have discounted as war with Germany was such a strong possibility, but Japan's advances through China had not yet assumed a serious threat in European eyes. At the time, Pound's ships included an aircraft carrier, HMS *Glorious*, but Pound was not sure whether she was an asset or a liability. He firmly believed that in the confines of the Mediterranean, with Italian bombers based in Libya, the Dodecanese, Sicily and Sardinia as well as the mainland of Italy, *Glorious* would not survive long. Yet, he knew that under his predecessor a plan had been drawn up at the time of the Abyssinian crisis, when British involvement against Italy had seemed a possibility, so that the ship could have one strike at the enemy's major naval base at Taranto before either being sunk or, hopefully, withdrawn to safety.

The commanding officer of *Glorious* at this time was Captain Lumley Lyster. Like Pound, he knew that an attack on Taranto had been considered in 1935, but the opportunity had passed as politicians failed to rise to the occasion. The secret papers had then been locked away in a safe aboard the ship. On being told by Pound to plan an attack on Taranto, Lyster sent for his Commander Flying and the ship's senior observer. The three of them then set about revising and updating the 1935 plans, while the crews of the ship's three Swordfish squadrons, at that time 812, 823 and 825, soon found themselves in intense training, with night take-offs and landings on the carrier's deck. They also mounted a series of dummy attacks on the Mediterranean Fleet in the Grand Harbour at Malta, where to add realism, the ships and the harbour operated under darkened ship and blacked-out conditions. Before long, Lyster was able to report to Pound that an attack was a possibility.

Such exercises meant that in many ways those living in Malta were fully aware that war was a distinct possibility and that Malta would be in the frontline.

Fear of a Bomber Offensive

No doubt the attitude of the Army and the RAF reflected the defeatist attitude to the bomber that prevailed throughout the 1930s, when the view was that 'the bomber will always get through'. This fear of a bomber offensive was obviously not to be taken lightly, as subsequent events were to prove, but it was overstated. It was a factor, together with a belated appreciation of their poor state of readiness, in the reluctance of Britain and France to go to war in 1938. Later, it was an excuse for the two Allies not initiating a bomber offensive during the Battle of France in 1940 because of French fears of German retaliation against French towns and cities.

Malta was just sixty miles from Italian airfields in Sicily, and only 180 miles from those in Libya. In practical terms, this meant that Malta was less than twenty minutes flying time from Sicily given the 200mph or so cruising speed of the bombers of the day.

Once again the threat of war receded, if only to buy time to build ships and aircraft and recruit and train personnel.

When Italy didn't enter the war at first, it seemed as if war in the Mediterranean was a distant prospect. At first little seemed to be happening, on the ground at least. Then the free world watched with alarm as German troops swept into Denmark and battled their way through Norway, before springing a surprise attack on the Netherlands and Belgium, both of whom had placed their hopes in neutrality. France was next. Despite the breathing space afforded by Munich, at the outset of hostilities the Allies were woefully unprepared. Both the Netherlands and

Belgium had earlier realized that in any conflict with Germany, they would have to fight alongside British and French forces, but no joint exercises were prepared. The Dutch had been saved by neutrality in the First World War, and hoped to do so again, but there was even less excuse for Belgium, which had been all but overrun by the Kaiser's armies in the earlier conflict.

By June, 1940, the UK was home to men who had returned from France, tired and exhausted, without equipment. The threat of invasion along the south coast of England was real, and the Battle of Britain was starting. The RAF was short of aircraft, and even shorter of pilots, having to borrow a number from the Fleet Air Arm.

There was little to spare at this dark time.

Italy continued to be neutral until German victory was certain, and then Mussolini finally declared war on Great Britain and France on 10 June, 1940.

The retreat and ultimate withdrawal of the British Expeditionary Force from France had at least saved experienced troops to fight another day. The RAF element, the Advanced Air Striking Force, was withdrawn earlier, and would have suffered heavily had it remained, as its early operations against the Luftwaffe had resulted in unsustainable losses, partly due to the obsolescence of many of its aircraft, but mainly because of delays in mounting offensive operations that allowed the Germans to establish anti-aircraft defences around key targets and the dispatch of aircraft on operations in such small numbers that enemy fighters and defensive fire could concentrate on them. Had they remained, while the surviving aircraft might have been flown to safety, experienced ground crews could well have faced capture.

No one really believed *Il Duce* when he claimed that if he ever had to attack Malta, he would use flowers rather than bombs. In fact, the Maltese and their British defenders had noted with alarm the Italian use of poison gas in Abyssinia. Maltese stone, they knew, was proof against high explosive, but gas was another matter.

Italy's Ambitions

The Mediterranean had been relatively peaceful during the Great War, with Italy amongst the Allies. Turkish warships had been bottled up beyond the Dardanelles, while the Austro-Hungarian Fleet had difficulty venturing out of its Adriatic bases. The only real activity had been the unfortunate and badly handled Allied landings at Gallipoli, although the threat of a Turkish thrust through Syria and Palestine to the Suez Canal had been real; it had provided a convenient excuse to ensure that the Gallipoli campaign was starved of resources that might just, under more active commanders, have made a difference.

When Benito Mussolini seized power in 1922, the threat had not been obvious at first. Despite having an important influence over Adolf Hitler during his rise to power in Germany, Mussolini had not portrayed the same expansionist attitudes. His one major interest had been the acquisition of an African empire, since the land of Marco Polo had missed out on the great explorations and resultant colonial expansion of the eighteenth and nineteenth centuries, primarily, it might be supposed, since Italy was itself a creation of the nineteenth century.

Italy already had some footholds in Africa. These were across the Mediterranean in Libya, and on the Red Sea in Somalia and nearby Eritrea. Somalia had been an Italian protectorate since 1889, the same year that Eritrea was taken from the Turks and became an Italian colony. Libya had been colonized by Italy in 1911 after being conquered from the Turks. Somalia had become an Italian colony in 1927, before being incorporated into Italian East Africa in 1936. Anxious to avoid war with the established colonial powers in Africa, Mussolini chose the one country that had never been colonised for his expansion, Ethiopia, known at the time as Abyssinia, which he finally invaded in 1935. Even so, Italy's claim on Abyssinia had not originated with Mussolini, and in seizing the country, he was renewing claims on Ethiopia that had dated from 1896, when Italy maintained that the country had asked to become an Italian protectorate, and then attempted an unsuccessful invasion.

11

The Abyssinian crisis should have been the first great warning signal to the governments of the democracies. Cinema audiences in the mid-1930s were treated to newsreel film of Italian bombers and well-equipped troops fighting ill-equipped tribesmen, many of them on horseback. The Italians used gas as well as high explosive. The popular feeling was that something should be done. The League of Nations was expected to mount sanctions against Italy, and approve military intervention. The sanctions were undermined by French refusal to support them. The British Mediterranean Fleet was told to observe Italian shipping, but to stop short of actually stopping and searching Italian ships to the dismay of its commander-in-chief, who had been convinced that his country would soon be at war with Italy. No attempt was made to stop the Italians using the Suez Canal, their only practical supply line for their forces in Abyssinia. Resolute action at this time could have sent a clear message to the dictators, but it did not happen. The League of Nations showed that it was virtually powerless.

The League's weakness sprang from many things. It was not as representative of world power as its successor, the United Nations, was to be. While the League was an American idea, and had been one of the proposals of Woodrow Wilson, the First World War President of the United States, for bringing peace, the inter-war isolationist USA was not a member. More important than the lack of representation on the League was the fact that the democracies were determined not to become involved in military action. Their economies had been undermined by the Great Depression, and none of them was ready for war, even though limited action early on might have saved far greater effort later. France was determined not to undermine trading arrangements with Italy. In the UK, the governing idea was the 'Ten Year Rule', in which the country expected to have ten years in which to prepare for war. The excessive optimism inherent in the Ten Year Rule can be judged from the fact that there were just six years of peace left between Hitler's seizure of absolute power in Germany in 1933 and the outbreak of the Second World War in 1939.

As early as 1930, a strong indication of Mussolini's intentions towards Malta came with a bungled assassination attempt on Lord Strickland, Prime Minister at the time and also owner of the *Times of Malta*. Malta's original link with Italy had been during the days of the Roman Empire, although from 1090 to 1530, it had also been part of the Kingdom of Sicily. Despite Mussolini's claims, the Maltese themselves were not Italian, but descended from Phoenician merchants and pirates, whose language they adopted and modified. Even so, there was a substantial body of pro-Italian opinion amongst many Maltese, especially the older and wealthier families, between the two world wars.

Malta Prepares

As the war clouds had gathered over Europe, many realized that they couldn't depend on Italy taking a passive role. Memories of that country's attack on Abyssinia were refreshed by the invasion of Albania. In mid-July, 1939, the Governor's Advisory Council devolved powers to a Central Committee. Soon after the outbreak of war in September, the then Governor, Sir Charles Bonham-Carter, addressed Malta's parish priests and urged them to form District Committees in the towns and villages so that if war did reach Malta, there would be an organization in place. This was an innovation, since Malta lacked the system of local authorities more usual in larger countries, with much of their role being handled by the 'government' – after all, the population was less than that of even a moderately large British city. While not exactly democratic institutions, the District Committees involved local people, usually including the all-important parish priest and the head teacher of the local school, as well as the district medical officer, and representatives of local organizations as well as one or two prominent figures in the local community. Their primary role was to recruit a local body of air raid wardens, who would also look after shelters, provide first aid and assist in casualty centres.

While peace lasted, the District Committees had the duty of recruiting adequate numbers of air raid wardens, ARWs, to ensure that they were adequately trained and then allocated an area, usually defined as a number of streets, within the District Committee's area. The work of the air raid wardens was supervised by the District Committee, while monthly reports to a Central Committee set up by the Governor were provided by each District, which was also expected to send a delegate. Although it seems that many Committee members were more concerned about food control and rationing at first, the work continued apace, and indeed in some areas, such as Paola and neighbouring Tarxien, the number of volunteers was such that extra lectures had to be arranged. By the end of the year, there were 365 men and 236 women ARWs. Inevitably, the degree of enthusiasm varied, and at Qrendi, the committee consisted simply of the chairman and secretary, the latter being the local headmaster.

The more active committees also sought suitable places for use as air raid shelters, including old caves, or identified areas where air raid shelters would be necessary.

Echoing British preparations for war, gas masks were distributed, and evacuation plans drawn up to take families away from the capital and the three cities and into country districts. Old passageways and tunnels in the bastions were opened up, so that there would be at least some shelter.

Once war did break out, the District Committees were also to help evacuation and billeting staff in their duties, as it was foreseen that some areas, such as the Three Cities lying so close to the dockyard, would have to be evacuated. A Food Control Board was also established, and the District Councils found themselves acting as a branch of the Board.

The authorities ensured that supplies of food and munitions were accumulated and stored ready for any attack. The difficult decision was taken to leave Gozo undefended, along with the small island of Comino, home to a monastery and a handful of farms. This was because access across the channel separating the islands could be difficult during heavy attack, and because there was so much to do on Malta itself, while Gozo was without military installations. Gozo's main role was to provide food for her

14

larger and more populous sister island, and it was recognized right from the beginning that even so, severe shortages were likely.

On the night of 2–3 May, 1940, a blackout practice was held from 22.00 until dawn the following day, with an air raid warning practice held at 19.00 on 11 May. The latter cleared the streets of Valletta in just under a minute, according to some observers, with cars parked immediately and black out precautions quickly observed. Apparently the only criticism was that a number of people re-emerged on the streets once the 'raiders passed' signal was sounded at 20.00, rather than waiting for the 'all clear'.

Sensing that time was not on their side, after the start of the German advance in the west, the Acting Governor, Sir William Dobbie, spoke to the people of Malta on 10 May, 1940, and declared his intention of raising a force of special constables, and five days later volunteers were sought for just this role. On 20 May, the newspapers carried an appeal calling for 'licenced sportsmen and other persons capable of using a gun' to join the Home Defence Force, to guard 'the countryside against possible landing of enemy parachutists'. Once again, the people were willing, and within three days there were 3,000 volunteers armed with shotguns and revolvers, and some antiquated weapons. The only contribution made by the authorities was the supply of brassards with the letter V, and steel helmets. The Home Defence Force was soon officially named as the Malta Volunteer Defence Force and organized on an area basis.

The atmosphere of impending conflict was further intensified with the imposition of a curfew from 23.00 to 05.00 starting from Monday, 27 May, with the threat that anyone who left home during the prohibited hours could be shot without warning. Four hospitals were prepared for casualties, including the two existing civilian hospitals, the Central Hospital at Floriana and the Blue Sisters at St Julians, with the addition of the Mater Boni Consilii School at Paola and the Bugeja Technical Institute at Hamrun. Three demolition gangs were created from the personnel of the Public Works Department, and these were based at ARP

Headquarters and at the ARP centres in Floriana and Cospicua – they were to prove to be well sited!

Individuals were also anxious to do their bit, including those Britons who planned to stay even if war did come to Malta, including the dependents of some of the service personnel.

'It was a mercy for Malta . . . it gave the Island a little more time to put her house in order . . .' recalled Kathleen Norman, whose husband was a naval officer.

> Lady Bonham-Carter was quick to realise the terrible shortage of nurses in the Island and threw herself heart and soul into the training of more women . . . She raised VA detachments and arranged with the military hospital to give a month's training to the volunteers so that they might have at least some practical experience. Many of us took that month's training, and very kind Imtarfa was to us, for our inexperience must have been a sore trial to sisters and orderlies. We were very grateful for that training in the years to follow.[1]

Lady Bonham-Carter was the wife of the then Governor, the ailing Sir Charles Bonham-Carter, who was about to be replaced by his deputy, Lieutenant General William Dobbie. Imtarfa was the Army hospital in Malta, a short distance outside Rabat. This was about as good a position as a hospital could possibly have in Malta. By contrast, the Royal Navy's hospital, Bighi, was in the dockyard.

Those army wives who had not drifted homewards during the first few months of war were put on six hours' notice to leave.

Vice-Admiral Sir Wilbraham Ford, the Vice Admiral Malta, provided Paymaster Lieutenant Robert Jackson, a young Australian, as an assistant to the Governor. The young man was credited by those present with much of the organization involved in stocking the island for a two-year siege.

'I have often wondered whether if we had husbanded the

---

[1] Kathleen Norman, *For Gallantry: Malta's Story by a Navy Wife.*

supplies we laid in a little more carefully we should not have survived the whole three years without hunger', reflected Mrs Norman.[2]

One precaution that was not taken was the construction of deep air raid shelters. These had been advocated five years earlier by Lord Strickland, but his advice had been ignored. Strickland couldn't do anything for the mass of the population in the face of such official indifference, but he did at least build a massive shelter under his newspaper offices, carving a bell-shaped pit out of the solid rock for his workers. As for the rest, the official advice was to hide under the stairs or under a table, unless, of course, they were able to use the old railway tunnel in Floriana or the crypt of their local church.

Italy Enters the War

In addition to attacking Malta, Mussolini had opened hostilities by sending troops into France, but his attempted invasion was countered successfully by the French Alpine troops. Had these *Chasseurs Alpins* not prevailed, France could have been overrun. As it was, despite having a strong air force, Mussolini asked for help from the hard-pressed Luftwaffe in his French adventure. When France formally surrendered on 25 June, Italy had gained no substantial territory.

Mussolini was by now damned in Hitler's eyes. He had earned German contempt, both for his delay and then for the poor performance of his troops. In Hitler's eyes, had Mussolini attacked France at the same time as Germany, the entire country could have been overrun. No doubt, taking Hitler's approach to Austria and Czechoslovakia as a guide, Mussolini could have demanded the return of Nice, which at one time had been part of the Duchy of Savoy, itself part of the Kingdom of Sardinia until 1760.

The news that Malta had been bombed reached Hitler later on

[2] Kathleen Norman, *For Gallantry: Malta's Story by a Navy Wife.*

11 June, during a late dinner at his headquarters in a small village in southern Belgium. The Führer was unimpressed. Hitler had been aware that Mussolini had been planning to enter the war for several days, and had attempted to dissuade his fellow dictator from entering just as it was clear that France was about to fall. Having managed to overrun five countries with slight losses, Germany didn't need Italian help. Hitler viewed Mussolini's late entry as a belated and opportunistic attempt to grab a share of the spoils of war. Cynical Germans soon coined a term for this late arrival on the field of battle, dubbing their Italian allies as 'the harvest hands'.

There was another reason for Hitler's attitude. His idea of warfare centred around *blitzkrieg*, 'lightning war'. A worthwhile ally would not be content with sending over a couple of handfuls of bombers. Instead, Malta would have been bombarded by the guns of Italy's six powerful battleships and their supporting cruisers, and blitzed by waves of bombers, while troops were readied to invade.

III

ISLANDS IN HISTORY

Today, many visitors to Malta include a visit to the Neolithic temples at Tarxien in their itinerary. They may also pass through St Paul's Bay, and see in the distance St Paul's Island, where the apostle was shipwrecked whilst being taken to Rome as a prisoner. What few will fail to appreciate will be the impressive fortifications around Valletta and the Grand Harbour, and the much older fortifications at Mdina, the old capital well inland.

These are just two surviving examples of a long history, from a time when Malta was close to the cradle of civilization and at the centre of the known world. The opening of the Suez Canal in the nineteenth century was to transform the Mediterranean from a backwater to one of the main commercial routes.

Malta

Malta consists of the mainland of Malta itself, the island of Gozo to the north, with that of Comino in between Malta and Gozo, with the latter providing much of the food for Malta's dense population. In 1940, the population was around 280,000, with the Maltese islands, including Manoel Island, virtually a suburb of Sliema, and the unpopulated islets of Cominotto, Filfla, St Paul's Island and Selmunett, having a total area of no more than 127 square miles. Even then, the population density was far greater than that of the Netherlands or Belgium.

Inevitably, Malta could not feed itself, but even so maintained a far higher standard of living than most other Mediterranean countries by virtue of its earnings as a major base for the British armed forces, including the major dockyard. The Royal Navy used the dockyard as its main naval base, but it also had ships moored on the other side of Valletta from the Grand Harbour, in the Marsamuxetto, with its offshoots such as Sliema Creek and Pieta Creek.

For those who have not visited Malta, there is an understandable tendency to look at the population density of Malta, in 1940, with an average of more than 2,200 persons per square mile, and imagine it to be completely built-up. In fact, the densely populated areas were extreme examples of urban development, with urban areas accounting for just 14.5 square miles and accommodating ninety-four per cent of the population. Around forty per cent of the population lived in what was known as the inner harbour area, effectively the 'Three Cities' of Vittoriosa, Cospicua and Senglea, the capital Valletta, Floriana and Sliema, including intervening areas between Valletta and Sliema such as Pieta and Msida. The outer harbour area accounted for another twenty-four per cent, and can be regarded as towns such as Birkirkara, Hamrun and Paola. The remaining 30 per cent lived in the other urban areas, such as Mdina and Rabat – which adjoin one another – and in towns such as Mosta or in *casals*, a cross between a town and a village such as Birzebugia or Mellieha. The remaining six per cent lived in small villages or on small farms.

At one time, Malta's small farms had produced the wide variety of food that any population needs for its survival. Imports were always important given the large population, for such small islands meant that Malta's farms could only provide at best less than a quarter of the food needed. Nevertheless, substantial changes in agriculture took place between the two world wars as Maltese agriculture began to specialize. The economic imperatives for doing so were clear, but the specialisation was to have tragic implications once the siege began. For example, in 1918, the Maltese had 20,000 acres producing grain, but by 1942, this figure was down to 12,000 acres, even under wartime conditions that dictated what farmers could grow and had converted additional ground to agriculture. The reason for this sharp fall in grain production was the decision between the wars for many farmers to switch to grape vines, a much more profitable crop.

Another profitable crop had been potatoes, and despite its need to import food, by 1938 Malta had been able to export 24,000 tons of potatoes, especially to the Netherlands where a type of large potato grown in Malta was very popular. The swings and balances of international trade are dictated not just by taste and opportunity, but what will grow. Malta's thin soil was useless for germinating potatoes, so the seed potatoes had to be imported, and every year some 4,000 tons were brought in, mainly from Northern Ireland, which had a climate far better suited to this particular crop.

The might of the naval base facilities and the dockyard was in stark contrast to the commercial port facilities. This was natural, for with a small population, smaller than that of many British cities, massive shiploads of supplies and extensive port facilities to receive them had been simply unnecessary, at least in peacetime. Traditionally, Malta had seen supplies arrive in small quantities, manageable for the limited port facilities, in small craft, many of them still worked by sail, from Italy, Sicily and Tunisia. The weakness of these arrangements were that in wartime they no longer existed, and convoys of large ships would have to be fought through to Malta from either Gibraltar, having first steamed through the Bay of Biscay from the UK, or Alexandria. Convoys dramatically reduced merchant shipping losses during both world wars, but they have the one disadvantage that ports are left idle between convoys, and then extremely busy and extremely crowded; in effect, too busy. This leads to another problem, for with supplies coming at intervals in substantial quantities, good storage is needed, and it needs to be safe from enemy action. Crowded docks and harbours are in themselves tempting targets for an enemy.

The British Army's main base was at St Andrews Barracks, but there were other barracks scattered around the island, including those for the Kings Own Malta Regiment and the Royal Malta Artillery, the two locally-raised regiments.

The Royal Air Force had its main air station at Hal Far, also used by the Fleet Air Arm when carriers put into the Grand Harbour. Close to Hal Far was the seaplane and flying boat base at Kalafrana. The RAF also had the new airfield at Ta'Qali, close to the walls of Rabat and Mdina. This had originally been planned as an airfield for Imperial Airways, already even in the late 1930s looking forward to the day when flying boats would be superseded by ever more capable landplanes on the colonial routes, and with Kalafrana was used by Italian commercial air services to Malta. Luqa was also under construction when war broke out in September, 1939.

History

It is believed that the Maltese archipelago was once part of a land link between what is now Europe and North Africa, and remains found in the caves at Ghar Dalam support this since they are of animals known to have migrated from Europe to Africa. More positively, it is known that Malta was inhabited by man as early as 4000BC, and that there was a Neolithic community on Malta by 3000BC. There are more than thirty Neolithic sites on the islands, and doubtless more have been buried under the extensive urban and village development.

A turning point in the history of Malta was the arrival of the Phoenicians. Their extensive trading activities spread along the entire coast of North Africa and to present day Italy. Whether or not they saw Malta as a trading centre, the Phoenicians would certainly have used the many harbours as places of refuge from the often severe Mediterranean storms.

Next came the Carthaginians, believed to have been the first to colonize Malta. When Hamilcar surrendered to Rome in 216BC, the islands fell into the fast expanding Roman Empire. Between them, the Phoenicians and Carthaginians provided the basis of the Maltese language, *Malti*, also sometimes known as Phoenician Maltese, although over the centuries, this has been modified with the addition and adaptation of Italian and English words.

When the Roman Empire collapsed, Malta remained nominally under Roman rule until the arrival of the Arabs in 870. Nevertheless, Christianity survived the Arabs until they in turn were expelled from Malta by Roger the Norman, Count of Sicily, in 1090, who gave Malta the red and white flag. Malta remained part of Sicily for more than 400 years, and as the ruling families in Sicily changed, so too did those of Malta, so that the Normans gave way to the Angevins and then to the Aragonese. Charles V of Spain gained Malta by marriage, and he then granted possession of Malta and Tripoli on the coast of North Africa to the Knights of the Order of St John of Jerusalem, after they had been forced to leave their island retreat of Rhodes, to which they had fled with the fall of Jerusalem to the Turks.

The Knights Arrive

Charles had commanded the Knights to defend Malta and Tripoli 'as an outpost of Christianity on the Barbary Coast of North Africa'. Notwithstanding this instruction, the Knights were later to lose Tripoli to the Turks in 1551.

The Knights had arrived in Malta at Birgu, now known as Vittoriosa, on the eastern side of the Grand Harbour, and it is not surprising that their first settlement was here. The Knights were accommodated in 'houses' depending on their nationality or *langue*, known as auberges, which have often been described as being akin to colleges at universities such as Oxford or Cambridge. Birgu had many fine buildings, even at this early stage, and seven of these were taken over as auberges. This even included an Auberge d'Angleterre, despite the fact that Henry VIII had dissolved the English *langue* in his reforms of what had been the Roman Catholic Church in England. To protect the Grand Harbour, the Knights established a fort at the tip of Monte Sceberras, Fort St Elmo, but lacked the time and the funds to construct similar forts at the Three Cities side of the Grand Harbour, or at the Sliema side of the entrance to the Marsamxett Harbour.

The Ottoman Empire was in the ascendant at this time, and the balance of power between Christians and Moslems was delicate indeed. The Knights appealed for additional men, and soon their number swelled to 641, with no less than 164 from Italy, with just one, Sir Oliver Starkey, ignoring official disapproval, coming from England. In their surge forward, the Turks attempted to take Malta, culminating in the Great Siege of 1565. The siege started on 18 May, when the winter storms were well past and with the prospect of making the defenders face the searing heat and water shortages of the summer months.

In a brutal campaign, no less than 8,000 Turks died attempting to take Fort St Elmo at the entrance to the Grand Harbour. It was not entirely one-sided, with 1,500 of those defending the fort also killed, including around 100 knights, whose corpses were beheaded and the heads tied to planks and floated across the harbour as a threat to those still resisting. The Great Siege lasted for four months, doubtless involving great privation in an island where water has always been a scarce resource, before the Turkish forces withdrew after losing around 20,000 men against 9,000 amongst the defenders, who then, as almost 400 years later, included many Maltese as well as the Knights and fighting men from other parts of Europe. The end of the siege was celebrated throughout Europe, with masses sung in all Roman Catholic churches.

It was not until the Great Siege ended that the Knights decided to create a new capital, Valletta, named after their new leader, Grand Master De La Vallette, and replacing the older capital, Mdina, or Notabile, in the centre of Malta. The choice lay between leaving Malta altogether or of finding a means of improving its defences. The Knights were unsure which to do, but La Vallette, and the majority of European Christian opinion, took the view that the Knights should stay, and Malta remain an outpost of Christianity especially after the fall of Tripoli. The construction of the new city, sometimes described as a 'city built by gentlemen for gentlemen', involved scraping the top of Mount Sceberras, which ran most of the length of the Sceberras Peninsula, which would be fortified so that a city could be built inside, commanding the entrance to both the Grand Harbour on the east, and the Marsamxett Harbour on the west. That this was to be no minor architectural adventure can be realized from the fact that the idea was supported by Francesco Laparelli,

Michaelangelo's assistant, and by Gabrio Sarbelloni, Philip II of Spain's assistant. Even so, the costs were overwhelming and La Vallette nearly abandoned the project, but the plan was saved by generous contributions from the Roman Catholic crowned heads of Europe, grateful for the valour of the Knights in resisting the Turks.

Laparelli drew up the outline plans, while a Maltese architect, Gerolamo Cassar, attended to the detail and the actual works. The new city included new auberges for the different *langues* of the Order. Work started in 1566, by which time the new city had already been named Valletta in honour of the Grand Master. Originally, it had been intended to flatten the ridge forming the top of Monte Sceberras, and use the rubble to build up the sides inside the city wall, so that basically the new city would have been flat, but the pressure of time and the cost of this work meant that the ridge remained, and in Valetta the streets running east-west from the top of the ridge, from what is now Republic Street and the parallel Merchant Street, fall away towards the fortifications overlooking the harbours on either side.

Meanwhile, as the Knights deserted Birgu, the town had the name Vittoriosa to commemorate the great victory.

This was the time of great glory for the Knights and for Valletta, which was the focus of attention throughout Christendom, but it was short-lived. A major setback to Turkish ambitions was only a short time away, at the Battle of Lepanto in 1571. After this, Malta was far less important, and Christendom seemed less in need of a bastion. In short, while the donations continued to flood in from the rest of Europe, Malta was increasingly forgotten, and instead of being the focus of attention was seen as a backwater, if it was remembered at all. This was before the construction of the Suez Canal, which once more put Malta on one of the world's most important trading routes.

With Egypt in his sights and realizing the strategic significance of Malta's position, Napoleon sent the French Army of the Orient to Malta, arriving in the Grand Harbour in June, 1798. In contrast to the determined resistance offered to the Turks, Napoleon's forces were able to take the island almost unopposed.

Not just the fortunes of the Knights, but also their morality, were at a low ebb at this time. They were no longer what might have been described as almost a caste of warrior monks, having neglected their military training and their vows of celibacy. Despite having provisions and water for eight months as a result of the lessons learnt during the Great Siege, little resistance was offered. The Knights had lost their previous Grand Master, the French de Rohan, the previous year, and his successor, the German de Hompesch, was distinctly lacking in warlike qualities. Worse still, there was internal dissent, the French Knights holding the new Grand Master in contempt. Even so, the failure to take action is hard to believe since the French Knights had lost their property in France during the French Revolution, and despite this reached an accommodation with Napoleon's generals. Just three days' debate preceded the admission of the French admiral, Brueys, and his fleet into the Grand Harbour. All of this might not have happened had the British not been in the wrong place. The then Rear Admiral Nelson had been hunting for the French, but his orders were to close the Straits of Gibraltar because the Admiralty had feared that the French would sail from Toulon and through the Straits to mount an invasion on the south coast of England.

The Maltese had exchanged one set of rulers, the Knights, for another, the French. The deeply religious Maltese resented the attacks of the French Republicans on the Church, and in particular the looting and despoliation of individual churches. Worse still, French officers were billeted on Maltese families, heavy taxes were imposed, and promises to pay pensions to the dependents of those Maltese impressed into French service were broken. When the Maltese saw the remnants of the French fleet, defeated by Nelson at the Battle of the Nile on 1 and 2 August, 1798, enter the Grand Harbour, they could see French weakness for themselves. An uprising followed, with the French garrison besieged in Valletta by the Maltese. Emissaries were sent to seek help from either Sicily or Naples, but instead they fell in with one of Nelson's captains, Saumarez, who immediately communicated with Nelson. By this time, the French were besieged by the Maltese in

Valletta. Siege and blockade by the British followed, albeit inter-mittently as demands on the British and the need to confront the French took ships away from Malta. Finally, in December, 1799, Nelson sent the 30 and 89 Regiments of Foot, the predecessors respectively of the Lancashire Regiment and the Royal Irish Fusiliers. The following year, the Maltese put themselves under British protection, asking Britain to take over their islands. At first, despite being in the full flood of colonial expansion, the British resisted taking Malta over, largely because the King of Naples maintained that he was Malta's original sovereign, and that the British were simply protecting it for him! It was not until 1813 that the British accepted their new colony, and this arrangement was formalized the following year under the Treaty of Paris, when Malta became a British colony. The first Governor and Commander-in-Chief, Sir Thomas Maitland, had been appointed in 1813. As probably the only colony to have positively opted for British rule rather than as the result of exploration or conquest, the Governor ruled on behalf of the Sovereign with the assistance of an advisory council composed mainly of Maltese citizens.

At the outset, the British made a major blunder that was to have repercussions more than 100 years hence. Maitland was ordered to issue his proclamation, placing Malta under the British Crown, in both English and Italian. The hope appeared to be that the latter would gradually fall into disuse, but instead, Italian became the language of the upper classes and of the courts, with many Maltese coming to regard Italy as a more suitable ruler, while the Maltese language became the tongue of the kitchen, of the farmers and fishermen. The British acquiesced in this process, even though, as Italy struggled towards unification, the implica-tions were increasingly serious given Malta's strategic position as a major British naval base.

The opening of the Suez Canal on 17 November, 1869, restored Malta's importance, although this time it was not as a bastion of Christianity, but as an important staging post for ships on their way to and from India, the Far East and Australia. Sailing ships could not easily use the Suez Canal, but steamships could, and steamships needed coal, so Malta became a coaling station, even though in Malta, as in many other places, such as Aden for example, the coal itself had to be imported. The Victorian Royal Navy took the defence of the Empire and of trading routes seriously, and from this time on Malta's vital strategic position ensured a strong naval presence and the dockyard became the largest employer on Malta.

Even though Italy was one of the Great War Allies, the conflict showed for the first time that Malta could be threatened. It was in many ways the saving of the British connection, as some 20,000 Maltese joined the Royal Navy and the British Army, seeing service in many of the theatres of this, the first global conflict. More than 25,000 beds were made available in Malta for sick and wounded Allied troops, doubtless many of the early arrivals having come from the ill-starred Gallipoli campaign.

The end of the war brought an economic depression to Malta, worsened by the cuts in the Royal Navy as the depression years began to bite, and the Treasury stuck rigidly to the ridiculous 'Ten Year Rule'.

It might be supposed that all was harmony in the time that followed. The Maltese obtained a limited form of self-government in 1921, but this was reversed when the constitution was suspended in 1930, restored in 1932 and suspended yet again the following year. The lack of harmony was caused by controversy over the relationship between the all-powerful Roman Catholic Church in Malta and the state, and by concern over the slow development of Maltese as a written language, partly as the result of Italian being used as the language of the upper classes and by the courts. The advisory council used English for its transactions and reports. In fact, during the first four decades of the twentieth century, Maltese had become the language of the kitchen. The use of Italian even extended to street names, with the main thoroughfare in Valletta becoming the Strada Real.

Meanwhile, Mussolini had taken power in Italy, and in 1933, Hitler finally took absolute power in Germany. The Abyssinian crisis of 1935 started to ring the alarm bells, and the Mediterranean Fleet was reinforced and plans made for attacks on the Italian Fleet. Had the League of Nations been more decisive, had it not been undermined by French reluctance to impose sanctions on Italy, or by British reluctance to stop the Italians using the Suez Canal to supply their troops in Abyssinia, modern day Ethiopia, the history of the twentieth century could have been different. As it was, unchallenged, the dictators became more belligerent.

While the Second World War delayed any further constitutional progress until 1947, it did finally resolve the language question, with Italian being replaced by English and Maltese. The Strada Real became Kingsway, and even after the adoption of the title Republic Street, some of the businesses based there still retained Kingsway in their titles.

IV

POWER IN THE MED

Important to the United Kingdom throughout most of the nineteenth and twentieth centuries, Malta eventually had the best maintenance and repair facilities for the Royal Navy between Portsmouth and Singapore, far more extensive than those at Gibraltar, where many Maltese had settled whilst working for the Crown. A posting to the Mediterranean Fleet was an attractive proposition for any naval officer, both socially and in the sense of advancing a career. It was one of the best postings away from the Grand Fleet, or later the Home Fleet.

Malta was far less attractive from the point of view of the professional soldier. There weren't for them the opportunities enjoyed by the sailors to 'show the flag', visiting foreign ports, while training facilities were constrained by the small size of the islands. A military presence was essential because of Malta's importance, but there were not the challenges of insurrection, inter-communal or tribal conflict, or possible invasion that were part and parcel of life elsewhere in the British Empire.

From the point of view of the airmen, Malta didn't figure highly other than for flying-boat operations from Kalafrana and, while it was under RAF control, Fleet Air Arm visits to Hal Far when the Mediterranean Fleet was in port. Malaya was far more important. Malta fitted into the chain of British air stations. It was an important staging post for military aircraft on the way to the Middle East and beyond, although bypassed by the mainstream of the Imperial Airways' services. Hal Far's importance was all the greater because of the lack of airport facilities at Gibraltar until the outbreak of the Second World War.

The Mediterranean was also important to France, the other

great European colonial power after the collapse of Spain's Latin American empire. Britain and France co-owned the Suez Canal. Like the Royal Navy, the French Navy, the *Marine Nationale*, had to divide its forces between the Atlantic and the Mediterranean and widely scattered overseas possessions.

Italy's entry into the Second World War coincided with the fall of France, so the French presence can be discounted. The forces that mattered were those of Italy, and later those of Germany, but only the former had major surface fleet units as German wartime activity in the Mediterranean was confined to submarines and motor-torpedo boats, or U-boats and E-boats.

REGIA AERONAUTICA

After Italy entered the Second World War, it soon became clear that the dominant force was the *Regia Aeronautica*, the Italian Air Force. As the British were soon to learn, control of the sea was dependent upon control of the skies.

By June, 1940 the *Regia Aeronautica*, had some 5,400 aircraft, of which 400 were elderly types based in Italian East Africa. Most aircraft were divided between Italy and North Africa, ready for a push into Egypt, with a frontline strength of 975 bombers and 803 fighters and fighter-bombers, more than 400 reconnaissance aircraft and 285 maritime-reconnaissance aircraft, but fewer than eighty transports. The remaining 2,000 aircraft were operated by flying schools and technical and specialist units.

Backbone of the Italian bomber force was the three-engined Savoia-Marchetti SM79 Sparviero, or Hawk. If the Italian Navy's warships had seen little action, the same could not be said of the SM79, used in the one-sided confrontations between Italian forces and Abyssinian tribesmen. The SM79 could carry up to 2,200 lbs of bombs or, in the anti-shipping units, or *Aerosiluranti*, two torpedoes.

Built mainly of wood, the SM79 had a low wing, limiting the size of bomb that could be carried. Three Alfa-Romeo RC34 engines each provided 750hp, with a cruising speed of 200 mph and a maximum speed of 225 mph. The three-engined configuration placed the bomb-aimer's position under the fuselage behind the middle engine. Defensive armament was poor, just four machine guns, with no provision for a tail-gunner. Thick armoured plating behind their seats protected the two pilots, but not the wireless operator or the engineer sitting behind them!

Other aircraft included the Fiat BR20M Cicogna bomber, CR42 and CR50 fighters, and the Macchi C200 fighter. The latter aircraft's 840-hp Fiat A74 radial gave it a maximum speed of just over 300mph, pitifully inadequate by this time. Worse still was its armament of just two 12.7-mm machine guns, at a time when British pilots felt that four machine guns were inadequate, eight machine guns, in the early Hurricanes and Spitfires, only just adequate, and that a successful fighter should have four 20-mm cannon.

As a defensive force, the *Regia Aeronautica* was weak and poorly organized, despite its large numbers of fighters, a situation not helped by the absence of radar, but as an offensive force, it was ideally positioned to cut the Mediterranean in two. The land mass of Italy, the famous 'leg' almost did this, added to which there were bases in Sicily and Sardinia, and to the east, bases in the Dodecanese taken by Italy from Turkey in 1912, as well as in present day Libya.

Despite their support for the Nationalists in the Spanish Civil War, the *Regia Aeronautica* gave the distinct impression of having had little experience of modern warfare against a determined, well-trained and well-equipped opponent. They repeated the mistake made by the RAF during the first year or two of warfare, sending bombers in relatively small numbers which meant that they did relatively little harm and were exposed to the full force of defending fire.

The Regia Navale

In June, 1940, the Italian Navy, the *Regia Navale*, was the single most powerful maritime force in the Mediterranean, with six battleships, seven heavy cruisers and fourteen light cruisers: under the terms of the Washington Naval Treaty, 'heavy' cruisers had eight-inch guns, and 'light' had six-inch guns. Supporting these major warships were 122 destroyers and torpedo boats and no less than 119 submarines, almost twice as many as the German *Kriegsmarine* had possessed in 1939!

These warships showed Italy's lack of experience in modern warfare. There was more emphasis on style and speed than on armament and armour protection. The Andrea Doria-class of battleships, which included the *Conte di Cavour* and the *Caio Duilio*, dated from the First World War, although reconstructed between the wars. These ships had a tonnage of 22,964 tons, were capable of 27 knots, and had a main armament of ten 12.6-inch guns, with a secondary armament of twelve 5.2-inch, ten 3.5-inch and nineteen 37-mm, the last being primarily for anti-aircraft protection.

The new Commander-in-Chief of the British Mediterranean Fleet, Admiral Sir Andrew Browne Cunningham, 'ABC' to his men, relates how, in 1938, the two Italian battleships, *Guilio Cesare* and the *Conte di Cavour*, under the command of Admiral Riccardi, paid a courtesy visit to Malta. The nature of such visits was that the hosts and guests embarked on a round of entertaining and inspections. In return for British hospitality, Cunningham and his senior officers were invited aboard.

> We lunched on board the *Conte di Cavour* with Admiral Riccardi, and came to the conclusion that he must have embarked the whole catering staff and band from one of the best hotels in Rome, so distinguished was his entertainment. Afterwards he took us round his palatial and highly decorated private apartments . . .[1]

In other words, the *Conte di Cavour* was really an admiral's yacht!

More modern and more impressive were the Littorio-class, built just before the outbreak of war to make full use of the maximum dimensions permitted by the Washington Treaty.

[1] *A Sailor's Odyssey: The Autobiography of Admiral of the Fleet Viscount Cunningham of Hyndhope.*

These were ships of 35,000 tons, capable of 30.5 knots. Their main armament consisted of nine 15-inch guns, with a secondary armament of twelve 6-inch and four 4.7-inch, twelve 3.5-inch, twenty 37-mm and thirty-two 20-mm. For comparison, the British *Prince of Wales* also weighed in at 35,000 tons, but was only capable of 28.5 knots. Her main armament was ten 14-inch guns, with a secondary armament of sixteen 5.25-inch, forty-eight 2-pounder pom-poms, a single 40-mm and twenty 20-mm.

The fatal Italian weakness at the outset of what was to be an increasingly sophisticated and technological war was the absence of radar, whether on the ships, ashore or in the air. Cunningham thought that the Italians 'were no further advanced than we had been at Jutland twenty-five years before'.[2]

The main bases for the Italian fleet were at Taranto in Italy's 'instep', Genoa in the north-west, and La Spezzia, slightly further south, as well as Trieste at the northern end of the Adriatic, close to the border with Yugoslavia. Taranto was closest to Malta, and as the war progressed, it was the base best suited for supplies to North Africa and to support naval operations during the invasion of Greece.

A weakness of the Italian strategic position was that in addition to forces in Libya, it also had forces in Eritrea and Somaliland, as well as Abyssinia, who could only be reached through the Suez Canal, a route controlled by the British.

Domination on paper was not the same as domination in reality. The Italian armed forces had done relatively little in the First World War and not been faced with a serious conflict since the Balkan Wars in 1912 and 1913. Italy's naval history, such as it was, was that of pre-unification Genoa and Venice, with the latter state having played a major role in the important Battle of Lepanto in 1571. The 'leg of Italy' created that unusual phenomenon of a country virtually surrounded by the sea, and yet not a maritime power in the true sense.

---

[2] *A Sailor's Odyssey: The Autobiography of Admiral of the Fleet Viscount Cunningham of Hyndhope.*

The British

The British had strategically-located bases in the colonies of Gibraltar and Malta, as well as in Egypt, theoretically an independent kingdom, but run almost as a colony, and on Cyprus. The British armed forces were even more stretched than those of France, with a combination of colonies and protectorates and there was hardly a continent without a British presence.

British defence planning between the two world wars was severely constrained, one might even say 'blighted', by the so-called 'Ten Year Rule', that decreed that the country would have ten years in which to prepare for war. The fallacy of this can easily be judged by the fact that Hitler seized absolute power in 1933 and war broke out in 1939, after a close shave averted by the Munich Crisis of the previous year. In fact, war almost came even earlier, as a result of the Abyssinian Crisis of 1935 following Italy's invasion, and the use of gas and the other instruments of modern warfare against tribesmen often armed with nothing more potent than old rifles. The poor state of Britain's defences may well have been behind the decision not to pursue the matter with the rigour that many members of the public would have liked, and which would have at least shown the Axis Powers that the democracies meant business. There were other reasons for not acting, of course, including the inadequacies of the League of Nations and French opposition to sanctions against Italy.

The extra time bought by the Munich Agreement was put to good use by the British in many ways. True, they continued to build obsolescent aircraft types, but they did at least complete the CH, for 'Chain Home', radar stations, and they ordered extra aircraft carriers and other warships. Earlier, the decision had been taken to transfer naval aviation from the RAF and back to the Admiralty. A new class of fast armoured aircraft carriers was already under construction, the Illustrious-class. Yet the years of neglect could not be resolved within a year or two. The defence of Singapore and Malaya was neglected, while closer to home, Malta did not have fighters, although the AA defences were reinforced and the island had radar.

The Royal Air Force had called for volunteers to take the first transportable radar station to be sent abroad to Malta in January 1939. Reginald Townson, then a corporal but later a flight lieutenant, was one of the volunteers, having known and liked Malta from a previous visit. He recalls being sent out on a British India liner, by then already part of P&O, with two lorries, one containing the transmitter and a Meadows petrol-engined generating set on one lorry, the receiver on another, and two trailers with Merryweather seventy-feet telescopic wooden masts to carry the two aerials.

'The site was already selected for us and we were put out at Dingli which . . . has a site height according to the ordnance survey map of 817 feet, the highest point of the island,' he recalled.

> As luck would have it, it turned out to be a very good site and particularly from the point of view of detecting Italians. I'm afraid the equipment was rather, well, it was well put together all right, Met-Vic (Metropolitan-Vickers) never put anything together unless it was like a battleship but as far as the radio frequency side was concerned it wasn't very brilliant. And we found that the transmitter in fact, we used to wind it up to put 25,000 volts on the final anodes, but when we got up to 5,000 volts instead of the transmitter putting out pulses it went into continuous wave which would trip out all the breakers and you'd have to start all over again.[3]

Fortunately, they had the services of a civilian engineer, believed to have been from the BBC, and with his help they effectively rebuilt the transmitter and got it to work. Many items of equipment had to be changed, for radar was in its infancy and this was the first time that a portable unit had been allowed so far from home. They also had problems with the transmitter overheating in the Maltese summer, and the Meadows generating set,

[3] IWM Sound Archive, Accession No.004600/06.

possibly the least sophisticated part of the whole arrangement, proved to be far less reliable than it should have been.

But by the time September 1939 came along we'd got it working reasonably well and we were in fact achieving one or two operational successes with the set but by no means could you say that it was in a state to hand over. And then of course . . . when September 3rd came along the war was declared and there we were, stuck with it. And so there we had to stay.[4]

Townson and his colleagues were seen as oddities by the people in the RAF's headquarters in Malta, who would try to get in to see the equipment.

'. . . they'd have a giggle among themselves about these funny people out at Dingli, you know, and telling us that they can see aeroplanes seventy miles away,' Townson continued.

Well, we fetched in three Blenheims . . . one night that had got themselves lost and were wandering around the Med. And fortunately we picked them up on the radar. And we had not W/T (wireless telegraph) to communicate with them and anyway it would have breached security if we'd gone on the air and told them which way to steer. But by hooking us up by landline with an ordinary D/F (direction finding) station at Hal Far we passed the information, the position information, to Hal Far. They would pass it up as a bearing which of course is a perfectly normal thing for a D/F station to do and this way the Blenheims were brought in. And that did produce a signal of congratulations from the AOC the next morning . . . By and large, HQ Med just did not believe what we could do . . . And it wasn't until the first hostiles actually appeared on the screen, we passed down the information that there they were and what

[4] IWM Sound Archive, Accession No.004600/06.

range they were and then gave the decreasing ranges as they came in, and lo and behold when we said they were nearly overhead there some Italians were, dropping bombs on us.[5]

The small radar team was headed by a flight sergeant, and when he was invalided home in late 1940, Townson was promoted first to sergeant and then to flight sergeant in his place.

More than any other single feature, the presence of radar on the island was to be the saving of Malta and of many Maltese lives. It helped too that the Italians did not have radar, and almost certainly could hardly understand it. This aspect of Malta's air defences was dependent on the work of just nine people.

> . . . there were nine of us altogether which we split up into three crews of three to operate over as much of the twenty-four hours as we could. The big snag was the Meadows generating set which was far from stable but then, you know, it had never been designed to do that sort of job. We had to have a stable mains supply which was never designed for it. We took it out of its van and stuck it into a little stone building that works and bricks put up for us in a hurry which made it a lot better but it still wasn't very good . . . we just felt that we just could not run that, or the transmitter come to that, for twenty-four hours a day. And so we used to shut down at night for a few hours, let it all cool off and start up again the next morning before dawn. And three watches of three to do that lot.
>
> We used to have one chap in the receiver, one chap in the transmitter, and one chap looking after the Meadows. As simple as that. And then swap them around. Hour on the tube and then change around and off they go.[6]

[5] IWM Sound Archive, Accession No.004600/06.
[6] IWM Sound Archive, Accession No.004600/06.

The Mediterranean Fleet

The state of the Royal Navy's Mediterranean Fleet in 1940 was such that the balance of naval power lay firmly with the Italians once France was out of the war. As Pound, who had been recalled home to become First Sea Lord, had hoped, ships were indeed brought back from the Far East to reinforce the British Mediterranean Fleet, but these 'reinforcements', including the elderly aircraft carrier HMS *Eagle*, recalled from the Indian Ocean, were in reality replacements, as his successor, Andrew Cunningham, had lost *Glorious*, recalled home to take part in the Norwegian Campaign. Cunningham's own flagship, HMS *Warspite*, was an elderly battleship that had been commissioned in time for the First World War and had seen action at Jutland. She and her sisters of the Queen Elizabeth-class had been some of the first major British warships to be fuelled by oil, something which many senor naval officers during the early years of the twentieth century regarded with suspicion, not out of any conservative attachment to coal, but because of the uncertainty over oil supplies. *Warspite* had been extensively modernized between the two world wars, and in 1940, she had a full load tonnage of 36,450 tons, and was capable of more than 25 knots. In addition to her eight 15-inch guns in four turrets that comprised her main armament, she had a secondary armament of eight 6-inch guns, eight 4-inch guns, thirty-two 2-pounder pom-poms, often described as the 'best close-in anti-aircraft weapon of the war' by many naval officers, and fifteen 12.7-mm machine guns. This was the one warship available to Cunningham on Italy's entry into the war that could fight on an equal footing with the Italian battleships and cruisers.

Cunningham also had two other battleships, but neither had been modernized to the same extent as *Warspite*. These two ships, *Malaya* and *Royal Sovereign*, were both too slow by the standards of 1939. Supporting these ships were five cruisers and a number of destroyers and submarines.

The Army in Malta

In Malta, on 3 September 1939, there were just four battalions of British infantry, some of them under strength, while a Maltese infantry battalion was forming and would in due course be the 1st Battalion of the King's Own Malta Regiment. The British battalions were the 2nd Battalion, Devonshire Regiment; 2nd Battalion, Queen's Own Royal West Kent Regiment; 1st Battalion, Dorsetshire Regiment, and 2nd Battalion, Royal Irish Fusiliers. There was also the 7 AA Regiment, Royal Artillery.

These forces were barely adequate to deter an Italian invasion. Urgent attention was already being paid to reinforcements. First of these were two territorial battalions of the King's Own Malta Regiment, which were ready by the end of September 1939, aided by the creation of the Malta Auxiliary Corps to provide reinforcements for the existing support arms on the island. Additional manpower arrived in November once the garrison was classed as a division. The following year saw additional resources provided, despite the desperate situation in France, with the 8th Battalion, Manchester Regiment, arriving in May 1940.

Meanwhile, additional AA defences were built up with the arrival of the 27 HAA, while the 7 AA Regiment was renamed the 7 HAA, reflecting the heavier calibre of its weapons. The Royal Malta Artillery was also expanded.

In the final year of peace, Colonel Martin Hastings was a second lieutenant in the 2nd Battalion, Devonshire Regiment. He had been posted to Malta in July 1938, where his unit practised beach and island defence roles until the outbreak of war in September 1939, when his role changed.

'I had an interesting job given to me which was to be a . . . recruit training officer of the Malta Artisan Section of the Royal Army Ordnance Corps, which I did and became temporary ordnance officer and earned an extra two shillings a day which was very fortunate for an impecunious second lieutenant,' he recalls.[7]

[7] IWM Sound Archive, Accession No.10453/6.

It was great fun and we enlisted, I suppose, about forty of them or so. They were now what you would call REME and they were the first lot of Maltese to be enlisted into the British Army outside Malta.

They were keen young men. Their main problems I think was English (sic) but they went off and they became good soldiers and I've often wondered what their eventual life was like in the army in Egypt . . . They were very keen. There was tremendous competition to get into the little unit. They had a very good colonel who was quite a character, called Colonel de Wolf, who was a bit deaf and everybody knew Colonel de Wolf in Malta. And he kept a very close eye on us and great interest and we finished up by marching through Valletta and we were inspected by the Governor on the Palace Square with the whole of Malta who seemed to be watching and cheering.[8]

Martin Hastings was soon promoted to captain.

The French fleet was coming in and out of Malta taking African troops to the south of France and we had a number of soldiers who went off with the Navy to provide guards on various ships which they would intercept and order into port. Other than that we hardly knew that a war was on.

It wasn't until Italy declared war that things changed . . . The Fleet moved out of Malta of course and went off to Alex and Gib and we had, as you know, just those basically three aeroplanes, *Faith*, *Hope* and *Charity*, the three small fighters, Gloster Gladiators.

When Italy came in, of course, the first day they sent over, I think it was, ten bombers and we all watched these bombers come over in a big circle high above the sky and our little planes were somewhere up there . . . But gradually it started to build up and we gradually started to build our defences and our role of beach defence and

[7] IWM Sound Archive, Accession No.10453/6.

airfield defence around Hal Far aerodrome, which was the Fleet Air Arm base mainly, and Kalafrana where the flying boats up to then had come in on their imperial lines of communication.[9]

Italy Prepares for War

While the Italian Navy must have understood that war was likely, and that the United Kingdom would be the most likely opponent from the start of the Abyssinian adventure in the mid-1930s, no official indication was given to the armed forces until April 1940, that Italy would expect to fight alongside the Germans. Mussolini listened to and consulted the army, who dominated the Supreme Command, leaving the sailors and airmen to do as they were told.

The Chief of the Italian Naval Staff, Admiral Domenico Cavagnari, also held the political post of Under Secretary of State for the Navy, and should have had great influence. He wrote to Mussolini, effectively complaining that entering a war once it had already started meant that any chance of surprise had gone. In the circumstances, Italy was in a weak position. He thought that Britain and France could block the Mediterranean at both ends and starve Italy of the fuel and raw materials needed to survive, let alone prosecute a war, or seek combat, in which case both sides could expect heavy losses. He stressed the difficulties inherent on being dependent on the cooperation and goodwill of the *Regia Aeronautica*.

This was a pessimistic forecast, and one that was overtaken by the collapse of French resistance. It was certainly more realistic about wartime conditions than the Italian Army. That the Army hadn't properly considered the impact of maritime strategy in wartime soon became apparent. On the eve of war, the Italian Army maintained that it had six months' supplies in Libya. Once fighting started, and especially after Marshal Graziani, Italy's commander in North Africa, invaded Egypt on 13 September, the demand for supplies of all kinds soared. A convoy system had to

[9] IWM Sound Archive, Accession No.10453/6.

be hastily instigated, but here the lack of Italian preparation and inexperience of modern warfare was soon to be seen, as often one or two small warships would guard a number of merchantmen.

British Preparations

As war drew closer, everyone knew that the situation in Malta was likely to be serious. Cunningham, who had spent much time on the island, was well aware of this. The British Mediterranean Fleet was moved from Malta to Alexandria in Egypt, a safer haven for the ships. This was a wise move, and as events were to prove, Cunningham had no choice, for within three days of Italy entering the war, Italian warships sank three British submarines, *Grampus*, *Odin* and *Orpheus*. Nevertheless, it did mean that the Mediterranean Fleet now found itself more than 1,000 miles from Malta, and twice that distance from Gibraltar.

A partial solution lay in creating what was in effect a fleet for the Western Mediterranean, Force H, based on Gibraltar and under the command of Vice Admiral Sir James Somerville. Force H also ventured into the Atlantic, as circumstances demanded, and included the still new aircraft carrier, HMS *Ark Royal*.

On the eve of war in the Mediterranean, the Mediterranean Fleet itself was, like Malta, without fighter aircraft, having just eighteen Swordfish for bombing, torpedo attacks, minelaying and anti-submarine operations. The Swordfish was a plodding biplane, much liked by those who flew in it, but despite training in defensive tactics, liable to be vulnerable to enemy fighters. Determined to do something about it, *Eagle*'s Commander Flying, Commander C. L. Keighley-Peach, found three Gloster Sea Gladiator fighters, the last biplane fighter and obsolete even when it entered service, and put these antiques into service, flying one himself and training two Swordfish pilots as fighter pilots. Such aircraft could cope with the enemy's reconnaissance seaplanes, hampered by the drag of their floats, but were scarcely able to handle the enemy bombers. It was fortunate indeed that the Italians did not have fighters of the calibre of the Messer-schmitt Bf109.

While the Admiralty was determined that the islands should be held, and Cunningham took the same view, he realized that there were many practical measures to be taken.

Before Italy entered the war, many British civilians and deped-dants had already been sent home aboard the Orient Lines ship *Oronsay*, on passage from Australia, while both the Mediterranean and the Bay of Biscay were still free from enemy attack. The fact that most of the army wives who sailed on the *Oronsay* felt that their departure was to some extent enforced led to her being called the 'slave ship', although it seems that they were well looked after despite the growing crisis in Europe.

Most of the remaining British civilians including the dependants of service personnel were evacuated in a convoy that departed on 10 July 1940, sending them by sea to Alexandria as a first step in what was to be a long journey home. A fast convoy carried the civilians, while a slow convoy carried the naval stores regarded as being superfluous in Malta and needed elsewhere as the fleet redeployed eastwards to Alexandria, out of range of enemy aircraft. These arrangements demonstrated the weakness of Malta's position. In normal times, the fast convoy carrying the dependants and civilians would have headed for Gibraltar and home, but with the whole of the coastline of North Africa between Malta and 'Gib' now open to the enemy's aircraft, it had to head for Alexandria, but even that course was not immune from enemy air attack.

The slow convoy would have gone to Alexandria anyway, as the Royal Navy built up that base to take the place of Malta. Creating what was, in effect, a new home for the Mediterranean Fleet was a major task. It even involved moving a floating dock from the UK because of the limited facilities at Alexandria, and the poor state of the floating dock already in Malta. Alexandria was too far away to provide an effective base from which to inter-rupt Italian supply convoys on their way to North Africa. Malta was ideally situated to harass Italian convoys across the Mediterranean, but 1,000 miles there and 1,000 miles back was too much for many of the ships, especially the smaller ones such as destroyers. The Royal Navy's warships were notoriously 'short-legged', a legacy born from the complacency of having so many well situated refuelling bases, such as Malta, in a far flung empire. Realizing that Malta would be a danger if the Royal Navy dared base warships or submarines there, the Italian Navy pressed for its invasion, but Mussolini held back.

For the passage to Alexandria, both convoys enjoyed the protection of the Mediterranean Fleet, with Cunningham hoping also to bring the Italian Admiral Inigo Campioni to battle.

In a foretaste of Italian strategy for the next three years, they didn't send their fleet, but instead sent *Regia Aeronautica*'s bombers to attack the ships. Those who had been living in Malta had already grown accustomed to this, but for many of the seafarers, it was their first experience of bombing. Dropped from 12,000 feet, the bombs screamed down, while the ships thudded and shook to the sound and recoil of their own AA guns. Ships disappeared from sight as bombs sent fountains of water, stained black by the explosive, high above their decks, while pieces of shrapnel struck the sides.

'It was a comfort to remember that there was always more water than ship,' commented Cunningham. 'But not very much, for a ship stood up huge, bare and exposed, above the absorbing flat acres of the sea.'[10]

Cunningham was one of the very small minority who believed that Italian bombing was excellent, later recalling that: 'It is not too much to say of those early months that the Italian high-level bombing was the best I have ever seen, far better than the German . . . I shall always remember it with respect.'

The three Sea Gladiators led by Keighley-Peach nevertheless accounted for five Italian aircraft that day, and before being replaced by Fairey Fulmars, these obsolete aircraft were to account for a further six Italian aircraft.

Only one British ship, the cruiser HMS *Gloucester*, received a

---

[10] *A Sailor's Odyssey: The Autobiography of Admiral of the Fleet Viscount Cunningham of Hyndhope.*

direct hit, but this was serious enough. She was hit on the bridge, killing seven officers, including her captain, and eleven ratings. Prompt action saw the fires extinguished and control regained as she was steered from her emergency position aft. Near misses also caused damage to the thin hulls of the destroyers, and the 'mining' effect of close underwater explosions caused internal damage.

The outlook that summer was bleak. The British Empire literally stood alone. The British Army had kept most of its men, but lost most of its equipment, and had seen nothing but defeat. The RAF was under pressure as the Luftwaffe tried to destroy it in the Battle of Britain, the outcome of which was still far from certain. The Royal Navy was under pressure and thinly stretched.

V

AN OUTPOST AGAIN

Within the space of one night, Malta had gone from peace to war. The island was once again an outpost, but this time of freedom in a world threatened by aggressive dictatorships.

During 1939 and the long months of the so-called 'phoney war', Malta was lightly garrisoned. Despite the substantial Italian forces present in Libya, the priority for both the British and French was to protect the Suez Canal. The collapse of France presented a major problem, for suddenly almost the whole of the North African coastline from the Egyptian border to Morocco was potentially available for Axis use. Even in Egypt, there were strong French naval and ground forces that had to be neutralized, while further east Syria was another outpost of Vichy. The full responsibility for defending the Suez Canal now fell on British shoulders.

The significance of this cannot be underestimated. The French Army in Egypt outnumbered that of the United Kingdom. The situation was resolved as French troops were repatriated from Egypt, while the French naval vessels in their North African ports were ordered to surrender to the Royal Navy or be attacked. They refused to surrender and at Oran and Dakar the Royal Navy found itself in the unfortunate position of having to strike at what had been so recently an ally, but even so, some ships escaped to Vichy France. At Alexandria, a stand-off was narrowly averted by the diplomatic skill of Cunningham and his senior officers, but it could have resulted in a naval gun duel in the harbour had not his wiser counsel prevailed, since the Admiralty was insisting on immediate surrender. In the end, some seventy per cent of the French naval personnel were repatriated, leaving the rest to maintain their ships ready for the day of liberation; meanwhile their guns were put 'beyond use'. No attempt was made by the Royal Navy to impress these ships into its service, as had happened in centuries past, partly because of a lack of manpower and partly because the two fleets had guns of different calibres. Soon, the Mediterranean Fleet was to find itself short of sufficient ammunition for its own weapons, so the logistics of having completely alien shells supplied would have been more trouble than they were worth.

A Thunderclap

For those in Malta, the defeat of France came as a shock, or as Mrs Norman put it, 'our really shattering thunderclap was the news of the fall of France. A Fleet and Air Force were at once lost to our aid. The sea, which was our lifeline became at once a narrow channel, infested with mines and submarines and within the range now of enemy airfields all the way from Gibraltar to Malta . . . '[1]

After the first attack, Malta moved almost immediately on to a war footing. There was resignation on the part of the British present on the island, for whom yet another theatre of war had opened up at the worst possible time, with 6 million French service personnel no longer in the conflict. Amongst the Maltese, there was anger and resentment that their larger neighbour had seen fit to attack them. There was also fear. The fear of the bombing, or of gas attacks, that had been widely predicted as the future of warfare between the wars, and whose consequences on the Western Front in the previous world war had become so widely known. There was also concern about invasion.

Everyone looked to the new Governor of Malta for a lead. Dobbie's first act was to cancel the six hours' notice for army wives. He had brought his own wife with him. Even so, those naval wives whose husbands were 'afloat' were ordered to leave,

[1] *For Gallantry, Malta's Story.*

while those whose husbands had shore appointments could stay or leave as they wished. Many naval wives accepted the 'offer' of accommodation in St George's barracks, even though this meant leaving their homes on the island.

'We were feeling very disgruntled at leaving our comfortable homes,' Mrs Norman remembers. 'But glad to see other families had not left in the exodus.'

> Strewn about the barrack grounds were funny little long shaped mounds – the slit trenches that were to be our shelter. I had an almost irresistible temptation to decorate each one of them with one of those large glass bulbs full of white artificial flowers and R.I.P. The whole place looked discouragingly like a cemetery.[2]

Given that the Maltese are almost 100 per cent Roman Catholic, it seems strange that the first wartime Governor of Malta was a devout Methodist. On the other hand, since Lieutenant General Sir William Dobbie had spent his military career in the Royal Engineers, the 'Sappers', whose members were supposedly all 'Mad, Married and Methodist', he was probably just conforming to type. Dobbie was a strict Methodist, austere and spartan in his tastes, and just perhaps that was one characteristic that endeared him to the Maltese, whose Roman Catholicism was devout and also puritanical, in contrast to the more liberal ways of many of the Continental countries. The best comparison with Maltese Roman Catholicism was probably that of the Spanish Basques.

Dobbie's first action was to send an Order of the Day to service personnel in Malta:

> The decision of HMG to fight on until our enemies are defeated will be heard with the greatest satisfaction by all ranks of the Garrison of Malta.
> It may be that hard times lie ahead of us, but I know that however hard they may be the courage and determination

[2] *For Gallantry, Malta's Story.*

of all ranks will not falter, and that with God's help we will maintain the security of this fortress.

I call upon all officers and other ranks humbly to seek God's help, and then in reliance on Him to do their duty unflinchingly.

During his time as Governor, Dobbie was also to make frequent broadcasts to those on the island, making them feel that he was taking them into his confidence and reinforcing his message with frequent invocations of the help of the Almighty.

Although well past the British Army's retirement age of sixty years, Dobbie had a dual role, acting as both Commander-in-Chief of Malta and as its Governor. This meant that he had the responsibility of defending Malta, and mounting operations against the enemy from the islands, while also being responsible for the health, safety and general well-being of the civilian population.

The threat of war had not envisaged such an early French capitulation, rather many had expected that the entire war would see intensive fighting in France, in effect a repeat of the experiences of the First World War. Even though Italian involvement had been regarded as possible, Germany's other potential ally, Spain, was weak and still struggling to recover from the effects of the Spanish Civil War. The Mediterranean, it was thought, could be kept secure by British forces at Cyprus, Gibraltar and Malta, an Anglo-French presence at Alexandria, and French forces at Oran, Tunis and Toulon.

Exodus

Casualties on that first day were light. One bomb killed six Maltese artillerymen at St Elmo, all of whom were bandsmen from 1 Coast Regiment posted to act as observers for the Harbour Fire Controls. There were seven civilian casualties, and inevitably during what must be regarded as 'total war', three of them were young children, little girls of five, six and seven.

The Italians did not seem to be working to a definite plan. The airfields and the dockyard seemed to be the primary targets, but bombing lacked precision. This could have simply been a reflection of the problems of high level bombing, or it could be that the heavy AA barrage was working well. In addition to the AA gunners of the Royal Artillery and the Royal Malta Artillery, there were also improvised AA defences in the dockyard, where the admiral superintendent had asked for volunteers, hoping for 400, and received 5,000 applications!

One of the early plans was for the evacuation of as many people as possible away from the areas most at risk, meaning effectively the three cities on one side of the Grand Harbour, and the capital Valletta, with its suburb Floriana, on the other. At the time of Italy entering the war, Valletta's population was around 24,000, that of Floriana, 7,000, and Cospicua had 13,000, Vittoriosa, 8,500, Senglea, 8,000, and Kalkara, 2,500. The numbers were not huge, but these were some of the largest towns. Many stayed put for the first night, and only started to leave in the morning, but the real spur to the mass exodus that followed was the start of the air raids.

'The road leading from Cospicua to Zabbar Gate presented a pitiful sight,' recalls J. Storace.

> Women with bundles on their heads or with bundles hanging from their arms, carrying babies, with one or two children holding on to their skirts, with a boy or girl pushing a pram loaded with the most essential belongings, crowded the road, walking without a destination in view, but leaving their beloved homes, abandoning their City, going anywhere as far away as possible from this target area. Buses, touring cars, cabs and other horse-drawn vehicles carrying the more fortunate families who either owned a vehicle or could afford to hire one, moved in this crowd of walking and less fortunate humanity in the direction of Zabbar.
>
> Some of the Cottonara ARP staff were detailed to control the walking refugees by making them keep to the left side of the road leaving the right side clear for traffic. As each

vehicle leaving Cospicua approached Silver Jubilee Gate, it was stopped and the driver ordered to load as many refugees as he could possibly carry, especially women with babies in their arms and without the escort of their menfolk. By also using for this purpose the ARP ambulances and trucks as soon as they returned from hospital, the congestion was gradually relieved so that by 11pm this vital main road was completely cleared.[3]

Matching pedestrians with motor vehicles, seemingly regardless of the destinations of either, seems a rough and ready method of evacuation, especially for those with a clear destination in mind, possibly returning to the country or coastal village of their younger years. People in small islands tend to commute far less and over far shorter distances than those living in larger countries. Small villages such as Dingli, by Maltese standards relatively isolated, suffered a large influx of refugees. A slightly larger village, Siggiewi, saw its population grow by more than 5,000, more than trebling its pre-war population. After the initial exodus, many stayed put, but on 26 June at Marsa, a bus crowded with passengers suffered a direct hit by a bomb, killing twenty-eight outright. Almost immediately, more than 8,000 fled the town in panic, leaving little more than 1,000 behind.

Strangely, the second day of war saw nothing more than a solitary Italian reconnaissance aircraft approach Malta, and this was shot down. On 13 June, there were four warnings, but only two air raids actually hit the island, the first striking at Kalafrana, killing two people and wounding another four. The second raid was attacked by the three Gloster Sea Gladiator biplanes, *Faith*, *Hope* and *Charity*, who forced the bombers to drop their bombs around the northernmost mainland village of Mellieha, with most falling in fields and some into the sea.

One farmer working in his fields as the bombs dropped knew what to do, throwing himself flat on his face. Neither he nor his donkey were injured, but when the air raid wardens reached him

---

[3] *When Malta Stood Alone.*

they found that he was furious, having spent the morning watering a crop of tomatoes, only to have it destroyed by the bombs!

On 14 June, air raids started around Valletta and Floriana, with some bombs falling on Pieta on the main road from the capital to Sliema. There were no less than eight separate raids that day. They ended at 19.25 with a raid that fell mainly on Cospicua, close to the dockyard, and in which incendiaries were mixed with the high-explosive bombs. A total of twenty-five aircraft came across on this raid in five waves. Cospicua was one of the most crowded areas, and casualties were heavy. Survivors struggled from the devastation, seeking safety, and many seeking shelter having lost everything except the clothes they were wearing. One man, who had been having a breakfast of fried fish when the first bombers had arrived that morning, sent his wife and three daughters to stay with relatives in Mellieha, in the north of the island.

'There was excitement in the Island that June, as you'd expect,' recalled Queenie Lee.

> All the families seemed to think that movement was the solution to all problems. Hundreds and hundreds of them packed up a few possessions and went to seek safety in the centre of the Island, and the squares near the coast and harbour were dead except for battalions of hungry cats. I remember going along the seafront between raids, and seeing no one but a solitary old man sitting on the edge of a bomb crater, serene in the belief that two bombs never fall in the same place. But our three planes worked miracles and must have frightened the Italians with their sheer impudence. In a few weeks, raiders were treated with contempt and returned to their homes and life became normal except for the inactivity in the creeks and harbour.[4]

Once hostilities started, the Governor moved quickly to remove those with strong Italian sympathies from prominent positions,

[4] IWM Sound Archive, Accession No. 1172.

and there really was only one, the Chief Justice, Sir Arturo Mercieca. He joined other pro-Italian Maltese in internment, initially in Malta, but later in East Africa.

Despite the fact that many refugees soon returned to their homes, by early August, the official estimate was of 81,540 refugees, more than a quarter of the population, with an incredible 16,939 billeted on Birkikara, while the much smaller towns of Qormi had 8,656, Rabat, 8,008, Mosta, 5,375, Zejtun, 6,312, and Zebbug, 6,317. Even little Safi, whose peacetime population was around 500, had 345 refugees, while Lija, with a population of 1,800, had more than 3,000 refugees. Many villagers welcomed strangers into their homes, while the wealthier landed gentry and Maltese nobility placed property at the disposal of the authorities, churches, convents and monasteries, and the band clubs opened themselves up to refugees, while local schools were often commandeered.

The Governor had spoken to the people of Malta on 15 June, announcing that each village would have an official, later described as the Protection Officer, who would work with the District Committee, the Police and the Special Constabulary, to ensure the welfare of the refugees, including food and accommodation. A Refugee Central Office was established at Birkirkara, usually known as B'Kara.

The importance of the church in Maltese life, and its strength, was to prove a blessing. In many places, the local church would attend to the feeding of the refugees, but if the church did not, or its resources were swamped by the sheer numbers involved, the Protection Officer had to open a community kitchen if there were more than fifty refugees. Archbishop Maurus Caruana had already ordered the churches to open 'Economical Kitchens' for those without food, and by 17 June, seven of these were in operation. Congregations pledged donations towards the cost of the kitchens, with at least one parish priest exhorting his congregation to give for this cause rather than for the repainting of the dome! The kitchens provided by the Protection Officers were known as the Communal Feeding Service, and while the Economical Kitchens closed down in September, the Communal

Feeding Service continued. A mood of austerity gripped the island, with sales of ice cream banned after 15 August: Malta's largest producer, the Wembley Ice Cream Factory, donated all of that day's proceeds to the Malta Relief Fund.

Eligibility for the Communal Feeding Service was by application to the Protection Officer, and successful applicants were given coupons for a fortnight at a time for hot meals from the kitchens and for other basic items that could be purchased through grocery shops. Those using a communal soup kitchen were given half a rotolo, about 400 grams, of bread and one hot meal a day. For children between three and eight years, this ration was halved, but supplemented by a pint of milk and an egg a day. For those without a kitchen meal, three pence (1.25p) of food was provided daily, including half a rotolo of bread and a rotolo of paste weekly, with children between three and eight years given a quarter rotolo of bread daily and half a rotolo of paste weekly . Children under three received a pint of milk and an egg daily. Any money not spent on these necessities could be used to buy up to half a gallon per head of paraffin each week, or could also be spent on oil, coffee or tea, sugar, fish, goats cheese or potatoes. All very well, but the increased demand in the smaller villages and towns meant that supplies in the shops quickly dwindled.

Unemployment soared in many of the villages invaded by the refugees, and many local evacuation committees looked hard to find work for these idle hands, but there was only so much demand for dressmakers or washerwomen. Yet, money was desperately needed, for those refugees fortunate enough to find accommodation, often at a very high price, still had to pay the rent on the property that had been abandoned.

Anticipating war, the Maltese authorities had spent £350,000 creating a reserve of essential commodities, and as soon as war broke out in September 1939, the government and the armed forces became the sole importers of such items.

Air Raid Precautions

After the first day's bombing, two things were clear. The threat of a gas attack had been wildly exaggerated but there was a pressing need for purpose-built air raid shelters. Even the large stretch of railway tunnel was not adequate for the population of Floriana, but those elsewhere on the island had nowhere, except in the dockyard where there was one of the largest shelters, with accommodation for more than 1,000 labourers, as well as the resident naval personnel.

Not surprisingly, many of Malta's reactions were based on the British model. This included a Home Defence Force and a Special Constabulary, for which 5,000 volunteers came forward, many of them reporting with their own weapons, mainly sporting guns for shooting wildlife. The Home Guard soon took over the anti-parachute duties of the police. The Maltese units in the British Army also expanded rapidly, with the King's Own Malta Regiment at one time enlisting two companies all of whom were former Boy Scouts.

The role of the Special Constabulary was no easy one. During one air raid, a bomb fell on to the Benedictine convent in Mdina, demolishing the top storey and sending two nuns, one of whom died immediately, crashing through to the floor of the storey below. The convent was a closed order with little contact with the outside world, and at first refused admittance to anyone, but eventually relented when faced with a forced entry. The rescuers were preceded down the corridors by a nun ringing a bell to warn the rest of the nuns to go to their cells, after which they were able to take the corpse of the bomb victim to the convent chapel.

At first, much of the island was without adequate warning of an air raid, and even in Valletta, the capital, the lower end of Kingsway could not hear the public Rediffusion speakers. Even in the dock area, often the first warning was when the AA defences opened up. In some places, maroons were fired, but at night these risked drawing the attention of enemy aircraft.

Realizing the urgent need for air raid shelters, the population set to with a will, helped by the fact that the limestone on which

Malta sits, and which is the ubiquitous local building material, is soft and easy to cut, but once exposed to the sea air it hardens. The local population was also encouraged to build their own shelters, even in the bastion walls, and in the large public shelters they could ask permission from the District Commissioner to excavate a private cubicle of their own. Permission for this was seldom refused provided that the work was completed within three months and that the tunnelling was level with the rest of the shelter. Cubicles were restricted to a width of six feet and could not have fixed doors. A right of way would also exist through these 'private' areas of the shelter and a fee of one shilling (5p) had to be paid annually. In the genuinely private shelters, it was not unusual for several neighbouring shelters to be inter-connected to allow for escape in an emergency, when one or more exits might be blocked. Attempts to create additional shelters in the cellars of the larger houses proved unsuccessful, however.

At first, a system of voluntary shelter supervisors was instituted, but this seems to have rarely worked well, with one or two exceptions, notable amongst them being the Very Revd Canon Publius Farrugia, Dean of the Chapter of St Paul's Shipwreck Church in Valletta.

Living in an air raid shelter, many families brought food with them, while some shelter supervisors managed to acquire small stocks for emergency use. Thefts did occur from time to time, especially as rationing became tighter during 1942. One of the worst cases arose when the entire emergency stock was removed from the food store in the air raid shelter under the Argotti. The food was removed through a ventilation hole that was large enough for cases of food to be lifted out.

'I know of three large public shelters in Floriana which were mostly excavated by voluntary labour,' recalls Emmanuel Tonna, who was in charge of the air raid wardens in Floriana. 'The one under the London Confectionery extending to the Lion Fountain in St Anne's Square; the one beneath the Seminary which was connected with the one in the Argotti and the one in Gunlayer Square . . . Volunteers also offered their services in the installation of electric light.'[5] A special prayer was written for those sheltering from air raids, entitled *Our Hope in The Lord*.

Quarrymen were ordered to register with the authorities, while water standpipes were quickly set up in those areas most likely to have large numbers of refugees.

Those who did not go immediately to an air raid shelter could be fined up to £2, but increasingly, people wanted to see the enemy being shot down.

Conditions inside many of the shelters were far from comfortable, and not always safe. Limestone is easy to cut and after exposure to sea air develops a hard skin, but until this happens, it crumbles easily. It became commonplace to have roof falls in newly cut tunnels, especially as the shelters shook under exploding bombs. In the wet seasons, mainly the spring and autumn, the walls would become moist and run with damp, even without rain as the scirocco blew across the islands. In heavy rainfall, the porous rock resulted in the tunnels flooding. Ventilation was often poor, and in many tunnels, clothing could start to grow mould in as little as a day.

It was bad enough trying to live like that, especially for those poor souls who had lost their homes and for whom the shelter was more than just a convenient temporary escape from the bombing. It was worse still for those who had to work in the shelters. These included those in the underground workshops in the dockyard, as well as those in the underground listening post at Lascaris, on the outskirts of Valletta, collecting signals intelligence of Axis moves both in Sicily and in North Africa. This was important work, stressful too, with so much depending on the ability of those involved to pick up clues to enemy intentions. Obviously, the listeners were waiting for signs that an Italian or German aerial attack was on the way, but such communication, at high frequency and *en clair* was not confined to the airmen, as it was also used by fast motor launches, including the German E-boats. Coded messages were indications that larger fleet units were at sea, or that important moves were afoot in the desert war.

---

[5] *When Malta Stood Alone.*

The position of Axis units, on the land or at sea, could also be found as in addition to intercepting messages, direction finding was also used. In so many ways, Lascaris was an offshoot of Bletchley Park.

Everyone attempted to continue as normal an existence as possible. The polo ground and golf course were turned over to food production, but otherwise a full social calendar was attempted. In order to economize on fuel, cinemas could still show films, but only the projection room had power, and film-goers had to find their own way in and out in the dark. Bars continued to ply their trade, but as stocks ran low, prices rose.

Curfews and Bans

The curfew was extended on the outbreak of hostilities from 20.30 to 05.00, on penalty of fifteen days imprisonment, but this was soon modified to allow people to move up to five yards from their doorstep. At the end of August, the morning end of the curfew was put back to 06.00, but with the concession that move-ment within a town or village was permitted up to 22.00. Then, after complaints that people could not attend early Mass before starting work, the restrictions were removed altogether within towns and villages, and shops, which at first had to close an hour before curfew time, eventually resumed their old opening hours.

Malta had the relatively high level of 585 buses for its popula-tion in 1940, although many had been commandeered by the military. There were 816 lorries and 170 vans, apart from those used by the military or by the government, and 1,875 private cars and 671 hire cars, as well as 341 motor cycles. From midnight on 13 July, hire cars, other than taxis, and private cars were banned unless with a special permit, so that immediately, almost 1,600 private cars and almost 300 hire cars were off the road. As the fuel shortages began to bite, taxis and other hire cars were banned on 13 October, while buses could only run between 05.30 and 09.00, 11.30 to 14.00, and 16.00 to 18.30. These changes caused serious inconvenience to those forced to commute due to their evacuation. Later, on 9 June, 1941, buses operating between 11.30 and 14.00 were withdrawn except at weekends, followed a month later by a warning that these too could also be withdrawn because of the large numbers of people using them! One man introduced a horse-drawn bus service between the Castile terminus in Valletta and Birkekara. The traditional horse drawn carriages, *karozzin*, reappeared, but were very expensive, and their drivers were noticeably more enthusiastic in the custom of service personnel who could both afford the higher fares and were more generous with their tips.

Most schools were closed on the outbreak of hostilities, and then re-opened in locations with quick and convenient access to shelters, but of course in many areas, the schools had been taken over as accommodation for evacuees, or by the military, or in two cases as hospitals.

There were to be 210 air raids over Malta between 11 June and the end of 1940. What was surprising was the low level of casualties during this first year of war, with few military casualties and less than 100 civilians. Part of this was due to the speedy preparation of deep underground shelters, and part also to poor accuracy by the Italians, faced with an increasingly well-coordinated AA barrage over the island.

The Forces Assemble

Despite the critical situation in the UK, on 12 August, a squadron of twelve Hurricanes had been flown to Malta off the elderly aircraft carrier HMS *Argus*. Malta had already become a base for offensive operations due to the presence of 830 Squadron of the Fleet Air Arm, although their aircraft, originally intended for training, lacked blind flying panels and long-range fuel tanks, the absence of which limited their offensive role and also made them more vulnerable.

September saw a more determined push to enhance the island's defences. On 1 September, the first convoy reached Malta, with three cargo ships and a tanker, cheered in, as so many were to be in the years ahead, by the delighted Maltese lining the battlements surrounding the Grand Harbour. Naval vessels brought another 2,000 troops to Malta by the end of the month. The RAF's strength in the island was boosted further by the arrival of 431 Flight, whose four Martin Baltimore bombers flew reconnaissance missions and whose operations greatly boosted the potential of the Mediterranean Fleet. The Baltimore was fast, and had a good range, and was soon to be the eyes of the Fleet as well as of Malta.

The state of the Mediterranean Fleet improved too, with the arrival of the brand new fast armoured aircraft carrier, HMS *Illustrious* accompanied by the recently refitted and modernized battleship *Valiant*, a sister ship of *Warspite*, and the two anti-aircraft cruisers *Calcutta* and *Coventry*. The arrival of these ships provided Cunningham with two other big advantages. The first of these was that he now had, for the first time, radar, which eased the amount of time his AA gunners had to stand to by providing early warning of an attack. The second was the arrival of the Fairey Fulmar fighter which, while slower than the Hurricane, largely due to its having a longer range and a two-man crew, then regarded as essential for naval operations, was still a big improvement over the *Eagle*'s three Sea Gladiators. The elderly biplanes had, however, acquitted themselves well, eventually accounting for eleven Italian aircraft – a tribute to the skill of their pilots.

Illustrious had also brought replacement aircraft for some of the losses suffered by Malta's 830 Naval Air Squadron and, at last, blind flying instrument panels and long-range fuel tanks to improve the capability of the Swordfish.

Attention had been paid to the defences of the Grand Harbour over and above anti-aircraft defences. For the protection of ships in the Grand Harbour, a form of boom defence had been created with a number of chains and nets positioned in the entrance. These included a double chain of cylindrical buoys and nets transferred from Alexandria after the Abyssinian crisis had passed; a guard ship, HMS *Westgate*; a second double chain linking St Elmo with the mainland; and a number of spiked rafts and underwater obstructions. Attention had also been paid to improving the anti-aircraft defences around the Grand Harbour

61

and at the airfields, with additional guns including the new 4.5-inch calibre weapons capable of shooting higher than 40,000 feet and intended to provide a box barrage to defend the port and dockyard facilities.

At first, the Italians had concentrated on high level bombing, but as summer turned to autumn, they introduced a new weapon, when on 5 September, five Junkers Ju87 dive-bombers appeared in Italian markings. This was the famous Stuka, but known to the Italians as the *Picchiatelli*. Their first raid was on Kalafrana. Further raids followed, with that on 12 September using twelve Ju87s to bomb Hal Far, and after dropping their bombs, the aircraft returned to making a strafing run across the airfield, which gave the gunners of the Royal Malta Artillery's 22nd Light AA Battery the opportunity of shooting down one of the aircraft.

An early tragedy occurred on 4 November, when a crippled British Wellington bomber crashed on to the roof of a house, trapping the occupants, parents with five children, and then splitting in two, with one portion falling down a forty-feet shaft with a surviving member of the crew. Prompt action saved the children, for which Captain Anthony Flint and Second Lieutenant Richard Lavington of the Royal West Kent Regiment were both awarded MBEs, and Constable Carmel Camilleri of the Malta Police received the George Medal for entering the shaft to save the trapped airman.

As the year-end approached, there were many reasons for being cheerful. Another convoy arrived early in October, and two convoys of six ships arrived on the night of 27 and 28th, and one more, with four ships escorted by the battleship *Malaya* and four destroyers, during December. While *Eagle* was by this time *hors de combat*, with her aviation fuel system damaged by too many near misses by Italian bombs, the night of 11–12 November saw the spectacular attack by Swordfish from *Illustrious*, augmented by six aircraft from *Eagle*, on the Italian naval base at Taranto. In little more than an hour, half of the Italian Navy's six battleships were lying on the harbour bed. The seaplane base and oil storage depot were destroyed, and several smaller warships badly damaged. All this, for the loss of just two out of the twenty-one aircraft that reached the target, and the crew of one of those was saved. This was the first time that an enemy fleet had been crippled by aircraft flying from an aircraft carrier, and marked the end of the age of the battleship. The lessons were not lost on another navy, far away in the east, for although the Imperial Japanese Navy had war-gamed its attack on Pearl Harbor, it now had confirmation that such an attack was indeed possible.

The attack on Taranto had been such a success partly because of poor reconnaissance by the *Regia Aeronautica*, and because of assumptions by the Italian Admiralty, *Supermarina*, that any British naval forces in the Mediterranean were trailing their cloaks in a desperate hope of drawing the Italian Navy into a major naval engagement. No one seemed to have been unduly concerned about the high attrition rate amongst Italian reconnaissance aircraft as they were shot down by the Fleet Air Arm's Fairey Fulmar fighters.

While the aircraft from *Illustrious* had been carrying out their exacting task, the Italians had also suffered an attack by the Mediterranean Fleet's cruisers, in part to distract the Italians from the developing attack on Taranto. Force H had also been involved, approaching the Italian coastline, and it was this force that the Italian Admiralty, *Supermarina*, had known about. Again they had assumed that the Royal Navy was 'trailing its cloak', once again hoping to tempt the Italian battle fleet out to sea. Force H had included the aircraft carrier HMS *Ark Royal*, but could not give additional weight to the raid on Taranto because its aircraft would have been vulnerable, with a long flight over Sicily and the toe of Italy to the target. There was another problem with *Ark Royal*; she had been built to provide the maximum size of ship within the limits of the Washington Naval Treaty of 1922, and in doing so, armour protection had been sacrificed. Her flight deck was so thin that on one occasion two 20-lb practice bombs fell off an aircraft as it landed and punched holes in the flight deck! The First Sea Lord in London, Dudley Pound, was fully aware of this weakness. Indeed, at the time of the Munich crisis, Pound had believed that any attack on Taranto would be best provided by shore-based aircraft, and that if a carrier's aircraft were used, it would be the ship's one blow at the enemy before she was either withdrawn for her own safety, or sunk by the enemy.

At this time, the situation in the Mediterranean was even beginning to look hopeful, and in stark contrast to the defeats elsewhere that had left the British Empire facing the combined might of Germany and Italy on its own. Malta had already become an offensive base for the Fleet Air Arm and the Royal Air Force; it now became a base for submarines. This was not without its difficulties, since most of the necessary supplies had been taken to Alexandria, but submarines operated from Gibraltar to Malta overloaded with torpedoes and other equipment until stocks were built up.

While the Italian Army in North Africa had invaded Egypt on 13 September, its advance had been held by General Wavell's forces, despite being the weaker in numbers. As the year ended, it was Wavell who was advancing.

In Malta, food seemed to be relatively plentiful as the year neared its close, and bars that had been closed were re-opened. In the areas most at risk from air raids, schools even re-opened.

Finally, as if to set the seal on the whole business, Cunningham dared take his flagship, *Warspite*, to Malta, where she steamed into the Grand Harbour during the early afternoon of 20 December, band playing, and crowds of Maltese cheering wildly. It had been the first visit of the ship since May.

'Our reception was touchingly overwhelming,' Cunningham wrote later. 'It was good to know that they realized that though the fleet could not use Malta for the time being, we had them well in mind . . .

'I went all over the dockyard next morning with the Vice-Admiral and was mobbed by crowds of excited workmen singing 'God Save the King' and 'Rule Britannia'. I had difficulty in preventing myself from being carried around . . .'[6]

[6] *A Sailor's Odyssey: The Autobiography of Admiral of the Fleet Viscount Cunningham of Hyndhope.*

VI

ONSLAUGHT FROM
THE SKIES

At the start of 1941, the outlook was hopeful. Four convoys had got through the previous year, and the island's fighting capability had been enhanced, not only by the reconnaissance activities of the Martin Baltimores, but also by sixteen Vickers Wellington bombers and two squadrons of Blenheims. Fighter defences were still inadequate, at just sixteen Hurricanes, but the bombers and 830 Squadron's Swordfish had bombed Bari, Brindisi and Taranto. The presence of the Wellingtons meant that the Italian Navy, having deserted Taranto for Naples, was still at the mercy of British air power. Damage to a battleship and a cruiser at Naples was proof enough, although, given the size of bombs at the time, conventional bombers could only damage, but not sink, a battleship as the bombs bounced off the armour plating on the decks and the large calibre gun turrets.

Not only was Malta becoming a base for offensive operations against the enemy, as the Admiralty had believed it would, it had also become a listening post, intercepting enemy communications and a link in the Ultra network, feeding information through Bletchley Park now that the German Enigma codes had been broken.

The dockyard was back in working order, although there were few warships in such an exposed position. The Italians had not even attempted an invasion. The much feared gas attacks had not materialized.

The feeling of surprise that the Italians had not invaded was shared by Berlin. The assumption by the Germans when Mussolini had belatedly rushed to join them was that he had a secret plan, a master stroke, to give him domination of the Mediterranean, including the invasion of Malta and possibly the French territories in North Africa as well. When nothing happened, a sense of anti-climax and missed opportunity had set in. It soon transpired that Mussolini's strategy was based on the assumption that following the fall of France, the British Government would sue for peace, and in the negotiations that would certainly follow, Mussolini wanted a seat at the conference table where he could extract the maximum territorial benefit from the situation for Italy's benefit. When the British continued fighting, and indeed showed every intention of intensifying the fighting, Mussolini found himself without a coherent strategy. When Italy's invasion of Egypt failed miserably, and his forces failed in Yugoslavia and Greece, Mussolini needed the Germans to help him out.

The Germans had watched with amazement and scorn at the destruction inflicted on the Italian fleet at Taranto. Losing half a country's battleships in a single night without a major fleet action taking place was unthinkable!

An appreciation of the strategic situation by the *Regia Navale* early in 1941, found that they had effectively lost control of the Sicily Channel and were barely able to use ports in Sicily, while they could not safely put warships into Taranto or Naples. Their forces in North Africa were under pressure from Wavell, while their main supply port at Tripoli was under attack and convoys between Italy and North Africa were subjected to repeated attacks by air and by sea. The coastal shipping routes off North Africa and the approaches to Tripoli were dangerous due to magnetic mines.

Now Mussolini wanted German help.

The Germans Take Over

Hitler and his generals could see that the Italian position was far weaker than they could have imagined. Having expended so much effort for so little cost in northern Europe, and having achieved so much, Hitler did not want his plans to be undermined by Italian failure, which would leave southern Europe as a soft underbelly. Staying at the Berghof in January, Hitler decided that he could not let Mussolini throw away the prestige of the Axis and the all-conquering German forces. Admiral Raeder pressed for an invasion of Malta, Hitler consented, but only after the Soviet Union had been invaded and defeated.

It was clear that if the Balkans were to be secured, German forces would have to do it. It was equally clear that if the British Army in North Africa was to be defeated, ultimately taking the Suez Canal, German forces would have to do that as well. The delay caused to the invasion of the Soviet Union by having to take Yugoslavia and Greece was to lead directly to the complete failure of German ambitions in the East.

First, however, Malta must be neutralized. Before that, the Mediterranean Fleet would have to be crippled, and to do this, the priority had to be the destruction of its most valuable asset, the aircraft carrier *Illustrious*.

The Germans wasted little time. Over the New Year, the Luftwaffe moved General Geissler's Tenth Air Corps, *Fliegerkorps X*, from Poland to Sicily. This was a battle-hardened force, numerically far smaller than the *Regia Aeronautica*'s 2,000 or more aircraft, but it had considerable experience in anti-shipping operations earlier during the Norwegian campaign. The Luftwaffe had its weaknesses. These included the absence until late in the war of heavy bombers, and although an autonomous air force, it was also committed, like the Russians, to close support of ground forces rather than true strategic air power as understood by the Royal Air Force and the United States Army Air Force. Nevertheless, the Luftwaffe, with its professional and experienced commanders, understood and believed in the concentration of power: the Tenth Air Corps, situated in Sicily, just sixty miles from Malta, was more powerful than the combined RAF and Fleet Air Arm strength in the Mediterranean, scattered over more than 2,000 miles from Gibraltar to Alexandria.

Geissler had 150 Heinkel He111 and Junkers Ju88 twin-engined medium bombers and the same number of Junkers Ju87 Stuka dive-bombers, as well as fifty Messerschmitt Bf109 fighters. Many have suggested that it was moved primarily to attack Malta, but its first priority, agreed with the *Regia Aeronautica*, would be British shipping, and especially the Mediterranean Fleet, with *Illustrious* as the prime target. Malta was second on the list, followed by the base at Alexandria. In addition, both air forces would sow mines in the Suez Canal and the Grand Harbour as well as in the approaches to both.

These plans had been decided with typical German thoroughness and a clear understanding of the order of priorities. It was understood that the raids on Alexandria and the mining of the Suez Canal would probably need to await the occupation of Crete. Most Luftwaffe aircraft were short in range and there were limits to the trade-off between fuel and the warload of bombs or mines if an effective punch was to be landed on the enemy.

It was this force that was to do so much to make the British presence in the Mediterranean barely tenable. It was also to show that Pound had been remarkably prescient in his predictions for the lifespan of an aircraft carrier in the Mediterranean once hostilities had started. For Malta, it was to be the start of a difficult year, and one in which those living on the island would come to understand the true force of modern air power.

Nevertheless, the next instalment in the war around and over Malta owed as much to British bad luck as it did to German thoroughness.

Operation Excess

The autumn and early winter of 1940 had seen convoys brought through to Malta at a reasonable frequency. At the end of December, another convoy was prepared. The usual practice was for Mediterranean convoys to sail from the UK through the Bay of Biscay to Gibraltar.

The convoy known as Operation Excess was no exception, steaming from the UK to Gibraltar in company with a far larger convoy for the Cape. There were five fast cargo ships, of which one, the *Essex*, carried 4,000 tons of ammunition, twelve Hawker Hurricane fighters disassembled and in crates, and 3,000 tons of seed potatoes for Malta. The other four were intended for Alexandria. The convoy sailed from the UK in December. On Christmas Day, while the convoy was still on its first stage, the passage to Gibraltar, the German heavy cruiser *Hipper* was sighted, and the convoy scattered. Force H left Gibraltar to provide support. Meanwhile, one of the heavy escorts, the elderly battleship *Renown*, was damaged by the heavy seas and was delayed in Gibraltar for repairs. The convoy reached the safety of Gibraltar without any further interference from the Germans, but one of the ships for Alexandria had been driven ashore in the bad weather, and had to be abandoned.

It was not until 6 January 1941, that the small convoy was finally able to steam eastwards from Gibraltar. The delay was to have serious consequences. As with the arrangements made for the arrival of *Illustrious*, Operation Excess was to involve both Force H and the Mediterranean Fleet, with Force H covering the convoy as far as Sicily, after which protection would pass to the Mediterranean Fleet.

On 7 January 1941, the Mediterranean Fleet sailed from Alexandria to meet the convoy.

Convoy protection was at its best when enemy ships could be kept well away, and to discourage the *Regia Navale*, Malta-based Wellington medium bombers raided Naples on 8 January, finding two battleships, the *Cesare* and the *Vittorio Veneto* there, and managed to damage the former, persuading the Italians to withdraw both ships northwards.

Once again, the Italians relied on air power to carry the war to their enemy. They sent ten Savoia Marchetti SM79s to bomb the convoy, although with little success and lost two aircraft to the *Ark Royal*'s Fulmar fighters.

The handover date was fixed for dawn on 10 January 1941, although in reality this meant most of Force H leaving the convoy at dusk on 9 January, with the exception of the cruisers *Gloucester* and *Southampton* and two destroyers, which were detached from the main force and sent with the convoy through the Sicilian Narrows in brilliant moonlight. They were challenged by a signal station on the Italian island of Pantellaria, and in changing course, they cut mine cables with their paravanes, being lucky not to explode any of them.

Had the convoy been able to keep to its original schedule, all might have been well, with a safe handover a couple of days before the end of the year. The arrival of *Fliegerkorps X* in Sicily was known to British intelligence, largely due to the signals monitoring station at Lascaris in Malta. What was not immediately apparent was that the *Fliegerkorps X*'s prime target was not Malta, for that unsinkable aircraft carrier could wait, but *Illustrious*. It was clear to the Germans that the ship and her aircraft would be a menace to Axis shipping in the Mediterranean, but with her out of the way, they could take their time over Malta.

Fliegerkorps X included many of the Luftwaffe's most experienced anti-shipping aircrew. On the broad reaches of the North Atlantic, such work was left to flying boats and the long-range Focke-Wulf Fw200 Condors and Junkers Ju290s, for which the Fulmar could prove a match, but over the 'Med', this was for the more manoeuvrable medium-bombers and dive-bombers.

As the Mediterranean Fleet steamed west, all seemed to be going well. One of 806's Fulmars shot down an Italian reconnaissance aircraft. The evening before the rendezvous, Italian bombers escorted by fighters had failed to find them. As usual, Italian air attacks had been poorly coordinated and sporadic.

Many had felt concern that *Illustrious* would be taking a risk operating within range of such a powerful force of enemy aircraft, and no doubt it had been made clear that the ship's aircraft could cover the convoy from a distance. They were all painfully aware that the handover would take place in broad daylight, and that on her last excursion into the area, *Illustrious* had enjoyed the benefit of darkness. Cunningham, nevertheless, was insistent that the carrier should be with the main body of the Fleet, mainly because of the beneficial effect her presence always had on morale aboard the rest of the ships. He had also concluded that aircraft carriers were at their safest when able to benefit from the protection of other ships, something that was to be proven during the war in the Pacific.

The morning of 10 January dawned clear and bright. It was not without incident, as a destroyer was seen by those aboard *Illustrious* to strike a mine that blew off her bows. The routine of flying off aircraft continued throughout the morning, with Swordfish on reconnaissance and anti-submarine patrols while Fulmars flew on CAP, combat air patrols.

Around 12.30, two Italian torpedo bombers made an unsuccessful attack on the carrier, missing her as her Commanding Officer, Captain Denis Boyd, successfully 'combed' the torpedoes, manoeuvring his ship so that they raced past. The attack had the effect of drawing the patrolling Fulmars down to low level. Relief Fulmars were being readied for take-off on the carrier's flight deck, so that the earlier patrol could return to the ship, when the carrier's radar spotted two large formations of aircraft flying from the direction of Sicily. Even as the Fulmars struggled to get off the flight deck, the Germans attacked, with forty-three Junkers Ju87 dive-bombers, the dreaded Stuka, giving the Mediterranean Fleet its first taste of the deadly accuracy of dive-bombing. One of the Fulmars was shot down as it took off, its pilot escaping but the observer, or navigator, behind him was killed outright.

The first bomb narrowly missed the ship, one of three near-misses that day, but over the next ten minutes, no less than six 1,000-lb bombs struck *Illustrious*. Of all the aircraft carriers operational during the Second World War, only *Illustrious* and her five sisters could take such punishment with their armoured flight decks and hangar decks, but the armour plating was meant to resist 500-lb bombs, and the lifts that moved the aircraft between flight deck and hangar deck were not armoured, and bombs fell through these. The hangar deck contained aircraft, many armed and with fuel in their tanks. It was also the action station for all off-duty aircrew, and many of them had assembled there. The bombs exploded in this space, the effect enhanced by the armoured top, sides and bottom of the hangar deflecting the blast through the aircraft and the naval airmen. Within seconds

71

of the first bomb entering the hangar, it was a blazing inferno. What one naval officer described as the 'vagaries of blast' meant that often those close to an exploding bomb survived, those further away were killed. One of two men in conversation had his head blown off, the other had to push him so that the corpse would lie down. An innovation in *Illustrious* was the fire-proof screens designed to divide the hangar in case of a fire. The screens shattered and their shrapnel added to that of the exploding bombs and ruptured aircraft. The ship's Master at Arms plunged into the hangar intending to drag at least one person to safety. They found his charred corpse the following day. The wardroom, the name for a warship's officers' mess, was no safer. A bomb crashed through into it, leaving barely a handful of survivors. Many of those who died in the wardroom had been wounded, then drowned as it was flooded by the water being used to fight the fires.

One of the ship's AA batteries had been put out of action by a bomb that had dropped through it without exploding, killing the gun crew, and plunging into the sea before exploding. All of the remaining guns continued firing. Aboard, everyone was doing what they could. Boyd manoeuvred the ship to avoid bombs before her steering was crippled, others led firefighting and damage control teams, while down in the boiler and engine rooms, temperatures soared to 140 degrees Fahrenheit while men struggled to keep the ship fully operational.

The ship was a blazing, crippled wreck. Boyd refused permission to flood her magazines while the threat of bombing remained. Had a bomb exploded in the magazines, or had one penetrated her aviation fuel system with its high octane gasoline, or had the pipelines carrying aviation fuel been damaged by the mining effect of near misses, the ship could have been blown apart, as happened to more than one carrier later in the war.

It took three hours before *Illustrious* was able to head for Malta, proceeding at just 17 knots, a little more than half her usual speed. Those of her aircraft in the air either headed for Malta or ditched. The fighters were welcome additions to those based ashore on the island, and their arrival was the first clue that something had gone wrong. Naval headquarters in Malta knew of the carrier's desperate plight, but could do nothing to help other than alert the dockyard to her arrival.

Meanwhile, the crippled carrier was attacked again by another twenty-five dive-bombers, and here Boyd's refusal to flood the magazines was fully vindicated, as her AA guns flashed into life. Her Fulmar fighters had refuelled at Hal Far, and returned to provide air cover, shooting down at least six Stukas.

It was not until 21.45 that evening that *Illustrious* finally limped into a darkened Grand Harbour.

Immediately, dockyard workers and naval personnel swarmed aboard to see what they could do, helping to douse the remaining fires, taking the wounded to hospital ashore. The grim hunt for the bodies of those who had not survived started the following morning. Many were missing, presumed dead, and at least one wounded man was believed to have been blown overboard by an explosion and lost while awaiting emergency treatment. The hangar deck was a blackened pit, reeking of cordite, burnt fuel and burnt flesh, with charred corpses plastered against the bulkheads. Identification was difficult.

For the living, life aboard the carrier was grim. Apart from the smell of cordite, burnt fuel and charred flesh, much of the accommodation had been destroyed, and most had lost their clothing and other personal items. They were exhausted.

The operation had not been completely in vain. The cargo ship *Essex* had reached her destination. Malta would be fed and reinforced. The three ships for Alexandria were also on their way.

Many have since questioned the wisdom of exposing *Illustrious* to such heavy aerial attack. Cunningham believed her presence was good for the morale of the Mediterranean Fleet, which still carried memories of being exposed to aerial attack without fighter cover, even the fighter cover that could be offered by the relatively slow Fairey Fulmar. Others maintain that she could have provided the fighter cover from a distance, and would have been far less exposed had she done so. Yet, there was another strand to Cunningham's argument for having the ship where she was on that fateful morning. The convoy had to be passed through, and so his major fleet units had to be there. Cunningham was probably one of the few naval commanders to appreciate so early in the war the value of having major fleet units operating with an aircraft carrier, so that she could benefit from the collective force of their AA fire. The truth may be either that the aerial attack really was so overwhelming that nothing could be done, or that tactics were still evolving and that the major fleet units were not close enough to provide the necessary cover. There is the inescapable feeling that aircraft carrier deck layouts of the day meant that two capable carriers would have been needed to provide the required level of fighter cover, something that was beyond the resources available to the Royal Navy so early in the war.

The *Illustrious* Blitz

The aircraft carrier *Illustrious* had survived, but was still in deadly danger. Now, so too was everyone anywhere near her as she lay alongside the Parlatorio Wharf in French Creek.

At daybreak on a dull, overcast morning, with the threat of rain, hundreds of Maltese dockyard workers swarmed aboard, ready to do all that was necessary to get the ship seaworthy. There would be no time for the thorough repair and refit that she desperately needed, and for which she would have to leave for safer waters. Meanwhile, her officers and senior ratings set about compiling a list of those who had been killed. After breakfast, the ship's company was mustered on the flight deck by divisions for a roll call. Amidst the noise and bustle of a busy shipyard, names were called out, and whenever no one answered, there was a moment's pause, then a chief petty officer (the naval equivalent of a staff sergeant) would ask if anyone knew anything. Sometimes, someone would answer that the person concerned was on watch, or killed or wounded.

No one needed to be told that the Luftwaffe would want to finish the job. It was a race against time as a ship in harbour was a sitting duck, virtually out of her element.

Illustrious was to spend two weeks in Malta. The first two days

74

were overcast with low cloud that kept the Axis aircraft away. The raids started on 13 January, and became a daily occurrence after that, with the Luftwaffe and the *Regia Aeronautica* operating jointly to provide what became known in Malta as 'the *Illustrious* blitz'. At first, once the air raid sirens sounded ashore, the ship's company uncovered the guns, while the dockyard workers, and those of the ship's company not needed, scrambled from their working place to the caves in nearby Senglea being used as air raid shelters. Getting from deep in the bowels of a large warship to safety ashore was no easy task.

The air raids reached a new peak for Malta on 16 January, described by many as the first really heavy bombing raid. The Luftwaffe sent forty-four Stukas, seventeen Ju88s and ten Messerschmitt Me110s, escorted by ten *Regia Aeronautica* Fiat CR42 and some Macchi 200 fighters. The Stuka pilots dived through intense anti-aircraft fire, with many flying below the high fortress walls of Valletta to deliver their bombs accurately. This first attack took just a few minutes, but was followed within fifteen minutes by a second wave. *Illustrious* suffered yet another hit during the first attack, but near misses left the dockyard around her burning and cratered.

A bomb hit the engine room of the cargo ship *Essex*, leaving fifteen dead and twenty-three wounded. Had it hit her cargo, the 4,000 tons of ammunition would have exploded and destroyed Valletta, the dockyard, the celebrated Three Cities, including the town of Senglea on the opposite side of the Grand Harbour, and, of course, *Illustrious* as well.

Aboard the carrier, the blasts of exploding bombs swept away the ladders, scaffolding and tarpaulins shrouding the ship. It was not just the intensity of the attack; the bombs were heavier too, with the Stukas struggling to lift 2,500-lb bombs, taking ninety minutes to reach 10,000 feet. The bomb that hit the ship caused further damage, and three near-misses fell into French Creek, flinging her against the Parlatorio Wharf.

Ashore, fifty-three Maltese civilians were killed, partly because of the intensity of the attacks, and partly because the poor performance of the Italian bombers had caused a false sense of security. In Valletta's Old Mint Street, bombs hit a tall block of flats, bringing it crashing to the ground. On the other side of the Grand Harbour, there was more serious damage, with the peninsula city of Senglea suffering the loss of no less than 300 houses. Rescue attempts were hampered as streets were filled with rubble, often more than ten feet high.

The attack was not without losses for the Luftwaffe, with ten aircraft shot down, with honours equally divided between the AA defences and the fighters.

With the arrival of the Luftwaffe, everything had changed. There was also some excitement about an attack. The full energy of the attack reached beyond the dockyard gates to the ancient city of Vittoriosa, as buildings, including the old auberges of the Knights of Malta, were reduced to rubble. In one especially tragic case, some forty people, sheltering in the sacristy of the Convental Parish Church of St Lawrence, were killed as a large bomb collapsed the building. The cost to the Maltese was great. In Vittoriosa, both churches had been destroyed, the second on 19 January, and the priest was forced to use a small chapel at the police station

'Only dire necessity forced us to use the shelters,' said Mrs Queenie Lee. 'Attacks were too exciting to miss. We groaned when our Hurricanes couldn't overtake the Messerschmitt 109; we cheered ourselves hoarse when gunners or fighters found their target, and blazing machines hurtled to earth followed by swaying parachutists.'[1]

Mrs Queenie Lee was the wife of a naval officer who lived in Malta for four years, two-and-a-half of them under wartime conditions. She was involved with war work, but her main job was as a teacher at the Royal Naval Dockyard School.

'The Germans set up a steady timetable of raids, dawn, midday and dusk, sometimes with a few extras thrown in . . . .'[2]

After the raid, it was decided to take all non-essential personnel, about 1,000 men, off the ship, leaving a skeleton crew

[1] IWM Sound Archive, Accession No.1172.
[2] IWM Sound Archive, Accession No.1172.

aboard. Even the AA gunners went to the temporary accommodation at RAF Hal Far as the Army wanted to test a new box barrage system, and found that the ship's AA fire got in the way.

There was some consolation that some ten aircraft had been shot down, without any corresponding losses amongst the Malta-based Hurricanes and Fulmars.

On 17 January, the Germans sent reconnaissance aircraft, and the next day, attacked the airfields, hoping to crush the troublesome fighter defences that rose to meet every air raid. On 19 January, the bombers returned to the carrier again. Another near miss exploded on the bottom of the creek damaging the hull and making more work before she could sail.

Remaining aboard, the engineering commander, Lieutenant Commander 'Pincher' Martin, worked unceasingly to repair the steering and get her ready for sea, for which he was later awarded the DSC. The engineers working on her were confident that they could get her back to sea since the engines were in reasonable shape, despite the battering that *Illustrious* had suffered.

She had not been abandoned by the Mediterranean Fleet, as the Australian light cruiser, HMS *Perth*, had stayed behind to provide extra AA firepower. They say in the Royal Navy that 'no good deed goes unpunished'. *Perth* was punished for her loyalty when a near-miss caused damage below her waterline during the raid of 16 January.

'Her officers and men came in and out of the tunnel (the dockyard air raid shelter) and the surgery,' recalled Mrs Norman, a navy wife, one of the few British civilians left behind in Malta.

> Their faces looked lined and grimy. They were dressed in old boiler overalls, in grey flannel trousers and sweaters – any odd garment they had managed to save from the wrecks of the cabins . . . It seemed impossible that *Illustrious* would put to sea again, but she was in Malta dockyard – the dockyard that just could not be defeated . . .[3]

[3] *For Gallantry: Malta's Story.*

The raids cost the Luftwaffe and *Regia Aeronautica* dearly. Malta's Hurricanes, reinforced with 806's surviving Fulmars, and the island's heavy AA defences, exacted a heavy price. Lieutenant Colonel Paul-Werner Hozzel, at that time a major in the Luftwaffe, later recalled that each day he expected to lose five or six of his best crews. One of his two squadrons lost all of its original aircrew during this period.

During the raid of 18 January, almost 100 enemy aircraft raided Hal Far and the village of Birzebugia nearby, killing and injuring many civilians.

Sunday, 19 January was another heavy raid, but it was another costly day for the Axis, with the Germans admitting losing ten aircraft while the Italians lost four, but the British claimed thirty-nine lost, another five probables and nine damaged. Seventeen of the Axis losses were attributed to the RAF's Hurricanes and the Fleet Air Arm's Fulmars, while just two British fighters were lost. The confirmed losses were not the total, as the *Regia Aeronautica* sent a Cant Z506 with Red Cross markings to patrol the sea between Malta and Sicily, looking for ditched aircrew.

Away from the ship, those ashore had no idea of the progress being made in getting *Illustrious* seaworthy. It was not until they were recalled during the afternoon of 23 January, that they realized that she was ready. Under cover of darkness, with the ship darkened and some repair stages still hanging over her sides, she left the Grand Harbour quietly and secretly. The Governor, Sir William Dobbie, was holding a session of the Council of Malta, the island's governing body, when a servant entered and drew the black out curtains before switching on the lights. Someone said: 'She's off – and safe.'

Illustrious reached Alexandria on 26 January, on the first stage in her journey to the still neutral United States and a complete refit at Norfolk, Virginia.

In London, a grateful War Cabinet sent a message of thanks to General Dobbie, who responded in his customary manner, 'By God's help, Malta will not weaken.' He didn't forget to broadcast his own appreciation to the people of Malta.

'The Dockyard is continuing, and will continue to carry on

giving their best work,' signalled Vice Admiral Sir Wilbraham Ford in response to the thanks and congratulations of the Admiralty. 'Let them All Come!'[4]

Meanwhile, the following month, February 1941, one of Hitler's brightest generals, Erwin Rommel, was warning Berlin that 'without Malta, the Axis will end by losing control of North Africa'. The noose was tightening.

After the *Illustrious* blitz had caused a further exodus from the towns in early 1941, and had also resulted in further great loss to the housing stock, people were asked to accommodate the refugees and the homeless. Initially, this was on a voluntary basis, but by the spring, those householders reckoned by the authorities to be using less than twenty-five per cent of the space available for habitation were required to set aside a room for a proportionate number of refugees. Then small families were encouraged to amalgamate with friends or relatives, sparing a house for the needy and avoiding having strangers billeted on them. The Communal Feeding Service was reactivated under the renewed pressures and a mobile canteen introduced.

There was some easing of the air raids from February 1941, with half of *Fliegerkorps X* moved from Sicily to North Africa to provide Rommel's *Afrika Korps* with the air cover it so desperately needed if it was to make an impact in the desert war and reverse the Italian losses. In March 1941, a convoy of four merchant ships managed to reach Malta, although two were badly damaged in subsequent bombing. The Hurricanes managed to shoot down nine dive-bombers during these aerial attacks, with another four being accounted for by the Grand Harbour's AA defences.

Meanwhile, the authorities, in reality the Governor's Advisory Council, introduced conscription in February 1941, with all males required to register for national service between the ages of sixteen and sixty-five, while within this broad band, there was military service for those aged between eighteen and forty-five years. This move stressed the importance of the direction of labour to those industries and areas of activity that required it

[4] *A Sailor's Odyssey.*

most. It also ensured that labour was in the right place at the right time, with gangs of stevedores ready to unload the supply ships as they arrived, and in between convoy arrivals, working elsewhere, filling in bomb craters on runways and roads, helping to demolish damaged buildings, and, of course, helping to build and then extend air raid shelters cut out of the soft limestone rock that was everywhere in Malta, and which was never more than a few inches beneath the thin soil in the fields. There were the inevitable, and necessary exceptions, including dockyard workers and farmers, quarry men and stonecutters, and government employees but, by the year-end, almost 4,000 men had been conscripted

During March 1941, the air raid precautions were eased, so that those not immediately in a danger area could continue with their work or their journey if they judged it safe during an alert, but in giving greater freedom with one hand, the authorities contrived to take away freedom with the other, with a much stricter curfew between 21.00 and 06.30 *even within towns and villages* other than to go to and from an air raid shelter. These changes provoked much public protest, especially since many judged that the police and ARP personnel were keeping them confined to air raid shelters for far longer than was necessary. This eventually became another factor in reduced use of air raid shelters as people preferred the comfort of their own homes and, most importantly, the chance to eat.

VII

GRIM REALITY

Within days, 1941, the year that had seemed to start so well, had turned into what one present described as a living hell. The worst of the raids disappeared with the departure of the *Illustrious*, but the Luftwaffe was to be an ever present menace, and this time marked the start of the darkest twenty months in the history of Malta. The necessary and successful raid on Taranto, coupled with Italian failings in Yugoslavia, Greece and in North Africa had forced the Germans to take an active interest in the Mediterranean. It was no longer '*Mare Nostrum*', 'Our Sea', to the Italians, as they held it only by courtesy of the Führer.

The Germans and Italians together had killed fifty-three Maltese civilians on 16 January. The Germans sometimes showed exceptional honour in their approach to the civilian population, but at other times did attack targets which they must have known were predominantly, if not entirely, civilian. They had after all inflicted heavy losses by bombing Rotterdam after the Dutch had declared it an open city in order to avoid civilian casualties. They had also bombed Guernsey and Jersey even though British forces had departed and surrender signs were displayed.

One indication of noble conduct by the Luftwaffe, or at least by a single German pilot, was seen on Gozo, which presented few worthwhile targets other than the ferry to Marfa on Malta. On one passage northwards to Gozo, the crowded ferry was spotted by a Luftwaffe aircraft, which remained in the area until it arrived at Mgarr. The aircraft remained around while the passengers disembarked, then the pilot pulled back his canopy and swooped low over the ship, waving his arm to show that everyone was to stay well clear, before returning to sink it. There were no casualties.

Of course, there is another side to this tale. Just how could an enemy aircraft take such a relaxed approach to its work? Quite simply, Malta's defences against air attack were overstretched. Just six Hurricanes and three Fulmars remained by this time, although some believe that there was still one remaining Gladiator. At least Grand Harbour had worthwhile AA defences. Sixteen Axis aircraft were shot down during the first three months of the year, while the air raids were at their worst.

'That was when the struggle for existence began,' recalled Mrs Queenie Lee.

> Not at first in the food sense – but in the problem of finding the time to eat. The Germans kept up a steady timetable of raids – dawn – midday – dusk and an occasional extra thrown in. When the day's work and meals had to be fitted in, these raids didn't leave much time to spare, but we've all discovered that bombs go down better when one is well fed. So we got up at dawn, and made sure of our breakfast before they came.[1]

Fortunately, the air raid shelter programme was advancing well by this time.

'By now we began to learn that two and more bombs can and do fall in the same place, and most people began to seek shelters under sixty feet of rock,' Queenie Lee continued.

> Many of the bigger ones had private cubicles. While the evening raid was going on, the mother and family would sit in the main shelter, while father chipped and chipped until a small alcove was cut out. Then mother and family moved into this and a shrine was placed in a niche. From that time, the family continued underground during the raids, whatever had been interrupted above ground.

[1] IWM Sound Archive, Accession No.1172.

Mother brought vegetables to prepare, while father continued to chip and chip.

Finally a comfortable room was ready and a few necessities were brought in. When night raids came in addition to daytime raids these underground homes were almost permanent dwellings. Even when paraffin was severely rationed the light at the shrine in the main shelter was kept burning by very small contributions from each family. Not everybody had these cubicles – much depended on types of rock and the numbers accommodated. As more and more homes were destroyed, hundreds of people had to live permanently in a hole in the rock.[2]

The soft yellow Maltese limestone was easy to work, and once exposed to the sea air its surface became hard. Even so, when hit by large bombs, it trembled and vibrated alarmingly, even though it didn't give way. One dockyard foreman described the feeling of the rock trembling as like 'a thousand snakes running around my stomach'. In the end, more than thirteen miles of shelter were dug.

On one occasion, fifty dive-bombers attacked a civilian evacuation camp. A surprise attack was followed by two more, the last coming as a number of people had left the air raid shelter and were helping to clear up the debris from the first two raids. There were about ten people caught in the open. There was no time to return to the safety of the air raid shelter, so they immediately split into twos and jumped into trenches, lying face downwards.

'Just as the familiar whistles and dives began, a small dog leapt into the trench, flew over the top of us and fixed himself between us and the walls of earth,' remembers Queenie.

I was afraid he would go mad with fright and bite us so I tried to calm him by patting him and speaking to him. His fur was literally standing on end and as stiff as hedgehog's

[2] IWM Sound Archive, Accession No.1172.

quills. I can feel it now. But I think his fear helped me to forget my own and saved me from abject terror as about 100 to 150 high explosives rained down around us. We all came out alive, although one trench was lost in a thirty foot crater.[3]

The heavy air raids continued by day and by night. The main targets remained around the Grand Harbour and the airfields, with an especially heavy raid on the runways on 5 March 1941. Attention was also paid to Marsamxett between Valletta and Sliema, with further damage to both, while magnetic mines were laid in the approaches to the Grand Harbour and Marsaxlokk. Unused bombs were often jettisoned over residential areas. Now careful to seek shelter from the air raids, there was little loss of life amongst the Maltese civilian population, but the damage was immense. Between raids, volunteers searched for unexploded bombs. The arrival of the Luftwaffe meant more than just more accurate bombing, and more frequent raids. It also meant that a new weapon of terror was used against Malta for the first time; the parachute mine, fused to explode some time after being dropped, but of course, no one knew for just how long that time would be!

Typically, when it exploded a mine could open a crater twenty-five feet across, but just five feet deep. In several cases, mines blew the roofs off houses, leaving the walls intact. There were other dangers, for the more commercially minded were anxious to catch hold of the parachute, since at a time of growing short-ages, a skilful seamstress could turn one of these into bed sheets. Often, local people did not recognize a mine for what it was, since magnetic mines intended for the harbours, often fell on the land and these often looked like some form of water tank, and it became a priority to keep the inquisitive, and the acquisitive, away! At night, observers could mistake a parachute mine for an airman from an aircraft that had been shot down, and would rush to the scene. The fact was that Malta was now being plagued by

[3] IWM Sound Archive, Accession No.1172.

1. Lieutenant General Sir William Dobbie, Governor of Malta when Italy entered the Second World War   *(IWM E490E)*

2. Commander-in-Chief of the Mediterranean Fleet, Admiral Sir Andrew Cunningham, known as 'ABC' to his men, aboard his flagship, the battleship HMS *Warspite*, in harbour at Alexandria.   *(IWM GM786)*

3. An early priority was to create as many air raid shelters as possible; fortunately the Malta sandstone was easy to work.   *(IWM GM906)*

4. Life in the air raid shelters was crowded, especially for those who had lost their homes and had to make the shelter their dwelling. *(IWM GM189)*

5. Eventually many private rooms became quite sizeable and furniture was moved in. *(IWM GM186)*

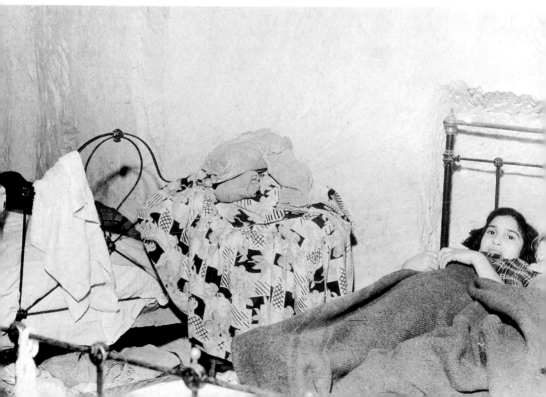

6. Many tried to make their own little alcove; here a rock cutter is hard at work. *(IWM GM178)*

7. Extensive bomb damage after the Baracca was hit is cleared up by soldiers. *(IWM GM285)*

8. The view across Grand Harbour from Valletta, with a fierce fire burning beyond the three cities. *(IWM GM75)*

9. Life returned to normal between the raids, presumably this was early on while there were still goods to buy in the shops. *(IWM GM418)*

10. An AA position high above Grand Harbour, with Senglea in the background.
(IWM GM946)

11. On the airfields, with the RAF having very few personnel, soldiers and sailors helped with servicing aircraft. Here an RAF Beaufort is loaded with a torpedo ready for an attack on enemy shipping. *(IWM GM1023)*

12. Troops help to prepare aircraft pens to protect parked aircraft from shrapnel, using stones from bombed buildings, while petrol cans filled with sand and stones were also often used in building these 'sangers'. *(IWM GM989)*

13. The SS *Clan Ferguson* arrives safely in Grand Harbour. Note the *dghajsas*, a popular means for seamen to get from ship to shore. *(IWM GM340)*

14. Communal living in the shelters was soon joined by communal feeding, with a queue for one of the Victory Kitchens where subscribers could collect a frugal meal either at 12.00 or 17.00 each day. *(IWM GM1746)*

15. In between convoys, supplies were brought in by submarine on the 'Magic Carpet' service, and by fast minelaying cruisers such as HMS *Welshmen*, seen here entering Grand Harbour. *(IWM GM1031)*

16. An open air Mass is held for men of the Royal Malta Artillery. *(IWM GM1253)*

17. Bombs blasted their way into the crypt of the Church of St Publius in Floriana, killing many of those sheltering there. *(IWM GM757)*

18. The end of the Opera House in Valletta. *(IWM GM663)*

19. As rescue workers sift through the rubble of a bombed home, a priest waits in case he is needed to administer the last rites. The man in the tin hat is a police officer.

(IWM GM527)

20. Many were killed
    when the Casino
    Maltese was
    blitzed.
    (IWM GM447)

21. South Street,
    Valletta, blocked
    by rubble from
    blitzed buildings.
    (IWM GM658)

22. A typical Maltese flat cart pulled by a donkey is used to remove possessions from a damaged building. *(IWM GM645)*

23. Few instances of bomb damage received higher priority than damaged water mains, essential for fire fighting and also for drinking in the hot Mediterranean summer. This is near the King's Gate in Valletta. *(IWM GM652)*

24. Lord Gort inspects bomb damage at Valletta's Porte Reale Bridge during a walking tour of the city. Closest to the camera is a Royal Naval Reserve officer. *(IWM GM1248)*

25. The Hon. Mabel Strickland, editor of the English language daily *The Times of Malta*, a daughter of Lord Strickland, who had urged the building of public air raid shelters five years before Italy entered the war. *(IWM GM2820)*

26. Buses damaged by bombs in Rabat. *(IWM GM330)*

27. As the fuel crisis began to bite, troops took to bicycles to ensure mobility. A battalion would receive less than thirty gallons of petrol a week, reserved for the quartermaster. *(IWM GM827)*

28. The lack of substantial port facilities meant that ships often had to discharge their cargo into lighters, although in this case, at least the ship's own derricks are working. *(IWM GM1068)*

29. To expedite the rapid distribution of goods away from the heavily bombed dock areas, destinations were allocated different colours, with signs by day and coloured lights by night. *(IWM GM1121)*

30. A rural supplies dump, away from the docks and the airfields that were the most frequently visited targets. *(IWM GM1128)*

31. The crippled tanker *Ohio* is helped into Grand Harbour with her precious cargo of fuel. She settled on the bottom after unloading and, after being refloated, she then broke her back at her moorings. *(IWM GM1480)*

32. An unexploded bomb is prepared for removal having been defused. *(IWM GM326)*

33. Presentation of the George Cross on 13 September, 1942. It was received on behalf of the people of Malta by the Chief Justice. *(IWM GM1587)*

mines from the air, on both the land and on the sea, with Grand Harbour and its approaches being steadily mined.

Radar Compromised

Even under these extreme pressures there could be examples of slow thinking and reluctance in adapting to changing times, and even changing needs and opportunities.

Reginald Townson recalls that the efficiency of the radar system was compromised by a still rank conscious RAF. The controller had to be a senior officer, as no one below the rank of wing commander was regarded as being experienced enough to control aircraft. Yet, it simply was not done for a wing commander to speak into a microphone to an aircraft, so this was left to a signals officer. Thus the situation was that the wing commander would pass his instruction to the signals officer, who would pass them on to an aircraft, and then the signals officer would pass the reply to the wing commander!

This charade continued even after war broke out. In Malta, the original transportable radar station was soon joined by three more with a much improved capability for catching aircraft flying at lower altitudes, although it was not until many years later and the introduction of airborne early-warning radar that the menace of very low-flying aircraft could be effectively countered. At operations control, the controllers and their staff worked on an ops table marked off with a map of the island with range rings and bearing lines, Townson believed at every ten degrees. Townson's station worked on range bearings. When the next stations were introduced, control didn't wish to change their table and replace it with one with a grid on it. This meant that the new stations had to pass their plots to the original station, that would convert them to its range and bearing and then, after this had been done, wasting precious time, pass them down to the ops room. This process would have taken minutes for every plot, and it was some time before control could be persuaded to have a grid.

The interception of incoming bomber waves while they were

still over the sea some way off Malta, later in the war would not have been possible using this system of passing plots through a central point for bearings to be allocated, before passing these on to control.

This story puts the lie to anyone who believes that the RAF, as the most junior of the three services and the one most involved with the newest means of warfare, was the least bureaucratic and most flexible!

The Easter Raids

The Axis air forces did not intend to show any respect for Easter. They celebrated Easter, 1941, by bombing for the first time the ancient capital of Mdina, the 'silent city', and completely without any military installations whatever. Some argued that it could have been hit due to its proximity to the new airfield at Ta'Qali, but the distance was sufficiently large for this to be untrue, and there was no way in which Mdina, standing on its hill overlooking the airfield, and with its walls, domed cathedral and very narrow streets, could be mistaken for anything like a military, or even an industrial or commercial, target. Easter that year saw the Germans victorious in Yugoslavia. Would Malta be next was the question? German invincibility seemed undiminished.

After Easter, there was a lull in the bombing that lasted until 27 April 1941, when a heavy daylight raid occurred. The night of 28–29 April saw another heavy raid, falling mainly on Valletta using bombs and mines. St John's Cathedral was very heavily damaged. A further raid on 29 April again struck at the capital, destroying a church, a theatre and a cinema.

On 28 April, the Dockyard Defence Battery was disbanded having given a year and 283 days of faithful service, with its role, and its guns, taken over by the now, much expanded, Royal Malta Artillery. Many of the Battery's members took up the option of joining the Royal Malta Artillery.

The death toll amongst civilians throughout that grim year varied. The total figure for January was sixty-five; February saw fifteen deaths; March, thirty; April, forty-seven; May, twenty-eight; June, five; July, forty; August, ten; September, one; October, ten; November, seven; and December, thirty-one; making a total of 289.

One raid in February had destroyed 200 houses in Valletta alone, although just three people were killed and eight injured. The homeless were given food and temporary accommodation in a Franciscan monastery until permanent accommodation could be prepared.

Many people left Valletta and the three cities to seek shelter amongst friends and relatives in the country, so that many families were grossly over-extended, with thirty or forty not unknown.

Hitler Divides His Forces

The fall in the death toll was due to more than improved defences and improved air raid shelters and better discipline in their use. Relief also came from other pressures on the Germans. Anxious to stop the British advance westward in North Africa, on 6 February, Hitler had ordered one of his best generals, Erwin Rommel, to North Africa, taking the 5th Light Division and the 15th Panzer Division, creating the famous *Afrika Korps* to confront Wavell's army. Modern warfare demands that armies need air cover, and half of *Fliegerkorps X* had been sent to North Africa. Unfortunately Wavell had been ordered to send substantial forces to Greece, weakening his grip on North Africa at a crucial stage.

A more effective move would have been to invade Malta first, but this idea was abandoned. Meanwhile, the Royal Navy had established a submarine base in Malta. The *Regia Navale* was desperate that Malta should be neutralized.

In Malta, Dobbie was anxious that the island should move to the offensive, and he ordered the Royal Navy to cut the Italian and German supply lines to Tripoli. The situation now arose where the British were attempting to attack the Axis convoys sailing north-south, while the Axis were determined to destroy British convoys sailing west-east to supply Malta. Increasingly, British forces in North Africa were receiving their supplies via the

Cape and Suez Canal. The Canal that was meant to cut the time and miles spent on voyages between Western Europe and the Gulf, India, Malaya, Singapore and Australia, was now a means of supporting North Africa, with the Mediterranean closed. The use of Malta as an offensive base was helped by the introduction of the new 'U' class of submarines, smaller than most of the other classes, but ideal for the clear waters of the Mediterranean in which, all too often, sonar is not needed to spot a submerged submarine.

The enemy air attacks intensified as winter turned to spring, and clear skies returned. The Bf109s would conduct sweeps over Malta several times a day, hoping to wear out the defending Hurricanes whom they outnumbered, or, better still, destroy the aircraft on the ground. Rather than looking for invading enemy paratroops, the parachutes seen by the Maltese were those of the Hurricane pilots after baling out. On occasion, farmers working in the fields would be machine-gunned by the Messerschmitt pilots. Air raids finally saw most of the RAF's Wellington bombers destroyed or damaged on the ground. The raids also spread beyond the communities surrounding the Grand Harbour, and in March struck at Sliema, across the Marsamxett from Valletta, in peacetime an elegant and prosperous seaside resort and dormitory town for the capital. In one raid, twenty-two inhabitants of Sliema were killed and another thirty-six injured.

Even at this difficult period, there was something over which to rejoice. On 28 March, the Battle of Cape Matapan was fought and won by the British, sinking three Italian cruisers and two destroyers. A new aircraft carrier, HMS *Formidable*, had been ordered to the Mediterranean within two days of the attack on her sister, HMS *Illustrious*, and she had eventually arrived despite the mining of the Suez Canal, with the two ships passing at Alexandria. Convoys were fought through to Malta in both February and March, with additional troops, while fighter aircraft were also flown in to replace those lost. This continued into April, with twelve Hurricanes delivered on 3 April and another twenty-three on 27 April, so that during April and May, no less than 224 Hurricanes were flown to the island. These were rare moments of success in what was probably the grimmest year of the war.

Aircraft Deliveries

In spring 1941, twenty Hawker Hurricane MkIIAs were ferried to Gibraltar aboard HMS *Argus*, and there transferred to Force H's carrier, HMS *Ark Royal*. They were flown off to Malta during the lull in the air raids on Saturday, 12 April 1941.

The arrival of the twenty Hurricanes, plus many more delivered on 8 May in crates for local assembly, meant that the RAF could now field three squadrons for the defence of Malta. The valiant 261 Squadron was disbanded into three new squadrons, with 185 at Hal Far and the other two, 126 and 249, stationed at Ta'Qali, where the officers' mess was in a hotel overlooking the airfield high up in the ramparts of Mdina. Luqa remained as the home for the bomber squadrons, with the surviving Wellingtons joined by 82 Squadron equipped with Bristol Blenheims, an aircraft that had not had a good war so far, with high loss rates in operations over enemy territory.

In May 1941, Air Vice Marshal Maynard was replaced by Air Vice Marshal Hugh Lloyd as Air Officer Commanding Malta.

By early summer 1941, there were sometimes two squadrons of Wellington bombers for night sorties against Italian and German forces, and especially against Italian ports. The Fleet Air Arm had also managed to move a second squadron of Swordfish to Malta. During one fourteen day period, between 30 June and 13 July, 1941, 122 bomber sorties were made from Malta.

Meanwhile, the Germans entered Athens on 27 April, and the invasion of Greece was completed by the end of the month, putting the Mediterranean Fleet under heavy pressure as it moved British and Greek troops in a smaller version of the Dunkirk evacuation from mainland Greece over the much longer sea distance to the island of Crete. While the Royal Navy was successful in rescuing more than 50,000 troops, once again the soldiers had lost most of their equipment. What was worse, to fulfil his pledge to defend Greece, as we have seen Churchill had ordered the necessary troops to be transferred from North Africa just as the Germans had entered this campaign. So, attacking on 31 March, a combined German and Italian army had been able to take Benghazi by 3 April and force Wavell's troops into another retreat.

Force H and the Mediterranean Fleet were to sail eastwards from Gibraltar and westwards from Alexandria respectively on 6 May. Departure from Alexandria proved to be difficult as the larger ships had to be preceded by minesweepers because the approaches had been mined the previous day. The problems were compounded by poor visibility from a sand storm that kept *Formidable*'s aircraft struck down in her hangar deck. On 7 May, the Vice Admiral, Malta, signalled that Grand Harbour had also been mined, which meant that his destroyers could not leave Malta to bring the convoys into port. By this time, those of Malta's minesweepers able to deal with magnetic mines had all been lost or seriously damaged. Cunningham ordered that a passage through the minefield be blasted with depth charges. This crude but effective method of minesweeping had already proved successful in clearing the Suez Canal. Even so, as the convoy's minesweeper entered the Grand Harbour on 8 May, she set off nearly a dozen mines!

Late spring in the Mediterranean usually means clear blue skies, but for once the ships arrived off Malta to find very low cloud, 'almost down to our mast-heads'. The enemy aircraft seen on the radar screens failed to see the convoys or the warships, although one Ju88 patrolling above the clouds was found by a Fulmar from *Formidable*, which shot it down, an act of some considerable skill given the German aircraft's superior performance.

Two of the ships bound for Malta were badly damaged, with one mined and another torpedoed, but managed to make it into Grand Harbour with their vital supplies. The rest of the convoy suffered relatively lightly.

On the return to Alexandria, having picked up the reinforcements and the military convoy, the Mediterranean Fleet came under heavy aerial attack, but again little damage was done as the attackers were driven off by heavy AA fire. Against the odds, Operation Tiger was a great success, prompting the warm congratulations of the Admiralty.

Typical of poor British planning, however, the tanks and aircraft on unloading in Egypt had to spend fourteen days being fitted with sand filters for desert conditions, during which time they were vulnerable to enemy air attack! Had the equipment been fitted before dispatch from the UK, they would have been ready for immediate use.

Many believe that Crete should simply have been used as a stepping stone, a holding position, before moving the rescued troops on to Egypt, but it was decided to defend Crete 'at all costs'. This was nonsense inasmuch as the British and Greek forces on the island were very badly equipped, and movement of troops around the mountainous terrain was difficult. The whole campaign in Greece, and now the defence of Crete, was being fought by forces that were being supplied from Egypt, putting demands on scarce merchant shipping and stretching the Mediterranean Fleet yet again, while detracting from its ability to fight an aggressive campaign against the enemy. Worse still, Operation Tiger apart, these supplies and any reinforcements were by now having to come from the UK not through the Mediterranean, literally a 'bomb alley', but round the Cape of Good Hope and through the Suez Canal. There was little air cover for the evacuation from Greece. There was also a strategic blunder by the defenders of Crete, who amassed most of their troops awaiting a seaborne invasion. What transpired was at once a disaster for, and although it was not appreciated at the time, a relief for Malta.

The invasion of Crete was given to the Luftwaffe, which included Germany's paratroops, without consultation with the other two services. A plan had been drawn up by General Kurt Student, commander of the German paratroop division, for the island to be invaded by paratroops and air-landed troops, with the latter using gliders. Occupation of Crete would give the Germans a forward base, making attacks on the Suez Canal easier, while it would become increasingly difficult and dangerous to send convoys from Alexandria to Malta.

Had the Germans depended on a seaborne invasion, the chance is that the invasion could have been defeated, for although the Mediterranean Fleet's mastery of the seas was increasingly challenged by Axis mastery of the air, the seaborne element of the invasion suffered greatly at the hands of Cunningham's ships. The Germans did not have specialized landing craft, but used invasion barges, basically captured Greek *caiques*, which were unwieldy and vulnerable.

Nevertheless, the airborne assault caught the defenders on the coast. Even so, the battle for the airfields was fiercely fought, and some analysts believe that had the British and Greek forces retained most of their equipment, and especially their communications equipment, the day might have been won. The invasion began on 20 May, with 500 transport aircraft and seventy-two gliders, supported by 500 fighters and bombers, an overwhelming level of air power. The airborne element of the assault took two days with 15,000 troops landed on the first day, a further 3,000 on 21 May. In fierce fighting around the airfield at Maleme, the British commander withdrew his forces to regroup so as to counter-attack the Germans, but the counter-attack failed and allowed the Germans to start to air-land troops on the runway even while it was still being swept by British fire, while the gliders landed on the beach nearby. On the night of 21–22 May, a German convoy with troops and heavy equipment was attacked by the Royal Navy, with the loss of many German ships and barges and much loss of life. Nevertheless, during continued heavy fighting, it was decided to withdraw on 28 May, but despite the best efforts of Cunningham, who continued to order ships to evacuate troops until 1 June, well past the deadline set by the Admiralty, almost half the British personnel in Crete were captured. The cost to the Mediterranean Fleet of defending Crete and evacuating troops had been heavy, with three cruisers and six destroyers sunk, two battleships and the sole aircraft carrier, HMS *Formidable*, another two cruisers and two destroyers all damaged so badly that they could only receive temporary repairs at Alexandria and would have to be sent away. When *Illustrious* had been crippled in the heavy air attack off Malta, within two days *Formidable* was ordered to the Mediterranean as a replacement. Such were the pressures on the Royal Navy by this time that no such relief was forthcoming.

At once, Malta's supply lines were still less secure than previously. Yet, the heavy losses of German paratroops so shocked Hitler that he forbade any further airborne operations. This saved Malta from the threat of invasion, but not from that of starvation.

As already mentioned, efforts to supply Malta were redoubled, and there was an attempt to push reinforcements through the Mediterranean, saving time and merchant shipping. This was code-named Operation Tiger, with five large cargo ships through the Mediterranean, carrying tanks for the British Army in Egypt and Hawker Hurricane fighters for the RAF. The escort for the convoy had also included reinforcements for Cunningham, with the battleship *Queen Elizabeth* and the cruisers *Naiad* and *Fiji* adopting what was by now the usual practice of sailing with Force H as far as the Sicilian Narrows, where they were handed over with the convoy to the Mediterranean Fleet. Cunningham's outward voyage on this occasion had also to provide cover for two convoys from Alexandria to Malta, one having four large merchant ships carrying supplies, and the other two tankers. The usual diversion had been mounted with an attack on Benghazi by cruisers.

Summer 1941, brought heat and a welcome relief from the dampness of the shelters, as these began to dry out. This was when the closure of the beaches hit hardest, since there were few ways of keeping the body sweet in the heat, with little water and little soap for those still fortunate enough to have a bathroom. While the water needs of the growing population and of a large fleet, had been kept in mind, at the time no one knew just how much was available, and an emergency programme of drilling was put in hand to see if underground supplies could be discovered. Later, a substantial underground supply was to be discovered, safe from the threat of evaporation in the summer sun, but at the time the damage to the reservoirs and underground water cisterns could not be fully assessed. Another pressing problem was the damage to water mains that meant that often supplies were interrupted for several hours, or that water pressure could suddenly drop. One could often be caught in the bath when the alarm went, announcing yet another air raid. Even so, there was some black humour in these circumstances, with the story going the rounds of one man who was even less fortunate, being found in the ruins of his house by an ARP party still sitting on the toilet seat. When asked what happened, the dazed man replied: 'I don't know. I just pulled the chain and the whole building went down!'

Further supplies reached Malta intermittently. On one occasion, the ships which fought through so valiantly were sunk in Grand Harbour before they could be unloaded.

One essential feature of efficient convoy operation is the return of the 'empties', and by July 1941, Malta was holding seven empty merchantmen, including the armed tanker *Breconshire*. Apart from being desperately needed elsewhere, with the use of the Cape route demanding extra ships, every day these ships stayed in Malta was another day at risk of being damaged or sunk in an air raid. Once again, the plan was to fight through a convoy to Malta, Operation Substance, and remove the empties. Cunningham's forces sailed west while Force H escorted a convoy eastwards, so that the Axis would be fooled into believing that the Mediterranean Fleet had sailed in order to collect a convoy for Alexandria. Passing through the Straits of Gibraltar on the night of 21–22 July, the convoy immediately suffered a significant loss in heavy fog as the troopship *Leinster* ran aground, carrying RAF personnel to help maintain the aircraft in Malta. Nevertheless, the other six merchantmen were able to continue, with a heavy escort including the aircraft carrier *Ark Royal* and the battleship *Nelson*, with her nine powerful 16-inch guns, arranged unusually in three turrets forward. A diversionary tactic was provided by two submarines deployed west of Crete making fleet signals to indicate that the Mediterranean Fleet was operating in the area, while the Fleet itself maintained radio silence.

At the cost of a destroyer sunk and a cruiser, a destroyer and a merchantman damaged, six ships reached Malta on 24 July and the ships already in Malta were able to make their escape. The damaged merchantman, *Sydney Star*, was crippled by Italian E-boats as she passed through the confines of the narrow Skerki Channel, but still managed to reach Malta, straggling alone behind the main convoy which arrived in Grand Harbour on 24 July.

Had the Italians sent their major fleet units to intercept the convoy, it could have been a disaster. The outcome might also have been less successful had the Luftwaffe still been around in force, but the German invasion of the Soviet Union, Operation Barbarossa, was as much a relief to the people of Malta as it was to those in the United Kingdom where it was a major factor in the lifting of the blitz.

Having failed to destroy the convoy whilst on passage to Malta, the Italians now decided to ensure its destruction whilst in the Grand Harbour. That they decided to use naval forces rather than airpower must be both a reflection of the efficiency of the AA defences surrounding the port, and of the poor accuracy of Italian bombing, contrary to Cunningham's views, which were not, in any case, shared by many of his officers.

Shortly after 04.00 on 26 July 1941, the people living in the communities around the Grand Harbour, having heard the all-clear after a nuisance raid, were shaken by intense fire, but this time it was not heavy AA fire with which they were, by now, all too familiar. Hurrying to vantage points, they saw searchlights pointing out to sea, beyond the entrance to the harbour, and caught in the searchlight glare was a small boat, weaving and try-ing to avoid the heavy barrage directed its way. The coastal artillery at Fort St Elmo and Fort Ricasoli fired with dreadful accuracy, and first one boat exploded, and then another as it too was caught in the searchlight glare and the 6-pounders from both forts concentrated their fire on it. The battle continued until first light, when RAF Hurricanes appeared on the scene and added their efforts to those of the shore batteries.

The attack had been made by small craft known as a *barchina*, effectively boat bombs with a single crew member who ejected from the boat as it raced towards its target. Like the human torpedo, that other Italian invention, these small craft were carried most of the way to the target by a larger craft, in the case of the *barchini* this was a fast tender. These craft were part of *La Decima Flottiglia Mas*, The Tenth Light Flotilla, commanded by Valerio Borghese. The actual operation was commanded by Commander Moccagatta, using the fast tender *Diana* with eleven small craft, with two MAS boats, *MAS 451* and *MAS 452*, to provide cover for the small craft and also pick up any of the pilots of the *barchini* who happened to survive. Moccagatta had to persist in persuading the authorities that the operation was viable, and in an attempt to persuade his superiors, he made two dummy runs with two *barchini* on two occasions, getting to within half a mile of Malta undetected. A human torpedo mother ship was also included in the operation. Known officially as the *Siluro a Lenta Corsa*, or 'slow running torpedo', but to their two-man crews as the *Maiale*, or 'pig', the human torpedoes were another rebuttal to anyone who doubted that the Italians were incapable of bravery. Ridden by their operators who sat on top dressed in frogmen's outfits, once inside an enemy harbour and under the target ship, the warhead could be detached from the torpedo and fastened to the hull. The idea was that the crew would then make their escape on the torpedo. Apart from the obvious dangers and difficulties of penetrating an enemy harbour at night, getting clear was important since the percussive effects of underwater blast meant that the crew were greatly at risk while close to the target. The two human torpedoes had specific tasks of their own to complete. One, ridden by Major Teseo Tesei and Chief Diver Pedretti, was to approach the viaduct on the breakwater by St Elmo and use its explosive charge to blow open the boom defence at this point. The second, ridden by Lieutenant Francesco Costa and Sergeant Luigi Barla, was to enter the Marsamxett Harbour and proceed to the Lazaretto, where it would attach its explosive charge to a submarine.

Top cover of Macchi 200 fighters was also provided.

Fortunately for the defenders, the whole operation was an

hour late in arriving off Grand Harbour. The air raid that had just ended had been intended to provide cover for the seaborne attack, but of course, it was over by the time they approached. Those ashore in Malta realized that something was likely to happen when their radar picked up the *Diana* while she was still more than twenty miles off Malta, but the radar operators then saw her stop for about fifteen minutes, before moving off in the direction of Sicily. Having alerted the defences, they assumed that the ship was simply playing games, trying to see if the Royal Navy could send ships from Malta, not appreciating that the *Diana* had stopped to launch her motorboats into the sea. When she moved off, the defences were stood down, but in the darkness, an alert machine-gun crew from the Cheshire Regiment spotted something out at sea moving across their sights. As the *barchini* approached Grand Harbour just before dawn was breaking, searchlights were switched on and the coastal batteries opened up, fighters were scrambled. The shore batteries had been waiting since the outbreak of war for just this opportunity, and did not let it pass. There was a combination of tracer and coastal artillery fire. The explosive-filled motorboats raced for the entrance to the Grand Harbour, like 'another mad charge of the light brigade' according to one witness. One after another, the small craft were hit, blowing up with little hope for those aboard. One at least blew up on hitting the viaduct, but whether it was this or Tesei's torpedo that brought down the span of the viaduct was not clear, but instead of opening up the boom into Grand Harbour, the collapsed span made penetration still more difficult. Four *barchini* that tried to escape were machine-gunned by fighters once outside the range of the coastal guns. The fighters also engaged the Macchi 200s, bringing down three of them for the cost of one Hurricane. The fighter pilot was shot down, but baled out, landing in the water. He saw one of the MAS boats and swam towards it, wondering why there was no response from those on board, and discovered why as he climbed aboard to find eight corpses! He raised a white flag, and the only Italian vessel left afloat was captured by an armed trawler.

Costa and Barla's human torpedo broke down, allegedly on the approach to the Marsamxett Harbour and was abandoned, with the two men captured a little later as they swam in St George's Bay. The torpedo was never recovered, and the distance between St George's Bay and the Marsamxett suggests that the crew may have entered the wrong harbour by mistake.

Only the *Diana* survived. The Italians lost sixteen boats, including the human torpedoes, with fifteen dead and eighteen taken prisoner.

Cutting Rommel's Supplies

The stranglehold that the Axis had on Malta's supplies had its counterpart in the stranglehold being applied to the Axis' own supply line between Italy and North Africa. Axis losses mounted during the second half of 1941. In June, according to the French *Revue de Defense Nationale* in 1954, the North African supply routes had 118,000 tons of merchant shipping available, of which just 8,500 tons were sunk or badly damaged, a loss rate of seven per cent. The tonnage available climbed to 153,000 tons in July, but losses more than tripled to 27,000 tons, or seventeen per cent. In August, 156,000 tons were available, but 39,000 tons were sunk or badly damaged, a loss rate of twenty-five per cent. By September, when no less than 163,000 tons of shipping was available, losses reached 63,000 tons, or forty per cent. Tonnage slumped dramatically in October to 50,000 tons, but losses reached sixty-three per cent, or 32,000 tons. In November, out of an available 37,000 tons, no less than 28,000 tons were lost, a staggering seventy-seven per cent.

This stranglehold on the Axis' arms flow was achieved by units based in Malta. The RAF bombed targets in Sicily and mainland Italy from Malta, while the Royal Navy maintained an assault on enemy shipping, including attacks by the Swordfish of 830 Squadron.

Italy's Foreign Minister, Count Galeazzo Ciano who, no doubt, held his position by virtue of being Mussolini's son-in-law, chronicled the changing situation in November 1941.

Since 15 September, we had given up trying to get convoys through to Libya; every attempt had been very costly, and the losses suffered by our merchant marine had reached such proportions as to discourage any further experiments. Tonight we tried it again; Libya needs materials, arms, fuel, more and more every day. And a convoy of ships left, accompanied by two ten-thousand ton cruisers and ten destroyers, because it was known that at Malta the British had two battleships intended to act as wolves among the sheep. An engagement occurred the results of which are inexplicable. All, I mean *all* our ships were sunk and one or maybe two or three destroyers . . . Under the circumstances we have no right to complain if Hitler sends us Kesselring as commander in the south.[4]

Foiled in their attempt to penetrate the Grand Harbour, and unwilling to risk a major fleet engagement, in December 1941, the Italian Navy tried again. This time the target was the British Mediterranean Fleet in its base at Alexandria. This was a less blatant attack, but it was also more successful. Several Italian submarines had been modified to carry the human torpedoes. On the night of 18 December, an Italian submarine surfaced in the darkness just over a mile from the entrance to the harbour at Alexandria, and released three 2-man human torpedoes into the water. This time the attackers were in luck, as the harbour defences were opened to let in Rear Admiral Vian's destroyers. The targets were the battleships. With some difficulty, one of the Italians, Luigi de la Penne, fixed his warhead to the bottom of the battleship *Valiant*, but he and his companion lost their human torpedo in doing this and had to swim to a buoy, from which they were rescued and taken prisoner by the British. Another pair, including Martellotta, managed to blow the stern off the tanker *Sagona* and also damage the destroyer *Jervis* lying alongside. Unable to escape through the closed dock entrance, they went ashore, but were soon spotted and arrested. The third duo,

[4] *Count Ciano's Diaries.*

99

Marceglia and his companion, fixed their charge to the bottom of the elderly battleship HMS *Queen Elizabeth*, and also attempted to escape, hoping to be picked up by the submarine. They were also spotted and arrested trying to spend English £5 notes which were no longer legal tender in Egypt. Even though he was detained aboard the *Valiant*, de la Penne kept silence until the explosion ripped open her hull and she settled on the bottom. The *Queen Elizabeth* suffered a similar fate.

It was simply the good fortune of the Royal Navy that both ships were in shallow water, and aerial reconnaissance showed them as if they were still lying undamaged at Alexandria. The crews of the two-men human torpedoes had failed to return, so there was little to show that they had been successful. The discovery of one of the torpedoes also caused the Royal Navy to embark on its own programme of torpedo development, although their crews used the far politer term of 'chariot' for their disposable craft. This was an instance of good fortune in misfortune.

As the year drew to an end with the Mediterranean Fleet having suffered heavy losses, despite its successes against the Italian Navy, for Malta, the one problem was that, as the German advance across the Soviet Union faltered and stopped under the crushing cold of the Russian winter, many of the Luftwaffe's aircraft were redeployed westwards where they could still operate. As winter closed in, the Luftwaffe returned to Sicily. Malta could not be allowed to continue to strangle Rommel's campaign in North Africa.

With *Fliegerkorps X* heavily committed in the North African campaign, and the Luftwaffe now heavily involved in the desperate dash to reach Hitler's objectives in the east, the burden of bombing fell once again on the Italians

The convoy of 25 July had brought, in theory, sufficient to keep Malta going for a further three months, but fuel and ammunition were being used at a higher rate than anticipated due to heavy operational demands. The harvest was collected, but in addition to the problems of land use mentioned earlier, increasingly farmland had been scorched and poisoned by high explosives. To eke out the grain, on 1 August, 1941 it was decided to knead potatoes with the dough for the bread, spoiling the usual crispness and lightness of the traditional Maltese loaf, often eaten with olive oil and tomato paste or puree. Worse, in the summer heat, the utility bread became stale within a couple of hours. A few days later, both olive oil and kerosene were rationed.

Other changes were also happening. The language was becoming Anglicized. People used the word 'fighter' rather than *ajruplan tal-glied*, 'bomber' instead of *ajruplan tal-bumbardament*, all of which was understandable in that the simple English terms rolled off the tongue more quickly and easily. Less easy to understand was the use of the word 'shelter' rather than the simple Maltese *kenn*.

Convoy GM2

In September, it was decided to run through another convoy to Malta, designated GM2. This was the largest so far with nine merchantmen with no less than 85,000 tons of supplies and 2,600 troops. The escort consisted, as usual, of Force H, with three battleships, *Prince of Wales*, *Nelson* and the flagship *Rodney*, the aircraft carrier *Ark Royal* and five cruisers, as well as eight destroyers. Yet again, the Royal Navy was hoping that, in addition to protecting the convoy, they would be able to draw the Italian Navy into a battle.

Passing through the Straits of Gibraltar on the night of 24–25 September, the convoy and the escort split into two groups to try to convince the enemy that it was smaller, with the heavy ships steaming to the northwards of the main body of the convoy, which sneaked along the coast of North Africa. This worked, convincing the Italians that there was just one battleship, and provoked Admiral Iachino to leave Naples with the two Littorio-class battleships, *Littorio* and *Vittorio Veneto*, and four heavy cruisers, *Trento*, *Trieste*, *Gorizia* and *Duca degli Abruzzi*, and fourteen destroyers, while sixteen submarines were also directed to the route of the convoy. The plan was that the *Regia Aeronautica* would attack the convoy and the escorts, which would be forced to scatter leaving ripe pickings for the surface fleet.

On the night of 26 September, Wellingtons from Malta raided the Italian air base at Cagliari in Sardinia, inflicting considerable damage to aircraft and the base itself, and severely cutting the *Regia Aeronautica*'s planned operation against the convoy. The Italians managed to launch a number of attacks from Sicily, but the only damage inflicted was to the battleship *Nelson*, flagship of Vice Admiral Somerville, which was hit on the stem by a torpedo and was operating at reduced speed as a result. On 27 September, at 14.30, aerial reconnaissance from Malta spotted Iachino's fleet, and reported two battleships, four cruisers and sixteen destroyers approaching the convoy and at a distance of less than eighty miles. Somerville sent his other two battleships to intercept and ordered *Ark Royal* to launch a torpedo strike. Flying in steadily worsening visibility and with the Italians making a change of course that was not immediately picked up, coupled with some confusion over communications, the Swordfish missed the Italians. Iachino had heard from the *Regia Aeronautica* that there was more than a single battleship sailing with the convoy – a rare instance of these two Italian services communicating well – and was under strict orders not to risk any major action unless he enjoyed overwhelming strength. He turned and took his fleet back to Naples.

The convoy's fighter cover and intense AA fire accounted for thirteen Italian aircraft, but another ten were lost out of fifteen Macchi fighters, which ran out of fuel when they failed to find the convoy, over which they were supposed to provide cover against the Fleet Air Arm's fighters.

As darkness approached, the weather cleared up. Somerville took his heavy units back to Gibraltar while the cruisers and destroyers escorted the convoy through the Skerki Channel towards Malta. The convoy sailed onwards on a clear moonlit night, to be attacked by Italian torpedo-bombers, attacking not in force but in ones and twos. The only casualty was a torpedo strike which sunk the merchantmen *Imperial Star*. The ship's cargo was typical of cargo for the Malta run, where cargoes were by this time always mixed, which was inefficient in loading and unloading, but reduced the consequences of losing a ship. The *Imperial Star* carried 12,000 tons, including several hundred crates of bombs, 500 tons of kerosene, as well as 500 tons of refrigerated meat, grain, flour and small arms ammunition. Given this dangerous cargo, it is incredible to learn that she also carried 300 passengers, since such cargo would not be regarded as safe for a passenger ship in peacetime! It was a miracle that she didn't blow up, but she remained afloat long enough for her passengers and crew to be taken off.

The remaining ships reached Grand Harbour the following morning to the usual tumultuous welcome from the crowds along the shore and thronging the battlements, with the cruisers' bands playing. Once again, Malta found herself with seven months' supplies, although kerosene and coal remained scarce.

In the euphoria, no one could have realized that it would be many months before the next convoy would reach Malta.

VIII

INVASION THREATENS

The big uncertainty hanging over everything was the threat of invasion, and whether this would be airborne, as in the Netherlands, or from the sea, or a combination of both. It was to be some time before it became clear that the *Regia Navale* had little intention of being caught away from its ports by the Mediterranean Fleet. British intelligence sources should have known about the *Regia Aeronautica*'s shortage of transport aircraft, although, of course, in an invasion they may also have been able to depend on the resources of the Luftwaffe. Even the Luftwaffe, with its vast fleet of Junkers Ju52 trimotor transports and gliders, could not always mount an airborne assault easily, since it usually manned transport aircraft by borrowing instructors from the bomber schools. The Italians did not have paratroops at this time. The threat of an airborne invasion was taken sufficiently seriously for the Police to form an anti-parachute section, a decision that seems odd since the Maltese Police were normally unarmed, and even if armed would not have been able to counter a large scale paratroop assault.

Despite the weakness of the garrison with so many demands on the British Army during the spring and early summer of 1940, efforts had been made to position coastal batteries from the Royal Artillery and the Royal Malta Artillery at strategic positions around Malta itself, which had ninety miles of coastline, although not all of it by any means would have been suitable for an invasion. Invasion was a threat, but so too was bombardment from the sea by units of the Italian fleet.

The usual precautions against invasion were put in hand. Beaches were covered in barbed wire, milestones defaced and direction signs removed. Some commercial concerns even removed their addresses from their vehicles. Nevertheless, as the rest of Western Europe saw the advance of German troops, marking the end of the phoney war, Malta had continued to trade with Italy. The Italian airline, Ala Littoria, continued to operate a seaplane service to Malta, using Marsaxlokk as a base, and there were also air services using Ta'Qali, although these moved to Luqa shortly before Italy entered the war. No doubt these aircrew and the seafarers on the cargo ships plying to the island provided a steady flow of intelligence for the Italian armed forces.

During the first year of war, attention was paid to strengthening the defences of the Grand Harbour, including both anti-aircraft and coastal artillery. Tank warfare was unlikely, and if an invader did land, there was the difficulty of him finding a suitable place. The south-west coast was protected by 400 feet high cliffs. The east coast had numerous shoals and reefs offshore. The best landing points were the beaches to the north of Malta itself, but those at Mellieha Bay and Armier Bay meant the steep and curved ascent to Mellieha itself, a natural defensive position. Even if troops could be landed at St Paul's Bay or Ghajn Tuffieha Bay, or if they landed on Gozo in readiness for a strike south to the mainland of Malta, they would be confronted by another natural defensive position at the Victoria Lines, north-west of Mosta and Rabat, with an almost vertical precipice along most of its length, with few roads running over it and a commanding view of the terrain northwards. At first paratroop and glider assault was ruled out, but the experience of the Netherlands immediately showed that this option was a distinct possibility.

Coastal protection against invasion was obviously a priority as Martin Hastings recalls.

> I think that the next thing that really happened was that we started to get masses of equipment . . . and every little beach post . . . all the way around Marsa Scirocco Bay, which was in the south of the island where we were, had a corporal and at least two machine guns and masses of

different forms of equipment that they were supposed to man, together with water and ammunition and food.

And it was quite a responsibility to train all these people and of course keep them fit because as soon as you put chaps in posts, of course, they get pretty static. Anyway a way of life developed fairly soon. I had to keep everybody happy and we took up games like basket ball and those sort of things and swimming in the summer in the sea and so on like that.[1]

Invasion Plans

A plan already existed for the invasion of Malta, known to the Italians as *Operazione* C3: Malta, but efforts to move this off the drawing board and into reality were intermittent. In its essentials, C3 called for invasion barges to move 40,000 Italian troops, including paratroops, with 500 combat aircraft to cover the operation and suppress the defences. There were to be protecting naval forces. The whole operation was planned to be over and done with in less than forty-eight hours, the time it would take Cunningham to arrive with the Mediterranean Fleet, so obviously no major naval engagement was ever envisaged. There would be landings at Mellieha Bay and St Paul's Bay, and a diversionary thrust at Marsaxlokk near the south of the island, although the roads out of this picturesque fishing village were narrow and easily defended.

There were no plans for an airborne assault simply because the parachutists did not exist, there were no gliders and just a relatively small number of transport aircraft, about eighty, and these were needed for the operations in North Africa.

Exercises were held with limited numbers of Italian troops as there were so few motorized barges, but many believe that these exercises were simply put on as propaganda, and as demonstrations for visiting dignitaries. The failure of the British government to seek peace terms with the Axis Powers after the surrender of

[1] IWM Sound Archive, Accession No.10453/6.

France, and the persistence with which Malta was being defended rather than surrendered, as Mussolini had demanded, had effectively called the Italian bluff. Rome did not have a strategy for the execution of the war, and from now on, the best that could be done was to support the Germans in whatever plans they advanced.

It wasn't just the paratroopers who didn't exist. No action had been taken to build landing craft. This was a serious weakness in Axis military planning. The seaborne element of the German invasion of Crete had to rely on barges, and suffered so terribly at the hands of the Mediterranean Fleet that, had the operation not been preceded by the airborne assault, it might have been defeated. Even with purpose-built landing craft, as the Allies were to discover, landings on enemy coastlines were still fraught with danger and the outcome far from certain; without them, these operations were far more difficult.

The true picture was that the Italians had an ambition, but no plans. Nothing had been coordinated. Communication between the different services, seldom easy or straightforward, was especially poor in all of the Axis countries. In Italy, the Army had the ear of Mussolini, in Germany the Luftwaffe had the same relationship with Hitler. Later, rivalry was to surface in Japan once she entered the war, between the strongly pro-war Army and the more pragmatic and realistic Navy.

Crete

After heavy air raids on 12 May 1941, and an exceptionally heavy one on 20 May, destroying two more of Valletta's churches and causing many casualties, the news reached the islands of the German parachute and glider invasion of Crete. This was a bomb-shell to the people of Malta, even though the military were well aware that the Germans had used similar tactics during the invasion of the Netherlands and Belgium. The Maltese were confident of the Royal Navy's ability and determination to defend them from invasion by sea, but the Germans and Italians had time and time again demonstrated their mastery of the skies.

The threat of invasion now seemed very real to those in Malta. It was also very real to those in Germany and Italy, with fresh plans drawn up involving only German forces based on a para-troop assault followed up by air landed infantry, with an invasion from the sea as a subsidiary operation. The attack would take place under heavy Luftwaffe cover by *Fliegerkorps X* and possibly heavy naval gunfire. No one was prepared to allow Mussolini a share of the action, still less of the spoils. In fact, despite earlier cooperation with the Italians, including the formation of a joint air command, the Italians were not even consulted over the in-vasion plans. General Erwin Rommel, Hitler's commander in North Africa, a general of supreme ability known as the 'Desert Fox', offered to lead the assault.

Sensing the public anxiety, Lieutenant General Sir William Dobbie, the Governor, spoke to the people at the beginning of July, saying:

> Not only will we not give up Malta, but we have no inten-tion of having it taken from us, whether by the Germans or the Italians. We have to face the possibility of invasion. Malta is immeasurably more capable of resisting attacks than was Crete. This opinion is fully shared by responsible officers, and I am saying this with the quiet confidence that I consider the circumstances justify. I know that Malta will rise to the occasion whatever is required of it. The Government and fighting services are leaving no stone unturned to ensure that Malta shall give a good account of itself and make its present history more splendid even than its past.
>
> With God's help I am confident that we shall succeed in so doing.

Martin Hastings recalls the fears of invasion increased after the Germans invaded first Greece and then the island of Crete.

> . . . there were various other things that happened, like the invasion of Greece and Crete and of course the use of

the paratroopers in that part of the world. And the sinking of a large number of British ships affected our way of thinking the Germans might try the same sort of assault on us.

However, while all this was going on, the aircraft from Malta, RAF and Navy, did some marvellous work intercepting the lines of communications to Tripoli and North Africa. And by sinking a large number of the merchant ships supplying the Italians and the Germans in North Africa they undoubtedly helped our military effort in the Western Desert. I often think that perhaps they didn't get the credit for all that they did to reduce the effectiveness of the Italian and German armies . . . which they undoubtedly did.[2]

Hitler Approves Invasion

Had the Germans been able to invade Malta shortly after their invasion of Crete, they might well have succeeded, but their losses in Crete meant that it would take time before a fresh operation could start, and there were the pressing demands of the invasion of the Soviet Union, Operation Barbarossa. The heavy losses in Crete also meant that at first Hitler completely forbade any future large scale paratroop assault.

Normally so thorough and practical, the Germans were also torn between the need to capture Malta and the temptation of pressing on through Egypt to the Suez Canal. At first, even Rommel was convinced that Malta must be occupied, but his early successes in North Africa and the appeal of outright victory securing Suez soon overrode everything else.

Hitler had appointed Field Marshal Kesselring as Commander-in-Chief South in 1941, with overall responsibility for the war in North Africa, where German forces were attempting to ease Italy's embarrassment in this campaign, as in the Balkans. By the

[2] IWM Sound Archive Accession No.10453/6.

following year, Kesselring was also convinced that Malta had to be taken. In April 1942, Count Ciano took up his diary again.

> The Duce informs me that Marshal Kesselring on his return from Germany brought Hitler's approval for the landing operation on Malta. It appears that the Island has been really damaged by aerial bombardments. This does not however alter the fact that the coastal defences are still intact. Therefore in the opinion of some naval experts, the undertaking is still dangerous and in any case would be expensive.[3]

The idea was put to General Cavallero, who prepared a plan, which Ciano noted the following month.

> Cavallero outlines our programme for carrying on the war in the Mediterranean. At the end of the month, Rommel will attack in Libya with the aim of defeating the British forces. If he can he will take Tobruk and will go as far as the old boundaries; if not he will limit himself to forestalling an attack by the enemy by striking first. Then all the forces will be concentrated for an attack on Malta. The Germans are sending a parachute division commanded by General Student and are furnishing us with technical material for the assault. It will take place in July or August at the latest. Afterwards it will no longer be possible because of the weather. Cavallero declares: 'I know that it is a difficult undertaking and that it will cost us many casualties, and I know too that I am staking my head on this undertaking . . . If we take Malta, Libya will be safe.' Cavallero does not conceal the fact that he hopes to derive a great deal of personal glory from this operation . . . but I believe he will never acquire it.[4]

[3] *Count Ciano's Diary.*
[4] *Count Ciano's Diary.*

As it turned out, the Italian Air Force did not concur with the conclusions of Kesselring and Cavallero, pointing out that Malta's AA defences were still very efficient and that the naval defence was still intact.

'The landing of paratroops would be very difficult; a great part of the planes are likely to be shot down before they can deposit their human cargo,' wrote Ciano.

> The same must be said for landings by sea. Again it must be remembered that two days of minor aerial bombardment by us only served to strengthen resistance. In these last attacks we, as well as the Germans, have lost many feathers. Even Fougier (head of the Regia Aeronautica) is anxious about a landing operation and the German General Lorzer did not conceal his open disagreement. The supporters of the operation are Kesselring and Cavallero, the latter going through his usual tricks to put the responsibility on the shoulders of others.[5]

The more realistic attitudes of the *Regia Aeronautica* and *Regia Navale*, who, after all, had not been consulted over the wisdom of entering the Second World War, were doubtless borne out by experience. One Italian pilot, Franco Pagliano, noted in his book, *Storia di Diecimilia Aeroplani*, that none of his comrades expected to survive more than seven sorties over Malta.

By June 1942, Kesselring had assembled the forces necessary for the invasion of Malta, but was waiting for Rommel to take Tobruk, after which he believed that he would be given the go-ahead.

Beach Defences

Expecting invasion, not only were the beaches in Malta cordoned off with barbed wire, but there were beach defences as well. The first line of defence was the beach posts, each identified by a letter

---

[5] *Count Ciano's Diary.*

and a number. The second line of defence lay in what were called depth posts, identified by the letter 'L', which were often two storeys with accommodation on the ground floor and designed to be fought from the upper storey. Both the first and second lines of defence were manned, but the third line, the reserve posts, identified by the letter 'R', weren't usually manned. Usually, each manned post would have two men on duty at all times under the overall command of a corporal, while all of the posts were connected by telephone, not only so that they could report any developments, but so that they could also be warned of exercises or air raids. All three lines of defence were heavily armed with machine guns, Bren guns and Lewis guns, some of which were fixed, others were on anti-aircraft mountings, Boyes anti-tank rifles and grenades, as well as stores of ammunition, food and water. The posts were often surrounded by mines, and a number had captured Italian anti-tank guns, a legacy of the early Italian failures in the desert war. Traps were laid for an invader, with one of the favourites being the construction of fougasses dug out of the rock and filled with explosives packed in behind rock and scrap metal, making an improvised mortar.

Of course, it is always a good idea if the enemy doesn't quite make it to the beach, so off many beaches, there were mines that could be electrically detonated. Each post had a Lyons light, a small but powerful searchlight, which could scan the sea in front of the post.

Life in the concrete pillboxes guarding the beaches was tough. 'There were bunks in these pillboxes,' Norman Travett remembers:

We had palliasses filled with straw, no sheets, but perhaps one or two blankets and sandfly nets. We used to do guard every night, two hours on and four hours off, every night, which was very wearing – you used to get run down considerably . . . We used to try and work it that possibly you did an early one so that you came off at say eleven o'clock then you could have four hours off which would bring you up to about three o'clock in the morning and then just have to do a short spell again at daybreak.[6]

Norman Travett was amongst the Devonshires and assigned to beach protection. Like the others in his unit, when they had been issued with tropical kit, they had thought that they were being sent to India. They reached Malta in a troopship via the Cape and the Suez Canal, arriving in Egypt only to be transferred to cattle trucks and taken to Alexandria, where they had a few days leave. The final leg of their journey to Malta was in the cramped accommodation of the cruiser, HMS *Gloucester*, arriving at night to be taken in hired local buses to a camp. Like the others, their spell on beach duty was interspersed with duties at the aerodromes.

The Devonshires were to defend the area around the bay known as Marsa Scirocco, and were headquartered in Tarxien, just outside Paola. On their left were the 1st Dorsets and to their right there were the 1st Hampshires.

'Food was exceptionally short,' Norman Travett recalls.

> For some six or nine months we had no fresh meat or potatoes. It was all tomatoes, pumpkins and a little bit of tinned steak and kidney and biscuit duff as we used to call it . . . army biscuits that were soaked with a little bit of fruit or something in it. We used to buy an egg occasionally on the black market . . . we used to pay half a crown (12 ½ p) . . . for an egg which in those days was a lot of money. We used to have it on Sunday morning.
>
> We lost many pounds, stones I suppose . . . we weren't at all fit.[7]

Travett remembers keeping chickens on the perimeter of his beach defence post, maintaining a supply of eggs for the occupants until food became so scarce that they could no longer keep

[6] IWM Sound Archive, Accession No.10462/5/1.
[7] IWM Sound Archive, Accession No.10462/5.

them. Their official rations were cooked centrally and brought around on a little Maltese flat cart drawn by a donkey. They didn't grow vegetables. When they had first arrived, they had a day a week off on which they would visit either Valletta or Sliema, while it was still possible to go to a café and be served egg and chips or steak and kidney pudding – conventional fare designed to satisfy British appetites. He also recalls that the forces were better fed than the civilian population, but that there were no attempts to beg food from the barracks.

Operation Hercules

Kesselring was still hoping for an invasion, with the German plan code-named Operation Hercules and scheduled for 10 July 1942. Two German parachute divisions had been gathered under the command of General Kurt Student, and these had been augmented by an Italian Parachute Division trained by the Germans. There were transport aircraft, including the large Messerschmitt Me323s for air lifting heavy equipment.

Besieged Malta had betrayed few of her secrets, and the Italians needed up-to-date intelligence, of the kind that could only be obtained by an agent on the ground. They found one in a twenty-six-year old Maltese, Carmelo Borg Pisani, who had become a Fascist while studying in Rome. A Maltese agent was ideal, knowing the island well and not having any language problems. Pisani was taken to a point just off Malta in a submarine, from which a dinghy endeavoured to put him ashore in a heavy swell, in which he was injured and his equipment damaged. At dawn, an army patrol found him, and assumed that he was either a Maltese soldier or an Italian washed ashore from a ditched aircraft or a sunken ship, and took him to the military hospital at Imtarfa. This was his undoing, as he was soon recognized by a Maltese military surgeon and detained for five months until he could be tried before a Maltese civilian court, which found him guilty and had him hanged.

Kesselring must have thought that his time had come when, on 20 June, Tobruk fell. Rommel, however, now promoted to

Field Marshal, had other ideas, and when the two men met in Tobruk, Kesselring found that Rommel had decided to press on instead with an attack on Sidi Barrani. In an attempt to break the impasse between two of the Reich's most senior military commanders, the decision was passed up to Hitler and Mussolini – it was the former who now took the decisions, and the Führer had no confidence in the Italians to fulfil their side of the operation. The invasion of Egypt was accorded priority. Ignoring the fact that the invasion of Egypt was being led by the Germans, Mussolini then flew to Derna where he prepared to make a triumphal entry to Cairo astride a white charger.

The forces earmarked for an invasion of Malta were not wasted however, as they were sent to reinforce the *Afrika Korps* when the British finally fought Rommel to a standstill at El Alamein. Nevertheless, the opportunity had been missed and Rommel was soon to find his lines of supply overstretched, while Malta-based forces had inflicted grave damage on the amount of material getting through throughout 1941 and into early 1942.

IX

OFFENSIVE AND DEFENSIVE IN THE SKIES

While the imminent entry of Italy into the Second World War had taken the Mediterranean Fleet away to Alexandria, the changing fortunes of war meant that not all of the movement around Malta was away from the islands. Sheer chance meant that Malta gained an offensive capability early on in the form of a Fleet Air Arm Squadron.

In November, 1939, the Fleet Air Arm's 767 Squadron had started using Hyeres de la Palyvestre in the South of France for advanced flying training with its Fairey Swordfish, making the most of the better Mediterranean weather and accompanied by the elderly aircraft carrier *Argus* for deck landings. Training continued as the Battle of France developed, but the squadron found itself in an impossible position once Italy entered the war. *Argus* was immediately recalled home for her own safety, but the squadron was left behind. In the Fleet Air Arm, squadrons with a number in the 700 series are non-combatant second line squadrons, including training units such as 767, with numbers in the 800 series reserved for combat squadrons. Its lowly number didn't stop nine of the squadron's instructors taking their aircraft to bomb the port of Genoa on 13 June.

This daring blow, flown without any fighter escort, was in spite of 767 Squadron finding itself in a difficult position. It was clear that their slow and vulnerable Swordfish couldn't fly home over occupied French territory and without a carrier they were faced with the bleak prospect of internment. Lieutenant Commander

Drummond, the squadron's CO, took his men and their aircraft to Bone in North Africa, from where the less experienced student pilots were sent home via Casablanca and Gibraltar. Whilst at the western end of the Mediterranean, the opportunity was taken to use six of the squadron's aircraft to top up the numbers aboard *Ark Royal*. The remainder of 767's aircraft, twelve in all, then flew to RAF Hal Far in Malta, to be redesignated as a new squadron, 830, with a new CO, Lieutenant Commander F. D. Howie. There was little delay in taking on an offensive role, although the squadron's aircraft lacked blind flying panels and long-range fuel tanks, the absence of which limited their offensive role and also made them more vulnerable. The early operations included bombing raids against both Sicily, starting with an attack on Augusta on 30 June, and Libya, while on 19 July, the squadron sank a U-boat.

Malta had already a limited air defence capability by this time. Four Gloster Sea Gladiators in a crate were discovered, left behind as spares for a carrier's squadrons. The senior RAF officer on the island asked Cunningham if he could use the four aircraft, and Cunningham readily gave his permission, realizing that without air cover Malta's role as a fortress and a base for offensive operations was doomed. All four aircraft were quickly assembled, but the first was lost on its first day of operations, Thursday, 13 June, leaving the famous trio named informally by the locals as *Faith*, *Hope* and *Charity*, to handle Malta's fighter defences. Flown by flying-boat pilots, these obsolete biplanes gave a good account of themselves as the air war developed over the island, but within a month or so, someone at the Admiralty, ignoring what was being done to protect their base and naval assets, demanded to know who had permitted Fleet Air Arm spares to be handed over to the Royal Air Force.

'I wondered where the official responsible had been spending his war,' Cunningham remarked.[1]

The Fleet Air Arm's Swordfish were not the only refugees from the fall of France to reach Malta. William Collins had been with

[1] *A Sailor's Odyssey.*

a Hurricane squadron covering the British Expeditionary Force in France. Escaping south to Marseille, they were joined by the remnants of two other units, so that eventually there were two Bristol Blenheim bombers and ten Hawker Hurricanes. The French in Marseille cautioned them against their original plan to fly out via Ajaccio in Corsica, where the local forces had thrown in their lot with Vichy, and suggested instead that they flew from Marseille to Tunis, a distance of 980 miles.

'We had overload tanks and we had approximately five hours thirty minutes flying time,' Collins recalls.'We set off and six of us made it and one of the Blenheims.'[2]

On arrival in Tunis, they had been interned, although they were put up in some comfort in a good hotel. Eventually they were released, told to refuel at a point in the desert, which they did, and then continued to Malta.

'But anyhow we went into Luqa in Malta on the day the Italians were bombing it. That's six Hurricanes and one Blenheim. And then for some unknown reason it was decided that the six Hurricanes would go on – should carry on with getting out to the Middle East.'[3]

The six Hurricanes would have been invaluable in the air defence of Malta at this early stage, within a fortnight of the start of the Italian air raids. It is not surprising that a later AOC Malta was to become notorious for hijacking aircraft and aircrew that caught his eye as they tried to use Malta as a transit point! Nevertheless, before leaving Malta on 24 June, William Collins had time to experience an Italian air raid.

'I'd just landed and was having a bath when there was a terrible crunch,' he recalls.

> And the bath left the floor. And I was rolled out. But Malta was a marvellous place. You know, stone buildings and they had air raid shelters which were perfectly safe because the Italians only used at the maximum 250 or 500 pound

[2] IWM Sound Archive, Accession No.006673/03.
[3] IWM Sound Archive ,Accession No.006673/03.

bombs. So basically other than to the runway the damage was very small until, of course, the Germans came in . . . later. And then Malta had trouble . . . Had we left those six Hurricanes there instead of just the three Gladiators the defence of Malta would have been more secure I think. You see they were never short of pilots in Malta. But they were short of aircraft.[4]

While the absence of substantial fighter defences for Malta was a serious weakness in British planning, the pressure on the United Kingdom itself was growing at this time, as the fall of France led immediately to the start of the Battle of Britain, the Luftwaffe's concerted effort to destroy the Royal Air Force and its aircraft. It was fortunate that the Italians never mastered the art of the massed bombing raid, overwhelming the defences, while the Macchi C200, despite the manufacturer's experience in the Schneider Trophy races, was one of the poorest fighters of the Second World War, worse even than the Curtiss P-40, and probably only just superior to the Brewster Buffalo.

Despite the critical situation in the United Kingdom, on 12 August, a squadron of twelve Hurricanes had been flown to Malta off the elderly aircraft carrier HMS *Argus*. The RAF's strength in the island was boosted further by the arrival of 431 Flight, whose four Martin Baltimore bombers flew reconnaissance missions and whose operations greatly boosted the potential of the Mediterranean Fleet. The Baltimore was fast, and had a good range, and were soon to be the eyes of the Fleet as well as of Malta.

There was another, far less unorthodox, set of eyes based on Malta, however. This was Wing Commander A. Warburton, who also arrived in Malta towards the end of 1940, bringing with him a Bristol Beaufighter which he had 'borrowed' in Egypt, stripping the aircraft of armament and armour and fitting vertical cameras for aerial reconnaissance. Warburton dismissed the Baltimore as being 'No bloody good', and staunchly maintained that his 'Beau'

[4] IWM Sound Archive, Accession No.006673/03.

was the fastest aircraft in the Mediterranean, able to reconnoitre 'any place at any time at any height', according to his friend, A. J. Spooner, who flew one of the Malta-based Wellingtons.[5] Certainly, Warburton was the stuff of boys' comic books, wearing unorthodox clothing such as sheepskin leggings acquired in Crete, and probably ideal for high altitude flying in an unpressurized aircraft. He did not have regular aircrew, but instead took two airmen whose job it was to change the film spools in the cameras, presumably taking just one of these at a time since the 'Beau' was a two seater, and a third person would not only have been uncomfortable, but would have offset some of the weight savings achieved in stripping the aircraft. Either way, he was never shot down even though he often returned to Malta chased by enemy fighters.

A few additional Hurricanes reached Malta on 17 November, when fourteen of these fighters were flown off HMS *Argus*, but only four reached Malta as the rest were lost, probably due to insufficient fuel since those that did make it to Hal Far arrived with very little in their tanks. Before the end of the year, a squadron of Hawker Hurricanes, No. 261, had been flown into Hal Far. Meanwhile, the offensive capability had also been boosted in November with the arrival of 37 Squadron operating Vickers Wellington bombers, the best that the RAF could provide at this early stage of the war, and augmented by some radar-equipped Wellingtons that were especially useful for guiding Swordfish on to their targets at night, although much later radar-equipped Swordfish did arrive. The Wellingtons were soon joined by two squadrons of Bristol Blenheim bombers.

Airfields were essential. Hal Far was in good condition, as was the new airfield at Ta'Qali. Luqa was newly completed. Kalafrana continued as a base for flying boats. None of these airfields had any protection against enemy bombing at the outset, showing that the impact that bombing would have on Malta was completely discounted. There were no protected dispersal bays for aircraft, no hardened hangars. At first, all that could be done

[5] *Siege Malta: 1940-1943.*

in the way of AA protection of these airfields was to detail Lewis gun crews to each of them. Only later would they receive significant AA batteries.

The Royal Engineers and the Pioneer Corps were given the task of improving the airfields, often with drafts of manpower from the infantry battalions, so that at times as many as 3,000 men could be at work. During the next two years they were to construct 300 aircraft pens to provide some protection from bombing, saving aircraft from all but a direct hit. Between Hal Far and Luqa, an incredible twenty-seven miles of dispersal area was provided, known as the Safi strip from the nearby village, and later this was developed into a new airfield.

For most of the siege, the RAF had few ground staff in Malta, so the Manchester Regiment provided the manpower to keep Ta'Qali operational, while the Royal West Kents did the same for Luqa and the Cheshire Regiment, the 'Buffs', looked after Hal Far. The Cheshires' 2nd Battalion of 1,000 men, more than fifty per cent more than the usual battalion strength, had arrived in February, 1941, with the 1st Battalion of the Hampshire Regiment. Given the confined space of Malta, and the barrier afforded by the sea, there would, in all probability, have been little for these infantrymen to do otherwise.

For Malta, there was some relief at Easter 1941, when on Holy Saturday, 12 April, twenty Hurricane MkIIs were flown off the aircraft carrier *Ark Royal* to boost the depleted strength of 261 Squadron.

On 21 July 1941, the RAF's Blenheims were alerted to the passage of a convoy of five ships, three of them Italian merchantmen and one German, as well as a tanker. The Blenheims went in at mast-top height, blowing up an ammunition ship and setting the tanker on fire, so that she was abandoned and drifted on to the Kerkenah Bank.

The attacks from the air, from the sea and from beneath it, meant that by October 1941, the Axis were losing more than sixty per cent of their supplies sent to North Africa, and the following month, this rose to an incredible seventy-seven per cent. Rommel was prompted to make nightly signals complaining about the shortage of supplies, blaming this on the Italians and also criticizing them for sending his supplies through Tripoli rather than Benghazi, and in so doing adding 500 miles to his already lengthy supply chain.

Throughout the summer and early autumn of 1941, more Hurricanes were delivered to Malta, so that by early autumn, there were about seventy aircraft. These were day and night fighters and fighter bombers, making offensive sweeps against Italian aircraft at their bases in Sicily, especially important as convoys approached Malta. Later, the Swordfish would be equipped with radar. Between May and November, 1941, mines laid by the Swordfish accounted for around 250,000 tons of enemy shipping, while the Blenheims accounted for another 50,000 tons, but suffered heavy losses in their very low level attacks.

Getting to Malta

Getting aircraft to Malta was hardly easy, especially for aircraft too large to be flown off an aircraft carrier. At Portreath in Cornwall, the RAF had a unit tasked with dispatching aircraft to the Middle East. Late in 1941, Air Marshal Sir Ivor Broom, then a sergeant pilot, found that with 230 hours total flying time he was the most experienced pilot in a group of six, which he was asked to lead. They couldn't fly over occupied France, and so their journey started with a seven hour flight from Cornwall to Gibraltar, where the runway built on the old racecourse was still quite short, and for the still inexperienced pilots there was the unnerving sight of wrecked aircraft which had failed to make a safe landing. The next stage of the journey from Gibraltar to Malta took seven hours, forty minutes. Flying a twin-engined Blenheim with a navigator was bad enough, since they hardly saw land between Gibraltar and Malta, so it is easy to understand the problems facing the solitary fighter pilots flying off from aircraft carriers, with limited navigational training and accustomed to fighting air battles within a radius of fifty miles or so from their home air station.

Broom recalls that, whilst maintaining radio silence, one crew decided that the absence of any landfall meant that the whole flight was lost, and decided to try their luck, peeling off from the formation, and eventually becoming prisoners of war. On landing at Malta, en route to Cairo, Broom's aircraft was the Blenheim hijacked by Lloyd to fill the gaps in the resident Blenheim squadron, No. 105. At this stage, Blenheim squadrons were detached to Malta from the UK for a three week tour of duty, before being repatriated. Broom spent a week with 105, before being transferred to 107, but found that the squadron had drawn the short straw, and spent more than four months in Malta before being relieved by 21 Squadron in January 1942. 21 Squadron was especially unlucky, spending just a couple of weeks in the island before being completely wiped out. The other Blenheim squadron in Malta during Broom's period there was No. 18.

'Our main role was to attack shipping taking supplies to Rommel in North Africa,' Ivor Broom explains. 'All daylight. And we'd go out searching for shipping and if we couldn't find any ships, and we were down by the North African coast, then we would go inland to find a target of opportunity, on the Tripoli-Benghazi road area. And we'd attack the target of opportunity and then back to Malta . . . .all at low level . . . fifty feet . . . '[6]

Not all of the attacks were in broad daylight, however.

The squadron was asked to attack some very important big ship in a Sicilian harbour . . . the harbour was so defended, that it was decided it had to be done at night. A moonlight night. And so they picked the two most experienced crews in the squadron to do it, and I was one of them. Now my total night flying was seven and a half hours. That included my training on Airspeed Oxfords, training on Blenheims . . . I hadn't flown at night since my training conversion six months earlier . . . in low level again . . . All this bombing

[6] IWM Sound Archive, Accession No.10981/3/1.

at low level was done at pilot release, not a navigator or bomb aimer . . . I remember the CO of the squadron said to me whilst at the briefing 'Would you like to do a couple of circuits and landings?' or circuits and bumps as we called them in those days, 'before you set course, so that you've had a look at what Malta looks like at night, with virtually no lighting'. And before I could answer my air gunner said, 'Not ruddy likely, let's do the op between the circuit and the bumps'. And so off we went. And it was a very successful trip.[7]

Promotion could be rapid, and because of Malta's isolation, what might be described as battlefield promotions were a necessity. Broom explains:

Now I was a sergeant pilot when I went to Malta, and we lost virtually all the officers, and we were left with a squadron leader who was due to go home, his tour expired. He was made acting wing commander until the new one came out. And I was commissioned in Malta. And one night I moved from the sergeants' mess to the officers' mess and that was my commission. I . . . bought myself a forage cap from Gieves . . . and a few inches of pilot officer braid, and took the sergeant stripes off my uniform. Pinned on, sewed on, the pilot officer braid, and that was commissioning in moving into the officers' mess.[8]

The squadron wasn't accommodated at Luqa because of the shortage of space. Instead, they lived in some barracks at Marsaxlokk. Nevertheless, the officers were accommodated at Luqa. On arrival in the officers' mess, Broom shared a room with a Canadian, who joked that he was his third room mate that week!

[7] IWM Sound Archive, Accession No.10981/3/1.
[8] IWM Sound Archive, Accession No.10981/3/1.

The big thing we noticed . . . we didn't get one ship come into Malta with supplies in the four and a half months I was there . . . we lived on Maconochies, which was meat and vegetables tinned, and we had it in every guise and form you can have it. The food was dull, and repetitive. We had this meat and vegetables fried, stewed, in pies, we had it curried, all sorts of ways . . .[9]

Night Fighters

The risk of being shot down by Malta's Hurricanes, and the heavy AA fire now amassed around the Grand Harbour and other key objectives, meant that most of the raids were now at night. A Malta Night Fighter Unit was established during the summer of 1941, initially using Hurricanes, although these aircraft were not at all well suited for their new role. The aircraft were guided onto their targets by searchlights and Malta's air defence radar. It was not until later that radar-equipped aircraft, initially Bristol Beaufighters and then de Havilland Mosquitoes, were to reach Malta, arriving in November 1942, after the real need for them had passed. The operation of the air defences over Malta at this time has been described as a 'three dimensional chess game'. It was not just a question of attackers and defenders, since as often as possible, the RAF and Fleet Air Arm would mount operational sorties against targets in Italy, Sicily and North Africa, and at sea, and often these aircraft would return badly damaged and unable to make the necessary manoeuvres expected of them. Added to this, there were night flights from both Gibraltar and Alexandria, flown usually by either BOAC or the RAF, and usually these pilots were complete strangers to the Mediterranean air war, and even those who were familiar with the situation, could find that changes had been made in the light of operational demands. Communication with incoming aircraft was difficult, since it

[9] IWM Sound Archive, Accession No.10981/3/1.

could only be made *en clair*, and therefore could reveal too much to the enemy.

To make use of the Hurricanes, the island was divided into two air defence zones, with a Hurricane patrolling each, and with Valletta as the dividing line. The two Hurricanes were kept informed of the course, speed and altitude of the bombers as they approached, until the attackers were some fifteen miles off Malta, when the Hurricanes would take a converging course to approach the targets on either side. The objective was to have the Hurricanes ready and waiting just as the bombers entered the searchlight zone. Experience showed that the defences had to be layered, with the Hurricanes responsible for aircraft above a certain height, and the AA gunners for all aircraft below that height. The system was ramshackle, but it worked, with subsequent analysis showing that out of every seven raiders flying over Malta, five were picked up by the searchlights, and of these, three would be attacked, of which two would be shot down. This meant that the *Regia Aeronautica* was suffering a far higher attrition rate than the RAF on its raids over Germany by this time. It was good, but not good enough, as a proportion of raiders continued to reach the airfields and the Grand Harbour, including one that sank the destroyer *Maori* with a direct hit.

Improving the Fighter Defences

Petty Officer Francis Smith of 828 Squadron remembers that the big air raids had started in December 1941, and that the number of aircraft destroyed on the ground soared from this time.

> But the real shock of Malta came over the Easter weekend, 1942. The Germans and the Italians hammered *hell* out of us. And by this time, because of the raids between Christmas and Easter, what few fighters Malta had left had either been shot down or been shot up on the deck (naval slang for the ground). And every month or so, the carriers used to come and fly off Hurricanes and Spitfires, from six

hundred miles away. Well those that got to the island got shot down when they got to the island, because the Mes were always waiting, all the time.

So come Easter-time, 1942, we had practically no fighters left, not many Swordfish or Albacores – because there was another squadron there, 830 – they were Swordfish, but they'd lost most of them as well.

. . . and there was practically no ack-ack ammunition left – that had all gone, because the convoys were no getting through. There was practically no food, there was no lights, there was no beer . . . there wasn't no anything. The island was really in an absolute desperate state, in May, 1942 . . .[10]

Queenie Lee also remembers those dark days.

Our red letter day was Sunday, 10th May, 1942: Spitfires had arrived . . . 36 enemy machines were brought down in an hour.

During these months fuel had become very scarce, and gas and electricity was cut off for five months.

During this time, I was teaching at the Royal Naval Dockyard School . . . one boy sometimes took 1½ to 2 hours to come to school, but come he did, and alone. They took the Oxford School Certificate and it took some time for the examination papers to arrive, but eventually they did, and they all passed.[11]

One of the RAF's leading fighter aces, 'Laddie' Lucas, a former journalist with the *Daily Express*, was amongst those based at Ta'Qali. Like the others, he had reached Malta having flown off an aircraft carrier.

'We were then flying the Spitfires off the carriers, and we had some disasters with that,' Lucas recalled some years after the war.

[10] IWM Sound Archive, Accession No.10476/4.
[11] IWM Sound Archive, Accession No.1172.

Mainly because they were sending pilots out who really weren't particularly well trained. If two pilots were asked to be sent out from a squadron, well, then, they sent people they didn't want, naturally. If you were a squadron commander and wanted to get rid of a couple of guys, send them out to Malta, so it was very rough on the people who were out there and surviving.

But any way, when the American aircraft carrier *Wasp*, was brought into play, which turned the battle in the middle of May, 9th and 10th May, for about ten days. It did two runs and it was fixed up by Churchill with Roosevelt, special concession, it could take forty-eight Spitfires, whereas the *Eagle* could only take sixteen.

And the first run, I mean, it went off very well, but within forty-eight hours, of the forty-seven aircraft, there was one which didn't go...they took off from a point about sixty miles north of Algiers, which was about 650 miles from the island, you couldn't get any closer, the Mediterranean Fleet wouldn't allow it. If the commander-in-chief said, 'That's quite close enough, you'll fly off from here with these 90 gallon tanks on', which we did, it was a fairly rough assignment. We did our own navigation and all that. And when this first forty-eight were flown off the *Wasp*, loaded up in Glasgow and just sent through the Straits, after forty-eight hours of course the Germans had been monitoring this all the way, and these raids came in one after another. And of course they beat these planes up on the ground, and I think there were seven serviceable aircraft after forty-eight hours . . .[12]

What had happened was that the USS *Wasp* had sailed from Glasgow with no less than forty-eight Spitfires for Malta, escorted by the battleship *Renown*, the anti-aircraft cruisers *Cairo* and *Charybdis* and a number of destroyers. Passing Gibraltar on 19 April, the ship launched her Spitfires towards Malta the following

[12] IWM Sound Archive, Accession No.10763/10.

day. She had not entered port at Gibraltar to avoid any delay and hoping to give no clue to the Germans about her intentions, but the Germans also used radio intercepts, could track the course of the convoy by its signals, and guessed that the *Wasp* was ferrying aircraft to Malta. They also managed to ascertain just when the aircraft were launched. Just one aircraft failed to reach Malta, but after the remaining forty-seven landed, roughly half each at Ta'Qali and Hal Far, a large air raid was mounted by Ju88s and Bf109s, catching the Spitfires on the ground, just twenty minutes after landing. Twenty of the aircraft were destroyed, and another twelve damaged.

Churchill managed to persuade Roosevelt to allow the *Wasp* a second run, this time in partnership with the *Eagle*, so that sixty-four aircraft were sent to Malta. This was still not enough to satisfy the AOC, Air Vice Marshal Hugh Lloyd. Lucas was amongst those who remembered Lloyd 'hijacking' aircraft intended for the Middle East.

Lloyd may have been something of a buccaneer, but he was also very practical. He ensured that a number of experienced fighter pilots were sent to Gibraltar so that they could lead in the aircraft from the carriers, keeping losses to the minimum. As for Lucas, he was so annoyed at the inaccurate coverage being given to the situation in Malta in his old newspaper, that he managed to send a story to them, circumventing wartime censorship by sending it via a friend during a visit to Gibraltar. Perhaps Lucas held such a high opinion of Lloyd for when the AOC heard about the story, he correctly guessed the identity of the culprit, and contented himself with telling Lucas: 'Well, it's a good story, isn't it, but you know you're not allowed to do that.'[13]

More important to anyone who has earned his living by writing, the newspaper sent Lucas a cheque for £50, which came in useful for a party in the officers' mess, and when the newspaper's proprietor heard about how much, or in his view, how little, had been sent, a further £50 followed!

Lucas had originally flown into Malta as a passenger in

[13] IWM Sound Archive, Accession No.10763/10.

February 1942, aboard a flying-boat from Gibraltar, landing at Kalafrana, alighting from the Short Sunderland just after dawn, and in time for the first air raid of the day. Lucas commented:

> And suddenly one heard the throb of sort of Rolls Royce engines, Merlin engines, and they sounded very rough I may say, and there were five old Hurricane IIs in an old fashioned vic formation which they'd given up in the Battle of Britain, just beginning to clamber up to gain height. And then about . . . nothing more than a minute or a couple of minutes later, high up, and you could just see it as the dawn was breaking on the haze, a lovely spring morning, February, there were these, probably a Staffel I suppose of 109s flying in that beautiful wide open nine abreast formation that they used to fly their Schwarms in. The rot (*Rotte*) the two aircraft was the . . . basis of their flying. But then they used to put them together in fours. And they were flying high up, high and fast.[14]

Lucas found flying the Hurricane was a great experience before the Spitfires arrived, and made him realize what the Hurricane pilots had suffered in the Battle of France, whereas the Spitfire V and the Bf109 were fairly evenly matched, with many pilots feeling that perhaps the Spitfire had a slight edge on the Bf109, although the Fw190 when it arrived was a far more potent aircraft. The Hurricanes had been cannibalised just to keep a few aircraft airworthy. He came to admire those who had been battling against the Germans in the Hurricanes for five or six months, and was glad when his own time with the aircraft lasted just a fortnight.

Lucas considered the real architect of the fighter defence of Malta to be his commanding officer, the then Squadron Leader, later Group Captain, Stanley Turner, a Canadian in the RAF. During the Battle of Britain, Turner had flown with Bader in the Tangmere fighter wing. He scrapped the outdated vic formations,

[14] IWM Sound Archive, Accession No.10763/10.

and taught the fighter pilots the technique known as 'finger fours'. The success of this technique was that the aircraft flew in line abreast, with the pilot on the right looking left and the one on the left looking right, covering the whole sky. It took Turner about a week to change 249 Squadron. Once the first Spitfires did arrive, Turner was rested from active flying, something that was long overdue as he had been flying in combat continuously from the start of the Battle of France in spring 1940.

The other great contributor to the fighter defence of Malta was 'Woody' Woodhall, credited by Lucas as being the best fighter controller that the Royal Air Force had in the Second World War. Post-war chief of the Italian Air Staff, Francesco Cavallera, who had been a fighter pilot based in Sicily during 1942, remarked to Lucas that, 'Your great advantage was that you had the radar and we didn't in Sicily and this made it very difficult'.

The role of the fighter controller was crucial to success. Watching the enemy aircraft assemble over their airfields in Sicily was simply the easy part of the job, the real skill lay in knowing when to order the fighters to take-off. Too early, and they could run short of fuel during prolonged combat. Too late, and they would not have time to get into position. It was also important to note the direction of any attack, as sometimes the attackers would try to work around the island and approach from a different direction hoping to catch the defenders off guard. It was important that the fighters should try to position themselves between the sun and the attacking force to maintain an element of surprise.

'These German raids used to come in like a railway timetable,' Lucas explained.

They used to come in at breakfast, lunch and dinner, just before dinner, sort of high tea time. And just occasionally they'd put in four but normally it was three (raids per day). And so if it was a morning raid old Woody'd get us up very high, twenty-five, twenty-six, twenty-seven thousand feet, south of the island. And then he'd start to bring us in and he would say, 'Now, the big jobs with a lot of little jobs

131

about and it's about eighty plus, approaching St Paul's Bay now. Suggest you come in now and come in fast.[15]

The fighters would dive down through the Messerschmitt Bf109s and straight into the bombers, but the shortage of fighters in Malta meant that these successes in breaking up the bombers had to be offset by the losses amongst the fighter squadrons after they had landed to refuel, when the Bf109s would come in fast and low in a strafing attack.

Much of the anti-shipping work continued to fall to the Fleet Air Arm's 830 Squadron with its Swordfish, later joined by the Albacores of 828 Squadron, stationed at what was then RAF Hal Far. Lucas recalls socializing with the Fleet Air Arm, and once again, food entered into the equation. The RAF had to make do with the uninteresting Maconochie's stew or bully beef, but the Fleet Air Arm seemed to be looking after themselves very well by comparison, and in the opinion of Lucas they probably had the best table on the island, better than that of the Governor, which was almost certainly true as he used the same rations as everyone else.

Many attacks by aircraft based in Malta were beyond the range at which fighter protection could be provided, but whenever fighters were available and an attack was within range, an escort would be provided. On one occasion, Lucas led a fighter escort for the Swordfish on a strike against two Italian cruisers off the coast of Tunisia near Cape Bon. Three Swordfish were flying very low. Staying high himself, Lucas sent a section of four aircraft down lower, as he watched the Swordfish start their attack. He saw two of the Swordfish hit by AA fire before they could release their torpedoes, but the third aircraft managed to torpedo an Italian cruiser.

On one occasion a Beaufort, believed to have been from 217 Squadron, flown by a South African, Ted Strever, was shot down, but the crew were rescued by the Italians and taken to one of the Greek islands, where they were given a good dinner with wine.

[15] IWM Sound Archive, Accession No.10763/10.

The next morning, they were loaded into an Italian flying boat to be taken to Taranto, guarded by an Italian corporal who had never flown before and who became very airsick. The hapless corporal was overpowered, and the Italian pilot forced to fly to Sicily where the Beaufort crew could plot a course to Malta. As they approached the island, they saw Spitfires coming to intercept the flying boat, at which point Strever ordered the Italian pilot to land the aircraft in the sea, some ten miles off Malta, although before this could happen the first Spitfire had made an attacking run. They were soon rescued. Before the Italians were sent off to a prison camp, Strever insisted that they be given dinner in the mess to repay them for their hospitality the previous evening, at the same time warning the Italians that they didn't have any decent wine. The Italians immediately offered the wine in their suitcases: they had been going on leave! Maconochie's stew or not, dinner that night was a decidedly jolly affair!

One point at which relations between the British and the Maltese came under some strain was when the Maltese found RAF pilots off duty in Valletta during air raids – they didn't realize that there weren't enough aircraft to go round!

When Lucas crash-landed in a field where Maltese women were packing potatoes into sacks, the three elderly ladies promptly emptied the sacks and filled them with earth before climbing onto the wing of his Spitfire and spreading the sacks on top of the smoking engine cowling.

'I have no doubt at all that the women had the most remarkable courage there.'[15]

'Speedfires'

The arrival of the Spitfires had been cloaked in secrecy, or so Sir William Dobbie had thought. He always made a point of visiting areas most seriously affected by the bombing raids. On 7 March, he visited a small village close to Luqa. Despite the heavy damage

[16] IWM Sound Archive, Accession No.10476/4.

to the village, most of the population had escaped, taking cover in the shelters. The nine fatalities had all come from the same family, who had their own private shelter beneath their house, but when this received a direct hit, the shelter collapsed into the cistern under the building, leaving those present to drown.

On this occasion, the Governor was in for a shock. Chatting with an elderly and very loyal Maltese, a veteran of the ill-starred Gallipoli campaign, he learnt that the man was expecting 'Speedfires' to be sent to the island soon: Dobbie had thought that only four or five people knew about the impending arrival of the Spitfires.

The man assured him that he had been told about the aircraft coming by the airmen at Luqa! Everyone knew about the aircraft, but no one knew when they would arrive.

Dobbie's next call that day was to Floriana. The old church of St Publius was still standing, although badly pockmarked by shrapnel and splinters, but the area around it had suffered grievously. He entered the main shelter, the old railway tunnel, and found those present in the vastly overcrowded tunnel, intent on their devotions.

As he moved on to his next visit, he was relieved not to hear the word Spitfire. He was soon to hear something else. As he left the shelter, shortly after 13.30, he heard the noise of aircraft engines, as aircraft raced in low, causing those around him to fear a German raid approaching beneath the radar coverage. People outside began to disperse and seek shelter, shouting warnings about the impending German attack. Suddenly, impervious to what seemed like imminent danger, a small boy shouted 'Hurrah . . . Spitfires'. Everyone turned, stared and started clapping, shouting hysterically, and offering prayers of thanks to the Almighty, Santa Marija and to the many favourite saints.

Fifteen Spitfires had been flown in from the deck of the veteran aircraft carrier HMS *Eagle*, some miles to the west, while south of the Balearic Islands.

That night, the fighter base at RAF Ta'Qali was bombed, something that was all too painfully obvious to those sheltering under the towns of Rabat and Mosta close to the airfield.

Several aircraft carriers played a part in these operations, including the veterans *Furious*, *Argus* and *Eagle*, the first two having been commissioned before the end of the First World War, and the modern *Ark Royal*, but the most significant contribution came with two deliveries by the USS *Wasp*, able to send forty-eight Spitfires at a time to the island.

On 10 March, the Spitfires saw action for the first time, climbing high before diving on to a small formation of three Ju88s escorted by Bf109s. Malta's AA gunners shot down one Ju88, before the Spitfires shot down a Bf109 and sent two others flying away trailing smoke. Once the score was tallied up later, it was found that the guns had accounted for one Junkers, with two definite and four probably Bf109s for the Spitfires, with another two probables for the Hurricanes.

On 20 April, forty-seven Spitfires were flown in off the *USS Wasp*. These aircraft never had a chance, as the new German air unit in Sicily, *Fliegerkorps II*, caught most of the aircraft on the ground, often as soon as they landed and before they could be refuelled and rearmed. The most any of them lasted was three days, due to the lack of protected accommodation. Kesselring was able to report to Goering that Malta was neutralized. On 9 May, sixty-one more aircraft were flown in from the *Wasp* and *Eagle*, and this time, the ground-crews had been rehearsed in what to do, turning the aircraft round so that many were back in the air in less than thirty-five minutes.

It was not surprising that Rommel was so enthusiastic over the idea of invading Malta in early 1941, but by June, 1941, the opportunity had gone following the debacle on Crete, and, the launch of Operation Barbarossa, Germany's invasion of the Soviet Union. It was Barbarossa that eased the Luftwaffe's pressure on Malta, just as it brought the blitz on British cities to a premature end. One of the objectives of Barbarossa was to secure oil supplies for the Axis; as it faltered and finally failed, the growing shortage of oil was to be felt most severely by Hitler's ally, Mussolini.

On 9 May, when HMS *Eagle* and USS *Wasp* between them had flown off a total of sixty-four Spitfire MkVs to Malta, three were lost en route. On arrival in Malta, some of the Spitfires were without their usual armament, carrying spares in their place. Meanwhile, the fast minelaying cruiser HMS *Welshman* was racing along the Algerian coast at her full 40 knots.

Francis Smith was with the Fleet Air Arm's 828 Squadron that had been sent to Malta ahead of its Fairey Albacore aircraft, pilots and observers, and found himself working with others to prepare for the safe arrival of the Spitfires. He recalled:

> . . . we knew they were coming, so what we did, we built pens of empty two-gallon petrol cans, filled up with sand, we built pens, and we organised everybody on the island – civilians, sailors, soldiers, everybody – into working parties, so many to an aircraft. All these aircraft came in, and I think about a third of them were left to use up their petrol in fighting the Mes, and the other two thirds landed.
>
> Well as these aircraft landed they were grabbed by a duty crew of eight or nine people, they were refuelled and rearmed, and they got airborne. And it worked – they got airborne in time to let the others come down, those that stopped up in the air. And this shook the Germans something wicked, it did. Because they knew that week before we hadn't got any fighters . . . so they got a nasty shock.[17]

The improvised aircraft shelters built in this way were sometimes known as sangers. The ready availability of so many empty fuel cans was the result of having fuel brought in small quantities aboard submarines and the *Manxman* and *Welshman*, the two fast minelaying cruisers. Ordinary merchantmen bound for Malta would also include some fuel amongst their cargo, although naturally this was nowhere near as efficient as using a tanker, but it did mean that some proportion of supplies got through if the tanker was sunk.

Good fortune accompanied the Maltese at this moment, since there was time to re-install the armament of the newly arrived

[16] IWM Sound Archive, Accession No.10476/4.

Spitfires, who went into battle on 9 May when there were ten air raids and between them, the fighters and the gunners accounted for thirty enemy aircraft.

No one could argue that the British were not trying. It was also clear that a cold calculation had been made. Malta could not unload so many big ships at once, so it was plain that not all were expected to reach the Grand Harbour.

Malta must have been a frustrating posting for Smith, since he was a TAG, telegraphist/air-gunner, and most of the operations from Malta dispensed with the TAGs, the flying being left to the pilots and observers since most of it was at night. Smith and his comrades had been told that they were going to the Mediterranean aboard two cruisers, but had assumed that their destination was Alexandria and were surprised to be put ashore at Malta, where no one seemed to be expecting them. He had to telephone the RAF to get transport to Hal Far. From October, with its aircraft and aircrew all together again, 828 operated with the resident 830 Squadron as the Naval Air Squadron Malta. Their arrival was not an unalloyed blessing. The Albacore had been intended as a replacement for the Swordfish, and although still a biplane with a fixed undercarriage, it did at least have a canopy. In fact, its Taurus engine was unreliable and the Albacore's successor, the monoplane Fairey Barracuda, was a maintenance nightmare, so Swordfish with its reliable Pegasus engine remained in service throughout the war in Europe. The Fleet Air Arm Songbook had something to say, or sing, about it:

> *The Swordfish relies on her Peggy,*
> *The modified Taurus ain't sound.*
> *So the Swordfish flies off on her missions*
> *And the Albacore stays on the ground.*

Back to the Offensive

Later we will see how the safe arrival of the tanker *Ohio* on 15 August 1942, saw Malta-based aircraft return to an all-out offensive, with the need for defensive sorties very much reduced as the Luftwaffe and *Regia Aeronautica* came under pressure. This was in complete contrast to the situation just a few months earlier, in the spring, when a final all-out attempt had been made by the Germans and the Italians to neutralize Malta in the run up to the planned invasion, and at times the island's defences were once more almost completely in the hands of the AA batteries, themselves running short of ammunition. This renewed blitz ended when the Axis bombers were withdrawn in May, but were renewed in July as soon as the RAF and the Fleet Air Arm resumed their attacks on shipping. The July bombing raids were less severe than those earlier. The priority throughout this period was to keep the airfields in Malta operational, filling craters and continuing to work, even when unexploded bombs or landmines made this hazardous.

The plight of Rommel's forces in North Africa because of the success of the aircraft based in Malta provoked another attempt to neutralize the island's airfields and squadrons in October, with Malta's Spitfires being scrambled up to six times a day. This final attempt was short-lived as the Luftwaffe and *Regia Aeronautica* losses were too heavy to be sustained. Finally, the Eighth Army's victory at El Alamein, followed soon after by the Allied landings in North Africa, marked the turning of the tide.

X

THE WAR AT SEA

Malta had already become an offensive base for the Fleet Air Arm and the Royal Air Force; in 1941 it became a base for submarines. This was not without its difficulties, since most of the necessary supplies had been taken to Alexandria, but submarines operated from Gibraltar to Malta overloaded with torpedoes and other equipment until stocks were built up. Submarines were also set to become an important link in the attempts to supply Malta.

Enter the U-Class

Throughout 1941, Malta continued to develop its offensive capability, helped in February by the arrival of the first of a new class of submarines, the U-class, while Grand Harbour also was the base for four destroyers. The destroyers were more powerful ships than earlier classes, marking the continuing evolution of the destroyer from the relatively small torpedo-boat destroyer of the early years of the century to a ship with broader potential, and included the 'J'-class fleet destroyers, HMS *Janus* and *Jervis*, and the Tribal-class fleet destroyers *Mohawk* and *Nubian*.

The clear waters of the Mediterranean had proved fatal for larger submarines, but the new U-class of smaller submarines was better suited to the Mediterranean, and of these, nine were deployed to Malta; *Undaunted, Union, Upholder, Upright, Utmost, Unique, Urge, Ursula* and *Usk*. The first two, *Usk* and *Undaunted*, nevertheless, did not survive long, but their place was soon taken by others of the same class. In addition to attacking Axis convoys and warships, these submarines were also ideal for landing raiding parties on the Italian coast, and on one occasion wrecked a railway line along which trains carrying munitions for the Luftwaffe bases in Sicily travelled.

The submarines were based at Manoel Island, which lay in the Marsamxett Harbour and was approached by a causeway just off the main road to Sliema, the island effectively dividing Sliema Creek from Lazzaretto Creek. Originally a fort designed to protect the outskirts of Valletta, which towered over the other side of the harbour, Manoel Island was now a naval base, with workshops and accommodation for resting submariners and for the artificers, the Royal Navy's skilled tradesmen. The submarines were moored alongside. Substantial AA defences were placed on Manoel Island, but being on the other side of Valletta from Grand Harbour did not spare the base from heavy aerial attack, and at the worst of the raids, the submarines found it safer to rest on the bottom, fully submerged.

The Malta-based submarines and Swordfish embarked on a campaign to sever the Axis supply lines between Italy and North Africa. The favoured hunting ground for the submarine commanders was the area off the Kerkenah Bank, even though it was heavily mined and contained many natural hazards to safe navigation. On the plus side, the Italians could only listen using hydrophones, but had nothing as effective as the British sonar, known at the time as Asdic, and also lacked radar. The campaign started in February 1941 with offensive patrols by *Unique*, *Upright* and *Utmost*. The first significant operation was in late February, when *Upright*, commanded by Lieutenant E. D. Norman, sunk the Italian cruiser *Armando Diaz*, one of two cruisers escorting a large German convoy. No doubt the Italians had committed two cruisers to this role to put on a show for their allies, but there were no major British warships in the area, and the cruiser, which posed no threat at all to a submarine, proved an ideal target. The effect on British and Maltese morale can be imagined!

Reconnaissance reports of large-scale shipping movements, received on 8 March, resulted in these three boats being sent to sea, even though *Utmost*, commanded by Lieutenant Commander C. D. Caylet, had only been in harbour for twenty-four hours. Despite this, the following day, *Utmost* found and sank the

Italian merchantman *Capo Vita*. On 10 March, *Unique* sank another merchantman, the *Fenicia*. Later in the month, these submarines were at sea again, with *Utmost* finding a convoy of five ships on 28 March, and torpedoing and sinking the *Heraklia* while the *Ruhr* had to be towed into port. The return voyage for the depleted convoy was no less eventful, when *Upright* torpedoed and severely damaged the *Galilea*, reported as being a straggler.

April saw *Upholder* join the flotilla, and for almost a year she, and her commander, Lieutenant Commander Malcolm Wanklyn, played havoc with the Axis convoys. From April 1941 to March 1942, this one submarine accounted for three large troop-carrying liners each of more than 18,000 tons, seven other merchant ships, a destroyer and two German U-boats, as well as damaging a further cruiser and three merchant ships. The first two troop-carrying liners had been in a convoy of three approached by Wanklyn steering on the surface, who then skil-fully fired a spread of four torpedoes at the ships. Two of the troopships managed to zigzag into the path of the torpedoes, with one sinking immediately, leaving the other to be finished off by Wanklyn when he returned the following morning. *Ursula* missed the third troopship, which managed to reach Tripoli safely. For his time in the Mediterranean, Wanklyn was awarded both the Victoria Cross, the highest British service decoration, and the DSO. It was a sad day when *Upholder* was lost off Tripoli with all of her crew in April 1942.

For a period of about a year, the Malta-based submariners exacted a high price from the enemy, but opportunities could be missed. Probably more than any other type of warship, submarines need to practise 'deconfliction', largely because of the difficulty of recognizing other submarines. 'Deconfliction' is the deliberate separation of friendly forces. In British submarine practice, this meant placing submarines to operate inde-pendently within designated patrol zones known as billets, and any other submarine found in that area was to be regarded as hostile. Yet, off Malta there were often so many British submarines that it was necessary to impose an embargo on night

141

attacks on other submarines because of the difficulty in accurate recognition.

During the early hours of one morning in 1942, HMS *Upright* was on the surface when her lookouts spotted another larger submarine on a reciprocal course, and it was not until they passed that they realized that the other submarine was a large U-boat. A missed opportunity! Of course, there were many U-boats off Malta at the time, and no one will ever know if the Germans were working to the same rules, or whether their lookouts failed to spot the smaller British submarine!

The Magic Carpet

The idea of using submarines to carry supplies was not new – it dated from the First World War when the Germans had established a company to operate merchant submarines to bring much needed strategic materials from the United States and bypass the increasingly effective British blockade of German ports. The siege of Malta presented an opportunity for British submarines to show what they could do, carrying supplies on what became known as 'Magic Carpet' runs. At first the Axis grip on Malta was relatively light, and losses on the early convoys were few and far between, but by 1941, the situation was increasingly difficult, and it became the practice for every submarine heading to Malta from both Gibraltar and Alexandria to attempt to carry at least some items of stores in addition to their usual torpedoes or mines. The 'Magic Carpet' submarines, however, were the larger submarines, and included the minelaying submarines *Rorqual* and *Cachalot*, the fleet submarine *Clyde* and the larger boats of the O, P and R classes. The tragedy was that had not an unfortunate accident deprived the Royal Navy of its sole aircraft carrying submarine, *M2*, some years before the war, that boat's hangar would have made an ideal cargo hold. In fact, the Royal Navy could have used the French submarine *Surcouf*, a large 2,800 ton boat also with a hangar, but never did so even though she was with the Free French rather than Vichy forces. Some have surmised that doubts over the reliability of her crew might

142

have been behind this failure, but it is more likely to have been a failure of the imagination, since the crew could have been taken off and a British one installed – but in any event, *Surcouf* was lost in the Caribbean.

The Porpoise-class minelayers and *Clyde* were especially effective as supply ships, with plenty of room between their casing and the pressure hull for stores while sometimes one of the batteries would be removed to provide extra space as happened on *Clyde* on at least one occasion, and the mine stowage tunnel was a good cargo space. *Rorqual* on one occasion carried twenty-four personnel, 147 bags of mail, two tons of medical stores, sixty-two tons of aviation spirit and forty-five tons of kerosene. Inevitably, there was much unofficial cargo, a favourite being gin for the wardrooms and messes in Malta, and even Lord Gort, Dobbie's successor as governor, was not above having a small consignment of gramophone records brought out to him in this way. Cargo was sometimes carried externally in containers welded to the casing.

The operation was not without its problems and the size of cargo that could be carried, while impressive in itself, could never compare with that of an average merchant ship, at this period around 7,500 tons. This was a measure of the desperation of Malta's plight! For the submariners, there were problems with buoyancy. On one occasion *Cachalot* had so much sea water absorbed by wooden packing cases stowed in her casing that her first lieutenant had to pump out 1,000 gallons of water from her internal tanks to compensate. Fuel was another hazard. In July 1941, *Talisman* carried 5,500 gallons in cans stowed beneath her casing, and on other occasions fuel could be carried in external fuel tanks. When carrying petrol in cans, submarines were not allowed to dive below sixty-five feet, while aviation fuel in the external tanks meant that fumes venting in the usual way constituted a fire hazard, so smoking was banned on the bridge and pyrotechnic recognition signals were also banned. Another problem was that the Mediterranean favoured smaller rather than larger submarines, with its clear waters and the lack of great depths, although, of course, these submarines were always too close to the surface anyway.

One disadvantage of the convoy system is that ships come in bunches, like London buses, rather than one or two at a time when port facilities can cope easily. The submarines were free of this inconvenience, the case of feast and famine, and made supply runs once every twelve days or so.

In addition to flying her 'Jolly Roger' at the end of a successful patrol, HMS *Porpoise* added a second flag flown beneath the Jolly Roger's tally of ships sunk – this was marked PCS for 'Porpoise Carrier Service', with a white bar for each successful supply run, and there were at least four for this one boat alone.

The 'Magic Carpet' submarines did not confine themselves to their supply runs. After unloading in Malta, they would take mines from the underground stores and proceeded north to lay them off the main Italian ports, such as Palermo, before returning to Egypt. On a number of occasions, these submarines also found and torpedoed Axis shipping, with one torpedoing and sinking an Italian submarine and then torpedoing an Italian merchant-man, which stubbornly refused to sink until the submarine surfaced and sank her with gunfire.

Meagre though the capacity of the submarines might have been compared with that of cargo ships and tankers, the steady trickle of supplies did at least stave off defeat. Their work was augmented by a tenuous air link with Gibraltar, operated by the newly-formed British Overseas Airways Corporation, formed in 1940 on the merger of Imperial Airways with its lively competitor, British Airways, which operated ex-RAF Armstrong-Whitworth Whitley bombers, modified to carry supplies.

Destroyer Actions

Meanwhile, the destroyers had not been idle. Typical of the early successes achieved by the destroyers was the night action of 15–16 April 1941. On 15 April, one of 431 Flight's Martin Baltimores discovered a convoy of five Italian merchantmen escorted by three destroyers, and on closer investigation, it was clear that the ships were carrying troops, tanks and other vehicles, intended for Rommel. A short but pertinent message

144

was immediately sent to Malta, where the destroyers *Janus*, *Jervis*, *Mohawk* and *Nubian*, were waiting. It took them just three hours to intercept the convoy, and on a brief but furious night engagement, all of the Italian ships were sunk, although one of the destroyers, *Tarigo*, managed to torpedo the *Mohawk*, sinking her before herself being sent to the bottom by the remaining British ships.

Then, just a few days later, on 21 April, the Mediterranean Fleet ventured west for a major attack on the Italian-held port of Tripoli. This operation was integrated with another, intended to ensure that oil and aviation fuel was fought through to Malta. This started on 18 April, with a convoy from Alexandria, and as usual in the Mediterranean, a sizeable and powerful escort was provided. Leaving 'Alex' at 07.00, the escort was headed by Cunningham's flagship, *Warspite*, accompanied by the Mediterranean Fleet's other two battleships, *Barham* and *Valiant*, and the new carrier *Formidable*, as well as two cruisers, *Phoebe* and *Cairo*, with a large destroyer screen. The difficulties facing Malta and the dangers for shipping approaching the central Mediterranean are amply illustrated by the fact that all of this was to provide cover for just one ship, the armed tanker *Breconshire*. It was also part of the plan for the escort to bring back four merchantmen from Malta. The *Breconshire* was left to continue her course into Malta safely shortly after nightfall on 20 April. That night, Tripoli was bombed by Malta-based RAF Wellingtons and Fleet Air Arm Swordfish. Oddly, *Formidable*'s own aircraft were limited on this occasion to flare dropping and spotting for the guns of the Fleet, rather than adding to the efforts of the Malta squadrons. Tripoli was mainly occupied by merchant ships and their escorts, usually nothing bigger than a destroyer. To ensure accurate shore bombardment, usually a great difficulty when attacking from the sea in the dark, Cunningham had the submarine *Truant* positioned accurately four miles off the harbour, showing a light to seaward as a navigation mark.

Joined by the cruiser *Gloucester* as they steamed south through the night, the Mediterranean Fleet sailed past the surfaced submarine *Truant* during the early morning of 21 April, just

145

before daylight, in what was literally the darkest hour before dawn, at least for the Italian defenders, when from 05.00 to 05.45, in Cunningham's own words, they 'pumped 15-inch and 6-inch shell into the harbour and amongst the shipping. The *Gloucester*'s sixteen gun salvoes must have been particularly effective.' In any such bombardment, those on the ships could see little of the damage being done, especially in this case as the air raids, which had only just ceased, had created clouds of dust and smoke from the fires started, but *Formidable*'s aircraft reported that five or six ships had been sunk, and it looked as if *Valiant*'s guns had set off an oil fire in storage tanks ashore.

This was another instance of the Italians not being prepared, despite, or perhaps because of, the air raids. Two consecutive attacks on one night seemed to have been beyond their comprehension. A full twenty minutes passed before the shore batteries came into action, and even then, their shells flew over the attacking warships, which suffered no hits at all. Inexplicably, the Luftwaffe also failed to put in an appearance, leaving Cunningham to surmise that possibly the radio station at Tripoli had been put out of action. Before the operation, with the agonies of *Illustrious* in January still fresh his mind, he had been expecting anything from the loss of a major ship in an enemy minefield to the destruction of several ships or heavy damage to all of them from a heavy Luftwaffe attack.

This was the Mediterranean Fleet operating at its best, for while Tripoli was under attack, Vice Admiral Pridham-Whippell took the Mediterranean Fleet's cruisers, with a destroyer escort, to attack coastal targets between Tripoli and Benghazi. After daybreak, as the Fleet started its return to Alexandria, three Junkers Ju88s attempted to attack, but Fulmars from *Formidable* shot down two of them and chased off the third.

During the first six months of war, from June to November 1940, the Italians had lost just four ships en route to North Africa, with a total tonnage of 11,104 tons. From December 1940, to the following March, they lost thirty ships with a total tonnage of 109,089 tons. Nevertheless, the two divisions of Rommel's new *Afrika Korps* managed to reach North Africa with few losses.

Effective control of the seas at this time would have done much to shorten the war and ease Malta's plight, but effective control of the seas now, as in no previous conflict, meant effective control of the air!

The work of the destroyers was reinforced by two light cruisers, HMS *Penelope* and *Aurora*, that were based at Malta from October 1941, and with the destroyers *Lance* and *Lively* formed Force K under Captain W. G. Agnew. At this time, Malta was also home to the cruiser *Ajax*, heroine of the Battle of the River Plate, although out of action. Less happily, after the evacuation from Crete, Cunningham no longer had a single battleship or, more important, an aircraft carrier. Had the Italians sent their battleships and heavy cruisers to sea, not to mention their substantial fleet of submarines that on Italy's entry into the war had far exceeded those of Germany in September 1939, the situation for Malta would have been hopeless.

The light cruiser *Penelope* was to be so badly damaged by shrapnel during her service in the Mediterranean and the stay at Malta, that she was nicknamed 'HMS Pepperpot'. The thin plating of a cruiser's hull was easily repaired, but repeated damage meant that she spent much of her time with her hull literally bristling with the small wooden plugs used by damage control parties to rectify small holes from shrapnel or machine-gun attack.

Force K was not long in proving its worth. Persuaded by the *Regia Aeronautica* that the two cruisers were so badly damaged as to be out of action, on 9 November the Italians sent a convoy of seven ships to North Africa with an escort of two cruisers and ten destroyers. Far from being confined to port, Force K turned up and in the engagement that followed, all seven merchant ships were sunk, as well as a destroyer, with another so badly damaged that she sunk later. On 20 November, another convoy was spotted with four ships escorted by two cruisers and eight destroyers. The two cruisers were badly damaged by torpedoes and the entire convoy beat a hasty retreat into Taranto. Two other ships were spotted steaming from Piraeus to join the convoy, and these were promptly sunk by *Penelope* and *Lively*. All this contributed to the loss of 54,900 tons of Italian shipping in November.

While spring and early summer 1942 saw a dramatic reduction in the Royal Navy's presence in Malta as the air attacks took their toll, the safe arrival of the convoy, Operation Pedestal, in August saw increased submarine activity. That was when the submarine *Saracen* arrived. Her First Lieutenant was Lieutenant, later Commander Edward Young,[1] who had started his career in submarines as a 'third hand' aboard HMS *Sealion* off Norway, attacking German coastal convoys.

From Gibraltar we were sent in convoy to Malta, which by this time was very much under siege. In order to get aviation petrol to Malta, two of our fuel tanks were cleared of diesel, and filled with aviation petrol. When we got to Malta, we not only had the petrol, but also other stores, including food. It was a relief to get all of this stuff out of the boat.

We then joined the flotilla of S-boats and . . . U-class boats.

We attacked a convoy, intending to sink a merchant-man, but the destroyers were too close so that we sank the destroyer instead, a German destroyer.

I don't think that we had very much trouble. There were a lot of planes going over all of the time, and we had constantly to go deep to avoid being seen. In the Mediterranean we did see an Italian submarine who appeared to be keeping no look out at all. We attacked him with three torpedoes and sank him. There were no survivors at all.

We didn't have much time for going into the town, everyone was very hungry, even we were hungry, although we were not as badly off as the Maltese . . . We weren't sent to get supplies for Malta, we simply brought some from Gibraltar as we were going there anyway.

[1] IWM Sound Archive, Accession No.12317.

We had a night encounter with an Italian submarine that flashed a long and unintelligible signal.

By October, 1942, the situation continued to be difficult, and there was even the renewed German air offensive in October, a last twitch of a wounded animal. Malta-based units remained on the offensive, with the submarines *Unbending*, *Unbroken*, *United*, *Utmost* and *Safari* attacking a convoy of five merchant ships, including a tanker, escorted by seven destroyers south of the Italian island of Pantelleria, coordinating the attack with aircraft from Malta.

XI

LIVING AMONGST THE MALTESE

'Malta was essentially a friendly place, with close links through marriage between the many families on the island,' recalls Queenie Lee. 'As for the English families, they drew together in the way that the English do when away from home.'[1]

This was essentially true before, during and after the war, but wartime put some aspects of the relationship under extreme pressure. This was not because the Maltese showed any resentment about being involved in the war, since they never forgave Mussolini for bombing Malta, but because of other pressures; being under constant enemy air attack, with interrupted sleep and with little food.

Not surprisingly, morale was crumbling, but it was not just because of the poor food situation and the constant attacks. Many Maltese felt that their own acts of gallantry were often overlooked while those of the British were exaggerated, typified by the saying, 'If a Britisher sneezes, he gets a medal for it'. It is tempting to suggest that this was rather akin to the widespread British belief that American servicemen were awarded the Purple Heart for simply being in an air raid, but there do seem to be some grounds for this resentment. A Maltese gunner hit between the shoulders by a shell splinter during a raid remained at his post, firing his gun, even though he was in great pain and unable to move his neck, had his heroism and devotion to duty simply recorded and did not receive any award. By contrast, a British

[1] IWM Sound Archive, Accession No.1172.

150

warrant officer received an MBE for saving pots and pans from a bombed out kitchen so that he could make his men a meal. Then, inevitably, there was the story of a British major receiving the Military Cross for swimming across the harbour to reach the batteries on the other side, yet those who knew him maintained that he couldn't even swim!

These problems apart, relations between the British forces on the island and the Maltese were for the most part very good. There was mutual respect on both sides.

' . . . I think the Maltese stuck it out very well, especially the gun crews, the Maltese gun crews,' recalls Francis Smith, a Fleet Air Arm telegraphist/air gunner based at Hal Far.

> Of course, the airfield got bombed, bombed out completely, and we moved down to the seashore, place called Birzebbugia, and we lived in a little hotel down there, for the sergeants' mess. And we had a gun-pit next door to the mess, and that got a direct hit one night, in August, and they . . . were in a shocking state, the gun crew. But they bore up very well. And so did the women. I had tons of time for the way they stuck it out, the Maltese . . .[2]

Gort did his best to establish good relations with the Maltese, not waiting for air raids to visit the towns and villages, but instead embarking on a programme of visits. At first he was hesitant about meeting the Bishop of Gozo, who was suspected of nursing anti-British sentiments. It soon became clear that the suspicions were ill-founded, especially after the Bishop accompanied the Archbishop of Malta to the George Cross award ceremony, and asked for a repeat performance for his people in Gozo.

Relationships with the Maltese were also often very good on another level. Young men, far away from home, were very susceptible to the charms of young Maltese girls. Any Maltese girl 'walking out' with a boyfriend or even a fiancé would be

[2] IWM Sound Archive, Accession No.10476/4/4.

chaperoned, but often more serious relationships developed. The prospect of marriage must have seemed attractive to both sides, but there were important problems to be overcome, and the chances of the marriage lasting were not good. One estimate was that, in 1940, there were some 2,000 abandoned Maltese women who had been 'navy wives'. Martin Hastings recalls attempts by the British Army to try to put a stop to the practice, not by banning it, which would have been unacceptable, but by making the young soldiers think ahead, and consider the differences. For a start, the order was made that anyone wanting to marry a Maltese would have to become a Roman Catholic, and undergo a course of instruction from their unit's Roman Catholic padre, so that the soldiers understood the Roman Catholic faith and accepted that any children would be brought up as Roman Catholics.

'So the policy was if possible delay and make the soldier think twice about how the Maltese girl, who was used to sun and quite a different way of life, being of a different religious faith, would get on in the grey skies of an English small town or village,' Hastings explained. 'But of course the soldier was free to do what he wanted to do basically.'[3]

There were, inevitably, those Maltese who saw their closest neighbour Italy as their natural partner. The fact that there were not more, despite the differences in language and ancestry, nevertheless speaks volumes. After all, many Maltese priests were trained in Italy, and that country provided the closest and least expensive location for much academic and professional training. The one thing that both Italians and Maltese had in common was their Roman Catholic faith, even more of a unifying factor then than now because services at the time were conducted in Latin rather than in the vernacular.

As mentioned earlier, the one prominent Maltese who was known to hold pro-Italian sympathies was the Chief Justice, Sir Arturo Mercieca. On the first morning of war, he was summoned to see the new Governor, the newly-promoted Lieutenant

[3] IWM Sound Archive, Accession No.10453/6

General William Dobbie and the Lieutenant Governor, Sir Edward Jackson. He arrived late because of the air raids. On entering the office he was immediately invited to resign from his position as Chief Justice and President of the Court of Appeal because of his Italian sympathies and the state of war that existed with Italy. General Dobbie continued to tell him that if he did not resign voluntarily, he would be removed from office without further delay since the King had signed an Order in Council on the 5 June authorizing his removal from office. Mercieca asked to see the Order and was promptly shown it. He told those present that he felt that his impartiality as a judge had been compromised by the Order and agreed to resign, on condition that he could make his resignation public and refer to the Order in the letter.

Initially, Mercieca was told that he and his family would face restrictions on their activities, but could stay in the family's summer home at Naxxar, near Mosta in the centre of Malta. Later he and others with pro-Italian sympathies were arrested and interned. Their internment, initially under the benevolent protection of the Maltese Major Walter Bonello, was initially fairly relaxed, and contact was maintained with their families. Early in 1942, most of the internees were moved to Kenya, and not allowed back until late 1944 and early 1945. Internment was undoubtedly essential, to avoid information being transmitted to the enemy or any acts of protest, but it may even have saved their lives as the full horror of the war developed. No charges were ever brought against them, and no one has ever suggested that they were criminals or spies, but the risk was enough, and they were probably some of the best treated internees in any of the combatant territories.

XII

THE HUNGRY SPRING

Compared with the hope that marked the beginning of 1941, the year 1942 started with a bleak outlook. The Royal Navy's main force in the Mediterranean had been crippled with the loss of its two battleships, following the earlier withdrawal of the aircraft carrier *Formidable* as just one element in the heavy losses and damage suffered during the invasion of Crete. At the beginning of 1942, the Mediterranean Fleet had four light cruisers and an anti-aircraft cruiser, and a number of destroyers, the latter being useful, but hopelessly out-gunned by the major fleet units of the Italian Navy

The situation was no better at the other end of the Mediterranean. HMS *Ark Royal*, mainstay of Force H, which had ferried aircraft to within flying-off distance of Malta and had provided combat air patrols and anti-submarine protection for convoys, was torpedoed by *U-81* on 13 November 1941, sinking the next day. The battleship *Barham* was torpedoed and sunk off Sollum by *U-331* on 24 November, exploding four minutes later and taking 862 of her ship's company with her. Earlier, she had survived two direct hits by 500-lbs bombs during the evacuation of Crete. The irony was that Cunningham had later rejected an Admiralty suggestion that she be scuttled in the entrance of Tripoli harbour to prevent Axis supplies reaching North Africa.

The following month, dismayed by Malta's ability to host the aircraft and ships destroying eighty per cent of the supplies being sent to the *Afrika Korps,* and with Luftwaffe units freshly back from the Russian front where the extreme cold of the winter made operations difficult, the aerial bombardment of Malta was stepped up once again. These heavier air raids resumed on 4 December 1941.

At sea, *U-557* torpedoed and sank the cruiser *Galatea*, while *Penelope*, *Aurora* and *Neptune* ran into a newly-laid minefield, with the first two damaged and *Neptune* sunk, while the destroyer *Kandahar* was so badly damaged that she had to be sunk. Force K's brief existence was at an end. Elsewhere, as mentioned earlier, the *Decima Flottiglia Mas* had pressed home a successful attack on the Mediterranean Fleet at Alexandria, leaving the battleships *Queen Elizabeth* and *Valiant* sitting on the floor of the harbour – it was simply fortunate that they remained upright and with the Italian charioteers who had inflicted the damage taken prisoner, the bad news was concealed from the Italians.

The September convoy had brought hope and some relief from the pressures of war, but bread still included twenty-thirty per cent potato, and most commodities were scarce.

Faced with heavier air raids and renewed Axis activity at sea, supplies started to be shuttled into Malta by the three minelaying submarines *Clyde*, *Olympus* and *Porpoise*, using Marsaxlokk as a port. This was some relief, but not a lot, as at the most they could only bring in 200 tons each at a time, and with priority given to aircraft fuel, there was little for the civilian population.

January 1942, saw honours for those who had done so much to keep Malta going. There was a KCB for Vice Admiral Wilbraham Ford; a knighthood for Major General S. J. Scobell and a CB for Air Vice Marshal Lloyd, as well as an OBE for Dr A. V. Laferla, Director of Education, and MBEs for Joseph E. Axisa, Commissioner of Police, and Emanuel Camilleri, Postmaster General. Ford was soon to be replaced by Vice Admiral Sir Ralph Leatham, while the Army also changed GOCs, with Major General Scobell replaced by Major General D. M. V. Beak. It is interesting to note that the naval commander was a rank senior to his military counterpart, and indeed to the AOC.

The Attacks Increase

'I've given up the number of raids we are getting. At the time of writing, 4pm, we have had exactly seven bombing raids since

9am, quite apart from a month of all-night efforts,' Vice Admiral Sir Wilbraham Ford wrote to Cunningham on 3 January.

> The enemy is definitely trying to neutralise Malta's effort, and, I hate to say, is gradually doing so. They have bust a sad number of our bombers and fighters, etc, and must continue to do so . . . Minesweeping is now difficult, and they appear to be laying them everywhere . . . Work in the yard is naturally very much slowed up as the result of the constant raids.[1]

Ford wanted modern fighters, meaning Spitfires, suggesting that they could be flown off a carrier.

His assessment was shared by Italian Intelligence.

> In consequence of the repeated air attacks on Malta, the population is profoundly depressed. Many a time the people are compelled to remain in inadequate cover for twenty hours and more. The attacks continue, fear, uncertainty and the tainted air produce among the individuals a sort of psychology of fear: they run out into the street simply to be able to breathe pure air and see the sky . . . aerodromes . . . are the objectives which have suffered most from these attacks. Also the Harbour has been seriously damaged; and in particular the basins of French Creek and Dockyard Creek have been rendered unusable. The hills surrounding the . . . airfields have been adapted as aircraft garages . . . from these, in the case of an alarm, the English pursuit-planes set out. Many times, however, so swift are the attacks, they are machine-gunned by low-level flying while they are getting ready to leave. Nearly all of what were at one time public shelters and have not been destroyed, have been requisitioned and adapted for use as petrol-stores . . . As a result of the continuous attacks, Malta has lost much of its importance as a naval and air

[1] *A Sailor's Odyssey.*

base . . . Malta lives today under the incubus of invasion. The opinion is that the conference which took place at Garmisch between Grand Admiral Raeder and Admiral Riccardi had as its object the details of the invasion plan. It is certain that the population will not be able to resist actual attacks . . .[2]

The idea that Maltese hillsides had been excavated for the construction of aircraft hangars was a persistent theme amongst the Germans and Italians throughout the war. The reasons for this are hard to find. It could be that they refused to believe that so many aircraft survived the bombing raids, or because they found it hard to believe just how many aircraft could be flown off to Malta from aircraft carriers.

While convoys were getting through, shortages were getting worse. Early in 1942, the ship bringing the seed potatoes to Malta was sunk. Substitutes were urgently dispatched from Cyprus, but did not prove suitable for Malta's poor soil. It was clear that the harvest was going to be thin.

The Luftwaffe's attacks increased in intensity. In January 1942, civilian deaths soared to eighty people, and then more than doubled in February to around 200, with even higher figures in March and April.

Not by nature a warlike people, the Maltese showed that they were equal to the challenge as the bombs rained down on them. On 11 January 1942, Lieutenant Gerald Amato-Gauci of the Royal Malta Artillery was in charge of the St Peter Battery, an AA battery, when a bomb dropped during one of several attacks that day exploded within five yards of his position, overlooking the Grand Harbour, wounding him in the chin and neck. The citation for his Military Cross stated that,

> Although shocked and in great pain, he carried on with the control of the guns, shouting out the necessary orders. He refused to receive first aid until the raid was over, when he

[2] *Count Ciano's Diaries.*

had to be helped to the post, subsequently admitted to hospital. This officer's staunch devotion to duty and great display of coolness set a very high example to all the men under his command. After his return from hospital, and during deliberate attacks by the enemy on his position he has always shown great initiative in dealing with the situation and his conduct has been an inspiration to all his men.

The intense air raids meant that many aircraft were being destroyed on the ground. It had long been an item of faith amongst the British aircrew based in Malta that they were safer in the air than on the ground. This had been especially true in the early days before a programme of constructing aircraft pens had afforded some protection, but not, of course, from a direct hit. Now, the Luftwaffe sought to destroy the RAF and Fleet Air Arm aircraft based in Malta, and those that could not be destroyed would soon run out of fuel and ammunition as the tempo of operations increased to meet the renewed German threat. A pattern emerged of daytime attacks using Junkers Ju87 Stukas and Ju88 fighter-bombers accompanied by Messerschmitt Bf109 and Bf110 fighters, and night attacks using Dornier Do17s. The RAF had noted that the Ju87s were vulnerable while coming out of their steep, screaming dive, and the Hurricanes now chased them down, catching them, too late perhaps to stop their bombs on their deadly course, but sufficient to ensure that this would be the last action for that particular aircraft, and, because of the low altitude, for that crew as well. Kesselring soon learnt of these tactics, and ordered the Bf109s to follow the Stukas down, so that they could catch the Hurricanes. The RAF then adopted a fresh tactic, sending the Hurricanes to 30,000 or even 40,000 feet, and then diving steeply through the German fighter cover. This was a hazardous business, since catching a Stuka at its most vulnerable meant going so low that the Hurricanes were flying within the levels reserved for AA fire, and many aircraft were damaged by what we would now call friendly fire. The risks were a measure of the increasingly desperate situation.

158

The first raids of the year had been on 1 January, when twenty-six people had been killed and another fourteen injured. On 2 and 3 January, attacks on the airfields lasted for a full thirty-six hours. This did not stop the Luqa Wellingtons attacking the airfield at Castel Vetrano in Sicily, destroying forty-four aircraft on the ground, including thirty troop transports. Overall, the number of air raids rose from 175 in December 1941, to 263 in January 1942, in which month a total of eighty-three people were killed and another 135 injured.

Life for the AA gunners was no picnic either. Eventually lookouts had to be posted, ready to blow whistles at which the gunners on a particular battery would lie flat to avoid the worst effects of shrapnel from near misses. As a last ditch defence against dive-bombers, shells were fired on No.4 fuse, exploding early to produce a 'porcupine barrage' into which the dive-bomber would fly and be damaged even if it wasn't shot down.

This terrible start to the year meant that the Grand Harbour was by now littered with wrecks, and anything daring to cross it was likely to be attacked. Some of the wrecks were relatively unimportant harbour craft, but they were joined by the destroyer *Maori* on 10 February, sunk in one of the ten raids that day. Even so, the submarines based on the other side of Valletta managed to account for 54,000 tons of Axis merchant ships between October 1941 and February 1942, as well as a destroyer and two submarines and two other ships near Taranto.

There had been one glimmer of hope at the beginning of the year. While a single ship arrived on 8 January, before the end of the month, on 19 January, three ships out of a convoy of four ships had arrived from Alexandria. There was to be one further ship arrive before the end of the month. This was not immediately seen as important as it should have been with hindsight.

In 1941, only one of the thirty-one ships sent to Malta had failed to arrive. Grim reality was not long in coming. Hunger was now beginning to bite, and then there was the question of fuel for the aircraft and warships, and ammunition for these and the

AA defences. It was time for another convoy. On 12 February, a convoy of three fast merchant vessels was sent from Alexandria, escorted by the anti-aircraft cruiser *Carlisle* and seven Hunt-class destroyers, with a distant escort provided by Force B under Rear Admiral Vian with three cruisers and eight destroyers; no aircraft carrier or battleship at this stage of the war. The following day, the *Breconshire* and three other merchantmen that had been waiting in Malta since the previous September, left escorted by the cruiser *Penelope* and six destroyers. The departing convoy carried those Maltese interned because of their Italian sympathies since the outbreak of war, on their way to internment in Kenya. The plan was for both convoys to meet and to exchange escorts. The ammunition ship *Clan Chatten* was bombed by German aircraft from North Africa, and had to be sunk by the convoy escorts before she exploded. The other two ships were also lost.

The situation was now rapidly becoming so bad that even the small craft plying between Gozo and Malta had to be discouraged for their own safety.

The one solution that occurred to the Air Officer Commanding, Air Vice Marshal Lloyd was to ask for Spitfires, and fast.

Off Duty Hazards

Opportunities for leisure were scarce, not least because the shortage of fuel meant that travel was difficult, especially for travel other than commuting to work. Even so, on 14 February many died watching the film *North West Mounted Police*, when the Regent Cinema in Valletta was hit, while the Casino Maltese in Kingsway also received a direct hit. Both were crowded with servicemen and civilians, and the true death toll was never published.

On 1 March, Floriana was the target. This town, an elegant dormitory for Valletta next door, had suffered little so far. The air raid sirens began wailing and the red flag was hoisted. E. S. Tonna recalls,

All of a sudden the skies rained death, and the heavy missiles hit one of the most thickly populated sections of the District. 'I instantly rushed to the stricken area to be met by a ghastly sight. I knew who the victims must be . . . Miss Pulo would not come to the school tomorrow and be bothered with the daily notes and shaping of figures; Joe a young pupil would not sing and relate stories to divert his young colleagues in the school shelter . . .'[3]

The effect of this sustained aerial bombardment and the throttling of Malta's supply lines was that Axis shipping losses fell from around eighty per cent in November, 1941, to less than thirty per cent by the following February. Kesselring was surprised by the continued resistance, and convinced himself that there were rock hangars close to Ta'Qali. Unfortunately, there weren't, although the idea had been considered and work had started, but then discontinued, possibly because of the distance there would be between the hangars and the airfield itself.

Kesselring raised the idea of an airborne assault on Malta once again, holding a conference with the senior officers of *Fliegerkorps II* in Sicily. He delegated to Air Marshal Deichman the command of an operation that would depend on first neutralizing the fighter defences and then the AA defences. Naturally, Rommel supported the plan. The actual airborne assault would now hinge on landings on the southern heights, from which it would be no great distance to seize the airfields at Hal Far and then Luqa. The main landings from the sea would be south of Valletta, with a diversionary seaborne assault at Marsaxlokk. At a meeting with Hitler and Goering, this plan was discussed. At first Hitler was against the use of airborne troops after the costly debacle at Crete, but eventually the Führer changed his mind.

---

[3] *Aspects of War in Floriana.*

Malta's Defences

Back in Malta, ammunition was beginning to run low.

Malta's AA defences at this time were controlled by 10 Heavy Anti-Aircraft Brigade, with the Royal Malta Artillery's 2 and 11 HAA regiments and two regiments of the Royal Artillery, with each of these four regiments having twenty-four guns spread amongst three batteries, each of two troops with four guns apiece. The AA gun batteries were positioned at Tigne (near Sliema), Manoel Island, Ta'Cejlu, Spinola, Ta'Gironi, Tal-Qroqq, Fleur de Lys, San Giacomo, Hompesch, Zonqor, Marnisi, St Peter, Xrobb il-Ghagin, Delimara, Ta'Karax, Gwarena, San Blas, Bizbizija, Gharghur, Salina and Wardija. These positions were for defence against high flying bombers, with the 7 Light Anti-Aircraft Brigade providing defence against dive-bombers or low-level attack, using Bofors guns. This was another mixed British and Maltese brigade, consisting of the 3 LAA Regiment of the Royal Malta Artillery, with 10th, 15th, 22nd and 30th batteries, and the 32, 65 and 74 LAA regiments of the Royal Artillery. The LAA regiments also had three batteries each, except for the 3, and each battery consisted of three troops, each with six guns.

Supporting these two AA brigades was the 4 Searchlight Regiment, another Anglo-Maltese unit.

The constant air raids meant that work came to a standstill throughout most of Malta whenever the air raid warning sounded. To attempt to minimize the disruption, a red flag system was introduced during spring 1942, with red flags being raised after the air raid warning sounded in those areas most at risk of attack, so that those outside these areas could continue with work, or indeed, their domestic chores. A red and white pennant was flown once it became clear that the raid might not develop into bombing. This system was used for the first time on 17 March.

As March 1942 passed, it became clear that another convoy must be fought through, while additional Spitfires were also needed. The timing coincided with plans to provide further support for the war in North Africa, now almost at a stalemate, but it also coincided with something else: Deichman gave the order for non-stop bombing of Malta, ready for an invasion. Part of the plan was to use Jabo bombs, essentially large rocket projectiles, to destroy the supposed Ta'Qali hillside hangars. All of these plans were set for 20 March.

That day started peacefully enough, but just as the working day got under way, the air raid sirens started their mournful howls, and around the dockyard, red flags were being raised. Six Ju88s could be heard, engines throbbing, as they neared the island, escorted by a larger force of Bf109s. The Ju88s were left to the AA defences while the fighters sought the Bf109s. One Ju88 burst into flames as the gunners found their target, but the others pressed home their attacks. The Spitfires soon showed themselves a match for the Bf109s, pursuing the German aircraft. In this and two further air raids, all with six Ju88s escorted by Bf109s, the defenders managed to score one Ju88 with two probables, plus one Bf109, but one precious British fighter was also lost. Down below, one Ju88 had managed to sink the submarines *Pandora* and *P-36*, although the Polish *Sokol* had been missed.

The morning's raids had been something of an opener. After a quiet afternoon, radar picked up a heavy concentration of aircraft as evening approached. The indications suggested more than 200 aircraft. The first wave of fifty Ju88s with a heavy Bf109 escort approached Malta, flying so that they had the setting sun behind them to make aiming difficult for the AA gunners, and headed for Ta'Qali. Wave after wave of aircraft attacked, dropping bombs, parachute mines, deep penetration bombs to split open hardened shelters, and anti-personnel mines. It was one of the last waves that was equipped with the heavy Jabo rockets, flying low and wasting their armament on the cliff face. Finally, Bf110s flew low, machine-gunning anything that looked like a target and dropping small bombs. Ta'Qali was a scene of devastation, so heavily cratered that some have compared it with a moonscape. Only darkness brought relief from the waves of attacking aircraft, while those on the ground left their shelters and attempted to provide room for the fighters, now with fuel tanks that were

163

emptying fast, to land. They worked around unexploded bombs – there was no time to wait for bomb clearance. No British aircraft were shot down, but many were destroyed on the ground.

Martin Hastings remembers that spring very well;

> . . . it was the spring of '42 that we really got our pounding and we had some tremendous tonnages of bombs dropped on us which were really frightening.
>
> But we all became very good. We had our radar of course which used to tell us that there was a formation forming up over Sicily of eighty plus aircraft, or something like this, and the little Maltese boys could spot these aircraft long before any of us could and say 'There they are'. Eventually, we got to know what the aircraft was, not only by sight but also by sound and we knew exactly when it was advisable to go down to a shelter.[4]

Hitler had indeed sent Kesselring.

Meanwhile, the convoys had left Alexandria and Gibraltar respectively.

That from Alexandria was code-named MW10, and consisted of four merchantmen including the tanker *Breconshire*, escorted again by the *Carlisle* and six destroyers, while once again Vian was close behind with three light cruisers and a number of destroyers. Once Admiral Iachino learnt of this convoy, he put to sea in the battleship *Littorio* and six destroyers, signalling to another squadron with three heavy cruisers and four destroyers to join him. This force heavily outnumbered, and even more important, outgunned the convoy escort and Vian's force, since heavy cruisers, defined by the 1922 Washington Naval Treaty as having 8-inch guns, were more than a match for the light cruisers, with their 6-inch guns.

The Gibraltar convoy was escorted by Force N, with the battleship *Malaya*, the cruiser *Hermione* and eight destroyers, while the aircraft carriers *Eagle* and *Argus* were carrying Spitfires for Malta.

[4] IWM Sound Archive, Accession No.10453/6.

In September 1941, Malta had supplies for seven months after the arrival of the convoy. Six months had passed since then. Both convoys were desperately needed; one would not be enough.

21 March 1942 started as the previous day had ended, with repeated heavy waves of aircraft attacking Ta'Qali. In all, the airfield suffered three attacks that day, with the second consisting of seventy-five Ju88s escorted by Bf109s and Bf110s. In these attacks, the Luftwaffe lost twenty aircraft. In a lull between the raids, sixteen Spitfires landed safely from the two aircraft carriers.

The following morning found Vian, aware of Iachino's presence, putting his ships between the Italians and the convoy, using a heavy smokescreen to provide cover for hit and run attacks against the Italians, then seeking cover behind the smokescreen before the Italians could find their aim. After a morning of heavy fighting, the engagement was broken off, only to resume that afternoon, when Vian succeeded in damaging the *Littorio* with a salvo fired from 10,000 yards, starting a fire on the battleship. His destroyers then appeared from behind the smokescreen and damaged the battleship further with a torpedo, and also torpedoed one of the cruisers, *Giovanni delle Bande Nere*. In what became known as the Second Battle of Sirte, the Italians lost two destroyers and the crippled cruiser was discovered and sunk by the submarine *Urge* from Malta.

After this inspired and heroic battle against the odds, the convoy came under heavy German aerial attack, with both the escort and Vian's ships closing up to provide heavy AA cover. Just fifty miles off Malta, the Luftwaffe's bombs struck the *Clan Campbell* and sank her. The convoy continued its fighting progress, and the following morning came within the air cover of Malta-based Spitfires. From 08.00 on 23 March, flights of Spitfires and Hurricanes patrolled over the convoy, and by 17.00, two Ju88s and a Heinkel He111 had been shot down, and another eight Ju88s so badly damaged that their ability to return to their base was in doubt. There were no losses amongst the British aircraft. A side benefit of this running battle was that the Luftwaffe was concentrating all of its efforts on the convoy, and giving Malta a welcome break.

With Malta within sight on 24 March, tragedy struck, as the *Breconshire* was hit by a bomb and forced to slow down. Vian made the destroyer *Southwold* take the tanker in tow, and put the cruisers *Carlisle* and *Penelope* to defend her while he hurried the remaining two ships towards Malta. In Sicily, as soon as he heard of the tanker's plight, Deichman sent thirty Stukas covered by a similar number of Bf109s to finish her off. The Spitfires attacked the Bf109s leaving the Ju87s to the Hurricanes, destroying two Bf109s and so damaging fifteen Stukas that their survival was unlikely. The *Breconshire* was not hit once in this attack. Then, just two miles from Malta, the *Southwold* struck a mine and sank. Meanwhile, two tugs sailed out from Malta and towed the crippled tanker *Breconshire* into Marsaxlokk, where she later sank in the bay.

The other two merchant ships, the *Pampas* and the *Talabot*, had reached Grand Harbour safely. Now the Germans started to attack the two ships, with barely two hours between air raids in what almost amounted to a re-run of the *Illustrious* blitz. Nevertheless, unloading started after midnight on the night of 24–25 March, and with the ships' own derricks out of action, the dockers unloaded 330 tons from the *Talabot* and a further 310 tons from the *Pampas*. Yet, not long after daybreak, more raids followed, with some making a feint towards Hal Far before sending half of their aircraft to the Grand Harbour, but the ships were still afloat at the end of the day, while the Luftwaffe had lost seven Stukas, four Ju88s and three Bf109s, while another thirteen aircraft were unlikely to have struggled home safely. Dockyard workers and soldiers were sent to help the stevedores struggling to unload the two ships, with a further 497 tons being taken off the *Talabot* and 310 tons from the *Pampas*. A further 145 tons and 289 tons respectively were unloaded from the two ships the following day before an all-out attack, notable for its sheer fanaticism, saw the *Talabot* hit at 12.30 on 26 March and set on fire, while two hours later the *Pampas* was also hit and started to sink, although despite this, on 27 March, despite eight raids, the hastily assembled unloading party managed to get a further 603 tons by day and 345 tons by night, from the slowly sinking *Pampas*, all by hand. Just five tons could be got off the *Talabot*, burning fiercely, with firefighters fighting to extinguish the fires, anxious that her cargo, which included ammunition, would not be lost. Despite further raids on 28 March, and a dockyard power failure, HMS *Avondale* was moved alongside *Pampas* to help with unloading cargo, and a further 243 tons were removed, often by men diving into flooded holds. Meanwhile, with her cargo of kerosene and aviation spirit now burning fiercely, the *Talabot* had seamen from HMS *Penelope* and a Maltese firefighting tug attempting to control the blaze. In the end, this saga continued for another three days and nights, with a further 905 tons being lifted off *Pampas* before she finally sank, while only another thirty tons could be taken off *Talabot* before, with her plates glowing red hot, she had to be scuttled to prevent her blowing up and destroying Grand Harbour and the communities surrounding it. The deed fell to Lieutenant D. A. Copperwheat of *Penelope* who swam out to the ship and attached explosive charges to the sea cocks, before swimming back to the shore to detonate them. For this, he received the George Cross. Two Maltese policemen received BEMs for their part in rescuing a dockyard worker who had accidentally been left aboard the blazing ship and who had found himself in difficulties after diving overboard into the harbour.

The other convoy had the five merchantmen accompanied by five cruisers and eighteen destroyers. This time three destroyers were sunk and three cruisers badly damaged, and just three of the merchantmen reached the Grand Harbour, where all three were sunk before they could be unloaded. Supplies were also carried on five submarines, one of which was sunk. In short, 26,000 tons of supplies were sent to Malta in the first three months of the year, but only 4,952 tons reached the shore.

It simply seems strange that no less than five ships were left so exposed in Grand Harbour with no attempt to provide a smoke-screen, which would have been especially effective in deterring dive bombing attacks. At no time did the Grand Harbour have barrage balloons, which if well-sited could have also helped to deter attacks and kept enemy aircraft high enough for the AA fire to have had a devastating effect. The heat of the Mediterranean sun could have made efficient operation more difficult than in temperate climes, but the Italians managed to provide a barrage balloon defence at Taranto.

The Luftwaffe once again applied an intensity to the bombing that the Italians had never managed to achieve. Each raid was heavier, but the frequency of raids also increased, with many aircrew making two or more sorties daily. It was also noticeable that the Luftwaffe pressed home their attacks with greater determination. The result was that Malta was raided between four and ten times a day, with formations of more than a hundred aircraft on each occasion. It was simply a relief that the Germans had foregone development of heavy bombers before the war, preferring greater numbers of light and what could at best be described as medium bombers. This was also a reflection of the German philosophy of *blitzkrieg*, lightning war, with air power carefully coordinated with fast moving armoured ground forces. The tight concentration of targets and the shortage of aircraft and the limited number of airfields in Sicily also meant that the Luftwaffe could not replicate the thousand bomber raids so beloved of the RAF. Even so, the damage was bad enough. Kesselring was desperate to subdue Malta, but he did order that civilian property was to be spared, although, with the best will in the world, this was difficult to achieve in many areas close to military targets, and not every member of the Luftwaffe was as determined to avoid civilian casualties as the man who waited patiently before sinking the Gozo ferry. The year was proving the worst yet, so that by the first week of April 1942, the damage was rising steadily, with 15,500 buildings destroyed, of which eight were hospitals and another twenty-two schools, while there were also seventy churches and eighteen religious communities, as well as ten theatres, eight hotels and the same number of clubs, five banks and six of the famous auberges of the Knights in Valletta alone, as well as others in Vittoriosa. One in seventy of the population had become a casualty, with 1,104 killed, 1,318 seriously injured and another 1,299 slightly injured. It was some slight consolation that the previous month, Malta's fighter and AA defences had together accounted for 177 enemy aircraft, an unacceptably high rate of attrition. The question was, which side would break first.

'People found refuge with their uncles and their aunts in the villages', recalled Mabel Strickland, editor of *The Times of Malta*.

> There were over thirteen miles of shelters. We ran like rabbits down into the shelters when the bombers were near. From the end of 1941 to April, 1942, was the worst bombing. There was 352 hours of AA fire in March or April '42, the equivalent of 15 days and nights of firing.
>
> We published seven days week, and tremendous credit goes to the newsboys for it wouldn't have been worth printing if we couldn't distribute.[5]

Easter Tuesday, 7 April, saw ten attacks after an incredible twelve the previous day, and marked 2,000 raids, with the Royal Opera House, just inside the Kingsgate, destroyed.

Amidst this mayhem, a welcome gesture of solidarity came from London. King George VI became Colonel-in-Chief of the Royal Malta Artillery. His message said it all:

> I have been watching with admiration the stout hearted resistance of all in Malta – service personnel and civilian alike – to the fierce and constant air attacks, in the active defence of the Island the RAF have been ably supported by the Royal Malta Artillery, and it therefore gives me special pleasure, to assume the Colonelcy-in-Chief of the Regiment.

The next day, 8 April, was the worst, with no less than fourteen raids, and for one of them, more than 300 bombers were sent over. Ammunition and fuel were now rationed to the defenders, with fighter sorties kept to the minimum and the AA gunners

[5] IWM Sound Archive, Accession No.1173.

rationed as well. A target date had been set, at which point Malta would have to surrender.

Meanwhile, that other stalwart of Malta's defences, the light cruiser *Penelope*, was attacked again while in dry dock for emergency repairs. She continued to put up a fight, and two Luftwaffe aircraft nearly crashed onto her as her guns shot them down. On one day, she was peppered by shrapnel, on another, her decks were covered with masonry, in each case from near misses. Not all of the bombs missed, however, and on 8 April, with seven of her crew killed and another thirty wounded, including her CO, Captain Nicholl, it was decided that she must try to leave Malta. That night, with her wounded CO in command having discharged himself from hospital, HMS 'Pepperpot' as she had become known, slipped away from Grand Harbour at 21.00 and headed for Gibraltar, steering on engines alone and with her hull bristling with wooden plugs, and just fifteen rounds of AA ammunition left. The Grand Harbour, so often the scene of bustle as ships came and went or had their needs attended to while in port, and so often displaying the might of British sea power, once again was deserted, except for the odd surviving tug.

A miracle was needed desperately. It seemed to the people of Malta that one did come when, on 9 April, a 2,000kg bomb crashed through the rotunda of the great church in the centre of Mosta, the third largest unsupported dome in Europe, just as the church was crowded with people praying. It failed to explode, and no one was hurt.

But it wasn't a convoy.

While Japan's entry into the war had brought the United States into the conflict, so that she was no longer a helpful and friendly neutral, but an active co-belligerent, it had also increased the pressures on the Royal Navy. Heavy losses had been suffered too, at the hands of Nippon.

The island's potential as an offensive base was seriously compromised as the Luftwaffe's *Fliegerkorps II* in Sicily brought maximum effort to bear on the island and its airfields whenever a convoy was being passed through from Italy to North Africa.

Every available acre was being cultivated.

The shortage of food affected everyone. Martin Hastings recalls:

> It was difficult because we had a new general come out called General Beak VC and he came out from England where everybody was rushing madly about, and the first thing he said was that everybody had got to go for a run every day. Well, this was all right, we all went for a run every day but we really hadn't got enough food to keep our energy going. It may have made our muscles fine but on balance I've always felt it was good for the spirit but it reduced our stamina, I think, probably because we overdid it a bit. He certainly stirred us up and sometimes his methods were not all that tactful and not always appreciated.[6]

Enforcing discipline and restraint under such conditions was of paramount importance. The British troops were not allowed to let any hint of their plight, on half rations, pass to the outside world for reasons of security. The population as a whole was listless, everything seemed to take two or three times as long to achieve because of the weakened state of the body. Making the best of a bad job, the troops were given 'sleep parades', in which they were told to lie down and sleep, rather than use energy or do anything that might make them more hungry.

In addition to this, the penalties for stealing food became draconian. The penalty for stealing a tin of corned beef worth 2s 3d (11p) was a minimum two years' imprisonment.

The penalties for running a black market operation were also heavy.

Malnutrition meant that sores wouldn't heal, and that people were prone to other forms of illness, but none of this was helped by the uniform still worn by many British army units. Hastings remembers:

[6] IWM Sound Archive, Accession No.10453/6.

. . . Things didn't heal. We got sores on our legs and all these sort of things which was partly due to the way we wore our uniform, with tight puttees and things like that.

I think people got things like jaundice. We had bed bugs in the wooden beds that we had, tier bunks, that we had in the huts and these sorts of things. I think that on the whole our health was fairly good but I think that these were the main concerns and of course food became the main topic of conversation and everybody watched everybody else to make sure that they didn't get more from the ration than they themselves got. Everything had to be split up exactly. The exact number of biscuits, the exact amount of butter or margarine or whatever it was to go and we always seemed to be hungry and as a result of that practically everybody started a little farm. So many chickens at each post and if we could get them to lay eggs then that was fine.

I remember at the town headquarters we got some eggs from the experimental farm and we borrowed a hatching thing to see whether we couldn't hatch them. Anyway, some of the eggs hatched and eventually I think I had about half a dozen white chickens and one cockerel . . . called King Pin. And these chickens laid us various numbers of eggs for the mess until the food for the chickens got less and less because there was less and less scraps and things to give them. So eventually, they got eaten too.

Then people grew a few of their own vegetables. And the local farmers . . . chaps were able to barter a few things.[7]

When it came to food, Hastings recalls that not everyone was treated equally, nor could they be. The diet for the service personnel was better than that of the islanders, but it was still poor.

We used to have a bit of a bone of contention because people who were pilots and aircrew that used to go out

[7] IWM Sound Archive, Accession No.10453/6.

172

used to get even better rations and so did the submariners and the Navy and people at sea, they got better rations. So sometimes we felt that we were all in Malta but some people got better rations than we did. But I suppose because they went into action and we sat there it was very appropriate that they should have . . . I also remember one of my friends had a brother who was commanding a submarine and we were asked to go and have supper or something on board. Well even this little submarine could produce a mighty fine meal to what we could do. This sort of thing we appreciated.[8]

It wasn't only the food that was scarce. Other items, normally regarded as essential, were in very short supply, including boot polish and toothpaste. Enterprising Maltese ground down some sandstone as a substitute for toothpaste, possibly one of the few commercial transactions left at this stage as many shops closed because they had nothing to sell.

Inevitably, with the shortage of fuel, transport of all kinds continued to be seriously affected. On 23 February 1942, weekend buses had been withdrawn completely and on weekdays many routes were severely curtailed, stopping far short of their stated destination, while other routes were diverted past many smaller towns and villages which effectively lost any direct public transport. Perhaps the least fortunate were the residents of Rabat, whose buses stopped a full twenty minutes walk from the town, close to the RAF fighter station at Ta'Qali, one of the targets most frequently visited by Axis aircraft! In mid-March 1942, passengers got off a bus at Ta'Qali and found themselves almost immediately in the middle of an air raid, and had to throw themselves flat on the ground. Maltese buses have been famous for overcrowding at busy periods, but by now, people would even sit on the mudguards. It was not as if the buses operated to anything like their usual frequencies during the permitted hours of operation. A good example arose at the small crossroads village of

---

[8] IWM Sound Archive, Accession No.10453/6.

Bir-id-Deheb on 8 March 1942, on a road that carried buses from Birzebbugia, Marsaxlokk and Zejthun, when ninety passengers waited from 08.25 to 09.00, but only two buses appeared, and could only manage to pick up fifteen passengers between them.

Many sought lifts, but there were few cars, although some service officers did follow official advice and offer lifts when this was practicable.

Life and Death Under the Bombers

In April, there were almost 6,000 bomber sorties against Malta, of which 1,638 occurred in just one week. The three airfields received 590 bombs on a single day, but this was surpassed on another day with 615 bombs. It was calculated that the 6,728 tons of bombs dropped on Malta that April was the equivalent to thirty-six raids on Coventry, the English Midland city brought to its knees when the city centre was ripped out of it on the night of 14–15 November 1940. Desperate for extra shelter, and in many cases having to move underground permanently after homes had been destroyed, the Maltese even cut shelters in the deep Rabat Fosse, a canyon separating Rabat from the old capital of Mdina.

The traditional Sunday Maltese custom of driving a light cart with a pony ended in tragedy for one family. A father and his eighteen-year-old son had set off under clear skies from the village of Gudja, and as they descended Paola Hill towards Marsa, the port and always a likely target in any air raid, they heard the sound of AA fire in the distance. They hurried onwards, and seeing Stukas preparing to dive on the Grand Harbour, hurried towards the abattoir air raid shelter. Reaching the shelter, the boy quickly tethered the pony to the iron gate.

'All of a sudden I heard the whistling of a descending bomb,' recalls Dr George Borg, a Maltese physician.

> Without a moment's hesitation I threw myself flat on the ground. Just as I was about to shout out a warning to my father I felt his body on me and his hands clasping me

174

tightly. My father was a six footer and his shoulders were over two feet wide.

I had no chance to utter a word to him because a tremendous crack and a bright blinding light flashed just on my right, only four yards away.

The acrid smell of sulphur and the TNT, the burning dry taste in my mouth, the blurring of vision with the smoke and the dust, the hissing loud noise in my ears were a terrible experience which still haunts my dreams . . . I then began to feel the weight of the stones and rubble pressing my legs and back to the ground . . . I thought that I was going to be buried alive like some people I had seen under the debris of a house . . . luckily my head and arms remained uncovered . . . with three or four jerks I freed myself from the heap of stones but found that my right leg was heavy and numb . . .[9]

His clothes had been blown off him, leaving him wearing a few tattered rags. There was no sign of the pony and cart, just a large crater in the street, while his father lay face upwards a few yards away, unable to stand. The young George Borg hurried to his father, and kneeling with him they started to say the Act of Contrition together, but his father stopped in the middle. George became agitated and called for help, and people left the abattoir shelter to hasten to his aid. As they reached him, more bombs started to fall, so they grabbed him and hurried him into the shelter – he didn't realize at the time that they couldn't bring his father as well. After the raid, which lasted about ten minutes, six men accompanied George to his father.

'When he saw me, he told me in a faltering voice: 'George, I am dying, I am dying. I did my best to save you.'[10]

They were both taken to the casualty department of a hospital, the journey taking an hour through the streets filled with craters and with rubble from collapsed buildings. George could hardly

[9] *The Siege Within the Walls*
[10] Ibid.

see or hear, his eyes filled with black burnt powder and his ear drums pierced. His father died soon after. George's own injuries were such that it was a month before he could be discharged from hospital.

The Luftwaffe did not have it all its own way all of the time. On Sunday, 10 May 1942, Junkers Ju87s and Ju88s arrived over Malta, fifty or so at a time, and were surprised by the latest batch of Spitfires that had been so carefully received.

'The sky was an absolute circus,' one witness recalls.

> Machines fell out of it like flies. Bursts of shell fire were so close that the sky looked like a wasp's nest and the seafront was lined with cheering crowds who forgot falling shrapnel and splinters in the sheer joy of witnessing a battle where we at last held our own and were superior; thirty-six enemy machines were brought down in an hour. Jerry got the fright of his life. That was the last of his mass attacks.
>
> And the spirit of the people never faltered, and the friendships of peacetime were more closely cemented by the hardships we all shared . . . Of course, we all grumbled at times and wished the bread would cut into just a few more slices, but the perils and courage of the men who brought it to us turned our grumblings into thankfulness and humility . . . Crowds always gathered at the public loudspeakers to hear every bit of news and to await the great day when North Africa would be freed, for this would be our salvation, too . . .[11]

The George Cross

At the height of Malta's travails, King George VI awarded the George Cross to Malta on 15 April 1942. The citation read:

'To honour her brave people I award the George Cross to the island fortress of Malta, to bear witness to a heroism and devotion that will long be famous in history.'

[11] IWM Sound Archive, Accession No.1172.

The delivery of the medal was delayed, of course, and it was not until 13 September that the new Governor, Lord Gort, who had succeeded Lieutenant General Dobbie, was able to present the medal to the Chief Justice, Sir George Borg, who accepted it on behalf of the Maltese people at a formal parade on the Palace Square.

Later, the George Cross with the citation, and the fuselage of the old Sea Gladiator *Faith*, were put on public display in the Governor's Palace.

The Maltese were delighted with the honour bestowed on them, the first time that the George Cross had not been awarded to an individual, and even today, only one other such award has been made – to another deserving body, the Royal Ulster Constabulary.

Another practical step was the order given to General Sir Claude Auchinleck to prepare for an offensive that would capture the airfields of West Cyrenaica, and to mount his attack no later than mid-June.

Yet, between 20 March and 28 April 1942, the Luftwaffe had mounted 5,807 bomber sorties against Malta, another 5,667 fighter sorties, and 345 reconnaissance sorties. The island had suffered from 6,557,231kg of bombs during this period, almost as much as the total dropped on the UK at the height of the Battle of Britain in September 1940, and of these, 1,869 tons had been dropped on Grand Harbour alone. This effort had been mounted by 2,150 bombers. A total of 297 people had been killed. The five fighter squadrons defending Malta had just seven Spitfires operational by the end of April, as well as a few Hurricanes. This was the sum total of surviving aircraft from 126, 249 and 603 Squadrons operating Spitfires from Ta'Qali, and from 601, Luqa's Spitfire Squadron, and 185, the Hurricane Squadron at Hal Far.

The 28 April was the day that Malta lost its electricity supplies, plunging the island into darkness until 2 May, an inconvenience felt most by those living deep in the underground shelters.

Early summer found Malta battered, and awaiting invasion. The heavy damage inflicted on the island meant that its offensive role was now limited. The British could no longer fight convoys through successfully to Malta, and the happy period when they had been able to cripple Rommel's supply route across the Mediterranean had passed.

This was total war with a vengeance. Increasingly, the Axis were prepared to give no quarter. In May 1942, the British asked through the International Red Cross, if the Axis would allow hospital ships to pass through to Malta. The *Regia Navale* raised no objection to this, doubtless bearing in mind Cunningham's generous treatment of the survivors of the ships sunk at Matapan, where he had signalled the position of the survivors to *Supermarina*, the Italian Admiralty, in Rome.

'The English would like to send some hospital ships to Malta,' Ciano noted on 19 May.

> Our Navy agrees in principle, but the Germans are against it. The Duce decides against it especially because his experience has taught him the many things it is possible to hide in hospital ships when the blockade would otherwise prevent their passage. Last winter we were able to deliver some timely supplies of petrol to Benghazi by making use of white ships.[12]

This was not simply an admission that the Axis had misused hospital ships in direct contravention of the Geneva Convention, it also was an explanation as to why the Axis powers had so often ignored the Red Cross markings on such ships in Allied ports.

May was also the month that finally the Royal Navy decided to withdraw its 'U'-class submarines that had operated with such good effect against Rommel's supply lines.

Those in Malta attempting to make the best of a bad job had at least a respite on 10 May when the deteriorating situation on the Eastern Front forced Kesselring to transfer the Luftwaffe back to the Soviet Union. Malta was saved by Hitler's obsession with the East just as much as the United Kingdom was when the need to

---

[12] *Count Ciano's Diaries.*

launch Operation Barbarossa ended the blitz on British cities. On the ground, the work of the radar station was augmented by the formation of an Anglo-Maltese RAF Observer Corps, with five Air Ministry Experimental Stations, or AMES, whose role was to plot the course of incoming aircraft to determine their likely target area. Later, a sixth AME was established on Gozo.

In mid-May, another seventeen Spitfires were flown in from the aircraft carriers HMS *Argus* and *Eagle*. The small numbers were doubtless due to the fact that the ships were also carrying their own aircraft, although *Argus*, originally laid down as a liner for Italy, never did have a considerable capacity. These were some of the few hopeful signs, but others were more ominous, with Rommel striking hard at British forces in North Africa on 27 May, and forcing British forces, poised for an advance, back. Relief through an advance in North Africa was still some time off.

The New Governor

Lieutenant General Dobbie, described by Churchill as that 'Cromwellian figure' was worn out. He had shared the same inadequate rations as the rest of the population, and had taken the stress of the responsibility of caring for everyone. To maintain morale, a new Governor had to be found. The choice was limited with so many senior officers engaged in the conflict. The mantle fell upon Lord Gort, the man who had done so much to ensure that the British Expeditionary Force escaped through Dunkirk, and who was in command of the garrison at Gibraltar.

Gort has been described as having been relegated to secondary posts after Dunkirk. He was certainly an embarrassment to the politicians and those military leaders who had urged him to stand firm in France, since he had the wisdom to recognize impending defeat, and the moral courage to order withdrawal and evacuation. Sending Gort to Gibraltar was a classic instance of sidelining a senior officer who had become an embarrassment. The 'Rock' was without doubt a key strategic position, but it would have been even more difficult to defend than Malta had Franco taken Spain into the Second World War. Fortunately, Franco had made it clear that he intended to remain neutral. Some have described Spain's neutrality as sullen, but escaping British prisoners of war managed to leave France through Spain, and so while Spain was not as well disposed towards Britain as neighbouring Portugal, it was certainly far from hostile. Officially, servicemen from the belligerent countries could expect to be interned on reaching neutral territory.

The posting to Malta put Lord Gort back in the frontline, although he did not appreciate this at the time.

Arriving in a flying boat at Kalafrana at dusk on 7 May 1942, in the middle of an air raid, General Lord Gort VC relieved Sir William Dobbie as Governor and Commander-in-Chief. He was welcomed by the three service chiefs, the Lieutenant Governor, the Chief Justice and members of the Executive Council. They all retired to a bomb damaged building nearby to meet Dobbie, but almost as soon as they had entered, bombs exploded quite close by. As they prepared to administer the Oath of Allegiance and the Oath of Office, they found that the Bible had been left behind and for a moment it seemed that Lord Gort could not take the oath. Dobbie saved the day, stepping forward and pulling out of his pocket his own personal Bible that accompanied him everywhere.

The rest of the transfer of power was accomplished quickly. There was no question of working the new man in, but simply a two hour discussion between the newly appointed Governor and his predecessor, after which Sir William and his wife and daughter flew out of the island to Gibraltar.

The new Governor placed the entire island on 'siege rations'. The siege mentality was enforced by a new term, the 'target date', used by those on Malta, and by those in London, Gibraltar and Alexandria concerned with the fate of the little Mediterranean island colony. The 'target date' was the date when the bread, fuel and ammunition would finally be exhausted. For those on Malta, it was an incentive to husband their resources and preserve everything possible. For those concerned with Malta's fate, it was a deadline, a deadly deadline, before which relief must be taken to the islands.

After the arrival of the two ships in the June convoy, the target date was a mere eight weeks away.

Gort brought a new energy to Malta's appalling situation. He also set an example, and instead of using his official chauffeur-driven car, he used a bicycle. Like his predecessor, he also had the same rations as everyone else.

On 10 May, *Welshman* sneaked into Grand Harbour where, at last, a hastily improvised smokescreen was installed using green canisters placed around the harbour and on some of the bastions. The Luftwaffe and the *Regia Aeronautica* flew over, doubtless knowing that the minelayer would be there, but could see nothing through the pall of smoke. Before they could carpet-bomb the area in the hope of hitting the target, they were set upon by two squadrons of Spitfires. This was the first air battle of the day. A formation of five Savoia Marchetti bombers, complacent and trusting in their fighter screen, were early victims, as the Spitfires attacked and shot down three, sending the two remaining aircraft running for safety but trailing smoke. There were eight raids in total that day, while the *Welshman* was being unloaded by hand, and sixty-three German and Italian aircraft were either shot down or badly damaged. Three Spitfires were shot down, but two of the pilots were rescued.

It seems incredible that it took so long before a smokescreen could be introduced to Grand Harbour. It would certainly have helped during the famous *Illustrious* blitz, and whenever ships had to be unloaded in the Harbour. True, it wouldn't have helped in the case of high altitude bombing, for although that would have been inaccurate, the bombs would still have hurtled down, into the Grand Harbour and anything sitting there, and into the communities around it. On the other hand, it would have stopped the deadly accurate dive-bombers. The Germans may have been skilful and brave, but they were not suicide pilots!

Meanwhile, the food situation on the islands was desperate. So much so that in June two convoys were sent to Malta, one from Gibraltar and the other from Alexandria, with the intention of dividing enemy attacks and hopefully converging on Malta together.

Operation Harpoon, the code-name given to the Gibraltar convoy, left the Clyde on 5 June under the command of Admiral Curtiss in the cruiser *Kenya*, with another cruiser, *Liverpool*, and ten destroyers completing the escort for five merchant ships. They would be joined at Gibraltar by Force T, with the aircraft carriers *Eagle* and *Argus*, the battleship *Malaya*, and the anti-aircraft cruisers *Cairo* and *Charybdis*, as well as another seven destroyers and four minesweepers. A sixth merchantman, the tanker *Kentucky*, also joined at Gibraltar, while *Welshman* also came, again in her role as a supply vessel rather than a minelayer. The convoy left Gibraltar on 11 June, at the same time as the convoy from Alexandria, code-named Vigorous, sailed.

Operation Vigorous was led by Rear Admiral Vian in the cruiser *Cleopatra*, with another six cruisers, *Arethusa*, *Birmingham*, *Dido*, *Euryalus* and *Hermione*, with the anti-aircraft cruiser *Coventry*. He also had twenty-six destroyers, four corvettes and two minesweepers, with which to escort eleven ships including a tanker.

The sailing dates for the two convoys coincided with the second anniversary of the first air raids on Malta, with the total on this day standing at 2,537 raids, which had killed 1,215 Maltese, while 590 Axis planes had been shot down over Malta.

The Alexandria convoy sailed into trouble almost as soon as it left port, being attacked by German aircraft based in Crete, demonstrating just what a valuable stepping stone across the Mediterranean this island had been. A cargo ship, *City of Calcutta*, was badly damaged in the first raid and had to run for Tobruk, while the Dutch merchantman, *Elizabeth Bakki*, also damaged, set back into Alexandria. Now the airfields in North Africa joined in, with aircraft sent from Tripoli sinking two more cargo ships, and the cruiser *Hermione*, which went down without any survivors. The Italian fleet, realizing that there were no battleships escorting this convoy, left port, but Malta-based torpedo-bombers attacked, sinking a cruiser and damaging the battleships *Littorio* and *Cavour* and two destroyers. Yet, the aerial attacks on the convoy continued, sinking three destroyers. Forced to face defeat, the convoy turned back. The terrible toll on merchant ships and naval vessels at this time can be attributed to the sheer absence of British naval air power. More than a year had passed and *Formidable* had still not been replaced.

Meanwhile, the Gibraltar convoy was attacked by U-boats, before the aerial attacks started from aircraft based in Sardinia. Two Italian cruisers and five destroyers retired in the face of the heavy escort, but the convoy then ran into a newly laid minefield. Several ships were sunk by air attack, including two destroyers. On 15 June, just two ships reached Grand Harbour along with the gallant little *Welshman*.

For this convoy, there were two innovations. Once again Grand Harbour was protected by a smokescreen while unloading took place, while a system of coloured signs had been established to allow for the speedy distribution of the cargoes to storage points across the island. The smokescreen was provided by portable smoke canisters. That these were effective can be judged by the fact that a customs officer complained that he often found that he could not find his way from a ship to the shore! The use of smoke meant that German and Italian bombers were bombing blind, and the dreaded and deadly accurate Stuka dive-bombers could not risk diving through the smoke.

The next move was to ensure that unloading was speeded up, and that urgent distribution of cargoes away from the heavily bombed port area to safer points elsewhere was also accelerated. Troops, mainly infantrymen, were drafted in to help the stevedores and ensure that no time was wasted. It was important to ensure that never again would a ship be sunk before she could be unloaded. Lorries were commandeered, and painted in colours that indicated their destination. Coloured signposts had been placed at junctions along the planned routes, and at night these were augmented by coloured lights.

In planning the new system of distribution, Gort had insisted, despite the shortage of fuel, that a trial run was necessary. Once a convoy arrived, it would be too late, and everything would have to work properly. The first night exercise was chaotic – the lights were removed by people living close by for fear that they would attract enemy bombers!

The next day, Gort had an official notice issued.

> The Public will have noticed a number of lights which were placed at intervals along certain roads on Saturday night. These lights were placed there in connection with an important military operation the successful outcome of which is essential to the defence of Malta. The exercise will be repeated on the night of Monday, 15th June.
>
> On Saturday night many of the lights were removed by members of the Public, either because they feared the glow of them would be visible from the air or because they wished to use the lamps in air raid shelters.
>
> Tests have proved that these lights are NOT visible from the air.
>
> It is essential that the lights are not removed or extinguished or the lamps borrowed or stolen. Anyone touching any of the lights in question will be 'Helping the Enemy' by lowering the efficiency of the garrison of the Island. The Police have accordingly been instructed to take severe action against anyone found touching, extinguishing or pilfering any of these lights.[13]

Ammunition Runs Low

The air raids continued, including six attempts to reach the two ships on 17 June. All in all, the two ships had bought 15,000 tons of supplies, but it was not enough.

In early summer, the failure of the convoys had another ominous effect. The supply of ammunition for the AA defences was running low. The fierce AA defence that had so upset the Italian bombers and that had given a feeling of comfort to those on the ground, was now reduced to intermittent bursts as ammu-

---

[13] *The Siege Within the Walls.*

nition was rationed to each gun. Spent cartridge cases had to be collected before fresh ammunition was issued.

' . . . because ammunition was so short we had to pick up our empties after (each raid) and say, "here's a hundred empties, sir, can we have a hundred fresh ones?" ', Norman Travett recalls.[14]

Fuel was so short that the bicycle was not simply another mode of transport, but also of warfare, with bicycle companies formed ready as a rapid reaction squad in case of invasion by paratroopers. Martin Hastings recalls that the Devonshire's weekly battalion ration of fuel was just twenty-one gallons, almost all of which was assigned to the quartermaster so that he could collect supplies and rations, with the bicycle being the normal form of transport for everyone else other than the CO, who rode around on a motorcycle, forsaking his usual staff car. Distribution of supplies to the defensive posts was by donkey and flat cart, and many company commanders found a pony and trap to be the ideal form of transport.

The sinking of so many ships in the two convoys meant that there was an imbalance in the supplies available in Malta. Wheat for baking bread was in short supply, but tinned fish was relatively plentiful, as were beans, but there was little milk.

[14] IWM Sound Archive, Accession No.10462/5/2.

XIII

RATIONING FOR VICTORY

Before the war, the Maltese authorities had spent £350,000 creating a reserve of essential commodities, including oil, lard, margarine, kerosene, tinned meat and tinned fish, and sugar. Once war broke out in September, 1939, it was decided that the sole importers of such items would be the government and the armed forces, and an Office for the Coordination of Supplies, or COSUP, was established. The officers of this department travelled more than 27,000 miles by air seeking supplies for Malta during the war years. Prices were supposed to cover the cost of the materials and transport, but to avoid inflation and also hardship to the poorer members of society, some items were sold below their true cost. The decision over when and how a convoy was fought through was taken in London – many Maltese believed that these decisions were taken by someone they called 'The Brain'.

Taking full control of imports may seem draconian, but it was an essential first step towards obtaining a clear picture of the supply situation. It was also likely that importers and wholesalers accustomed to the small size of frequent pre-war shipments would not have been able to cope with or afford the infrequent large shipments that were inescapable with the convoy system. In any event, it also overcame the problems that could have arisen if one importer had lost all of his supplies as a ship was sunk.

Gradually, some order was created out of the chaos, with a Food and Commerce Control Officer reporting to the Council of Government that 'staple articles of food are available . . . in sufficient quantities to render rationing unnecessary'. Even so, the level of supplies that the FCCO allowed wholesalers to release each month were set just below the demand of the average consumer, prompting action against hoarders and control of food prices, enforced between 21 September and 21 October when the police inspected 1,268 shops, and found 375 grocers guilty of overcharging. Overcharging was punishable by fines of as much as £400, while one wholesaler lost his licence for a month.

One difference between Maltese practice at first and that in the UK, was that hoarding by householders, as opposed to wholesalers and retailers, was not at first discouraged since it was felt that some reserve of supplies could be allowed, especially if distribution arrangements were to break down following an invasion.

It soon became clear that a system of rationing was needed, but even before this was officially sanctioned, many Protection Officers instigated local rationing schemes, but inevitably this led to substantial differences in the ration between different communities. Depending on where they lived, a family of four might find that they were entitled to one, two or three bars of soap each fortnight. The supply of kerosene, still the source of heat for cooking even in the 1950s for most households in Malta, and also used for lighting by many in the country districts in the 1940s, was often badly interrupted, with many not receiving supplies for up to fifteen days. Protection Officers also sorted out this problem, enforcing it with escorts for the kerosene cartmen. At Lija, for example, the ration was a gallon and a half of kerosene weekly.

The desire to establish a seven-month reserve of the most essential items arose with the safe arrival of a convoy in September 1940, and this, more than anything else, was behind the decision to introduce rationing, but this was not announced until February 1941.

In the air raid shelters, many families brought food with them, while some shelter supervisors managed to acquire small stocks for emergency use. Thefts did occur from time to time, especially as rationing became tighter during 1942. One of the worst cases arose when the entire emergency stock was removed from the food store in one air raid shelter. The food had been removed through a ventilation hole that was large enough for cases of food to be lifted out.

Rationing

Before rationing was introduced, a Food Distribution Office, FDO, was created. The FDO established the entitlement to supplies of wholesalers and retailers. Another essential pre-liminary was to require the head of each family to register at a post office, stating the number of people in their household, specifying how many were under the age of three and how many were between the ages of three and eight years. He was also required to provide the name of the retailer from whom rationed goods would be purchased. Rationing officially started on Monday, 7 April 1941, and rations became due on 6 and 21 of every month. The first goods to be rationed were sugar, matches, soap and coffee. Sugar was on a standard scale of a rotolo, or 28 ozs (800g), per person, the other items were on a tapering scale since it was felt that larger families did not need much more of these items than smaller households. For matches, families of five or less were entitled to four boxes of matches, but larger families had just six boxes. A single person got one bar of soap, a family of four or less got two bars, those with five to eight persons got three bars. Less easy to understand is that families of three or less had ¼ rotolo of coffee, those with four or five persons had ½ rotolo, and those of six or seven ¾ rotolo of coffee. By August, lard, margarine and edible oil were also rationed. A single person was allowed ¼ rotolo of lard or margarine and one terz, 0.32 litres, of oil, while a family of five received a rotolo of lard or margarine and four terzi of oil.

Before introducing kerosene rationing, people were en-couraged to build up a small reserve. In December 1940, the government ensured that there was an abundance to allow these reserves to be created, and this policy was maintained until 2 April 1941, when once again kerosene carts were put under police supervision. At first, the system was haphazard and not so much a ration but a restriction on supply, since no individual was allowed to buy more than a half gallon at a time. It was not until May that a formal kerosene rationing system was introduced, with a family of three or less receiving a half gallon weekly, with ¾ gallon for a family of four or five, and of six to nine, not uncommon in Malta, one gallon. The Food Distribution Office also looked after kerosene.

Kerosene rationing proved time and time again to be one of the most controversial and difficult. Housewives argued that they could not cook one hot meal a day with a weekly ration of ½ gallon, and the situation was worse for those who had to use kerosene for lighting as well. Worse still, there were several recorded instances of the ration not being delivered, and this no doubt found its way onto the black market. The authorities eventually tightened up, and in addition to the policeman, an official of the FDO also attended and supplies were issued carefully, street by street.

These moves still left many items off the ration. Fresh fish was becoming scarce due to aerial attacks on the fishing fleet, while no fishing boat was allowed to go more than six miles off the coast and all fishing at night was banned, so the supply of tinned meat and fish, especially sardines and tuna, was becoming important, but prices were soaring. There was little or no fresh imported meat after July 1941, so frozen beef was imported. By late 1941, the Food and Commerce Control Officer banned the sale of meat in restaurants and hotels twice a week, and soon followed this by a blanket ban on the sale of beef in any catering establishment. While the food situation eased during summer 1941, with the arrival of two convoys so that the seven month reserve was re-established, it was already apparent that the safe arrival of convoys could not be counted upon, and after September, 1941, only two convoys got through during the next seven months. Local meat, mainly goat or chickens, was by this time also becoming scarce.

By spring 1941, sugar, coffee, tea, margarine, lard, matches and rice were all rationed. Cows were not introduced to Malta until after the Second World War – the poor pasture available could not sustain them – and at first goats' milk was still available. Cows' milk came to Malta either as powder or in tins, and in the latter form was much favoured by the Maltese for tea or coffee drunk from glasses, but as the shortages began to grow, even this pleasure was to be denied them.

Of the basic commodities, during summer 1941, butter was still plentiful, although the Maltese themselves were not great consumers of dairy products. Bread wasn't rationed at this stage, but this staple of the Maltese diet was often expensive, forcing the poorer members of Maltese society to waste much time shopping around, looking for the best price. The average wage for a Maltese worker was around five shillings a day, no more than half that in the UK. Olive oil also continued to be available. It was possible to augment the diet with fresh fish caught with rod and line off rocks, but the easiest positions were wired off to prevent invasion. Taking a boat, no matter how small, out to sea was a dangerous business.

Inevitably, rationing created a black market. One such black marketeer was Fredu Schembri of Vittoriosa. Times were hard even for the black market. The few who could afford his goods were able to snap these up immediately they became available, while there was always the risk of exposure by the majority who could not afford it, and had simply to tighten their belts. Supplies were intermittent, and the gaps between became longer and longer. Schembri eventually bowed to the inevitable and joined the Home Defence Force, which kitted him out with a helmet, armband and a rifle.

The authorities decreed that the entire potato crop would be bought by the Government, buying these at a good price to encourage production and overcome any temptation to keep produce to be sold on the black market, where a sack of potatoes could easily fetch £5. The Government then sold the potatoes at a lower price, but with strict rationing. Bread rationing was something that the authorities were reluctant to introduce as this was a staple of most Mediterranean diets, but people were initially forced to buy bread from the baker with whom they were registered and, from February 1942, the making of cakes and pastries was banned. Nevertheless, by April, bread rationing was necessary, and took effect from 5 May. The daily bread ration was 10½oz (300g), about a third of the usual adult Maltese consumption, meaning considerable hardship for many adults. One advantage was that the price of bread was halved. Bread rationing was difficult to enforce, with no fewer than 223 bakeries in Malta. Initially, to eke out the ration, wheat was being mixed initially with maize and barley, producing a dark coloured loaf rather than the white crusty bread to which the Maltese were accustomed. Later, it became necessary to include a proportion of potato in the island's bread, due to the shortage of grain, which proved unpopular as it affected both the taste of the bread and it seemed to become stale much more quickly. The cut in the acreage devoted to grain mentioned earlier was beginning to be felt. At one time, grain not so much unloaded as salvaged from a sinking ship had been badly soaked, but it still had to be used.

Malta before the war and for a couple of decades afterwards, had large flocks of goats wandering with a goatherd from one piece of grazing to the next. By 1941, seventy per cent of the goats had been killed and eaten.

Wood was still available for baking bread, but increasingly this was having to be scavenged from the ruins of bombed buildings – a hard task since traditional Maltese architecture uses little wood other than for doors, window frames, furniture, such as cupboards, and for the wooden covered balconies that adorned the front of most houses. As shortages grew, many houses that had not been damaged were to lose their balconies in a programme that mirrored the drive for scrap metal in Great Britain, and had seen large houses and public parks lose their railings.

The cost of living was an important factor, with most government employees earning less than five shillings, 25p, daily, less than half the UK figure at the time. Some factory workers earned between three and four shillings a day. Many Maltese worked for the British armed forces, with the RAF and the Army seeing their Maltese civilian workforce rise from 1,900 in 1939 to 8,800 at the end of 1941. Government employees rose from 2,600 to 8,200 over the same period. Price controls and food subsidies were necessary, and appeared in November 1941, in an attempt to return to the prices prevailing on the outbreak of hostilities. Bread was to be sold at 3d for a rotolo instead of 3½d; paste 6d instead of 9d; sugar 4d instead of 6d; coffee 10d instead of 1/2d and lard and margarine, 1/- instead of 1/8d. Matches were reduced from 2d to a penny; soap from 4d to 3d; a bottle of oil from 8½d to 6d; a tin of milk from 9½d to 7d and a gallon of kerosene from 1/3d to 1/-.

The arrival of three out of the four ships in a convoy from Alexandria in March 1942, simply prolonged the agony. Gort's other concerns were coming to dominate his every waking moment. He already had the garrison on half-rations, and had organized sleep parades so that the soldiers would not waste energy or build up a healthy appetite. He now had to start to reduce the rations of the civilian population, a far harder task even in wartime. Already, safety matches had been rationed to two boxes per fortnight for each family. Now, all remaining food-stuffs had to be pooled to provide everyone with one meal a day using communal kitchens. It would stretch the food as much as was humanly possible, and also offer considerable savings on fuel – these were the Victory Kitchens.

The almost complete failure of the two convoys in May 1942, finally brought Malta to the brink of starvation. In June, two offi-cials were seconded from the Ministry of Food in London to report on the 'Food Situation in Malta'. By this time, they noted, the paste ration had been cut completely, and the bread ration reduced. The sugar ration had been cut from 28ozs per head to 21ozs and then to 14ozs (half rotolo). Further ration reductions were announced to the population by the Lieutenant Governor, Sir Edward Jackson, on 20 June 1942. For a family of five, this meant a monthly ration of 2½ rotolos of sugar, 4 terzi of oil, ½ rotolo of cheese, ¼ rotolo of tea, 1 rotolo of fats, ½ rotolo of coffee, three bars of soap, four tins of corned beef, four tins of fish and four boxes of matches. This reduced the average daily calo-ries from the pre-war figure of 2,500 to less than 1,500. The bread ration would be maintained until mid-October. All brewing was stopped and the grain stocks in brewers' hands requisitioned.

'It was in June, 1942, when the siege really settled down on Malta, grim and cruel. From May to November the island faced up to ever tightening rationing', recalls Mabel Strickland, Editor of *The Times of Malta*, and daughter of Lord Strickland.[1]

Generous prices were offered for grain from farmers and commission paid to brokers to ensure that as much home-produced food as possible was put into the economy, but these measures were not announced until the harvest had been threshed to ensure that surplus food was not fed to the animals. Fodder rations were reduced and generous payments offered for pigs and goats, which were initially intended to be distributed through the retail trade but before this could happen a change of plan saw the meat thus gained sent to the Victory Kitchens. A farmer or goatherd received a bonus of thirty shillings for each animal slaughtered, but unwittingly, rather than take the animals to the abattoir themselves and receive the money, many sold them at far less than this to intermediaries who pocketed a sometimes substantial difference! The scale of this can be gathered since in May 1942, there were 44,426 goats in Malta, and that summer more than 12,000 sheep and goats were slaughtered, and by the end of the siege about half of the sheep and goats had been slaughtered. At one time, the authorities were considering allowing each goatherd to keep just four goats.

Having earlier encouraged families to lay in stocks of food, possibly against the threat of invasion, on 1 July 1942, everyone was ordered to declare their stocks of essential commodities. The excess of oats, bran, wheat or flour, or paste, barley, sugar, maize, carob beans, cotton seeds over and above twenty rotolos had to be declared, while anyone with more than four rotolos of butter, margarine, lard, cheese, coffee, tea, rice or tomato paste had to declare it. No one was allowed more than twenty tins of corned beef, fish or milk, and no more than ten bottles of edible oil, five gallons of kerosene, twenty bars of soap or fifty boxes of matches. All reserves of petrol and coal had to be declared.

[1] IWM Sound Archives, Accession No.1173.

On 20 June 1942. the Lieutenant Governor, Sir Edward Jackson, made a broadcast to the people of Malta. He held little back. He quickly squashed hopes for an increase in the bread ration, although he didn't mention that had bread not been so fundamental to the Maltese diet, the ration would have been reduced. The ration of tinned meat would be maintained, and that for tinned fish would be increased. The ration for most other items was cut in half, including kerosene. This bad news was tempered by promises to improve the food provided by the Victory Kitchens, and to provide additional Victory Kitchens.

The vagaries of the convoy system meant that there was now suddenly a certain amount of wool for knitting, just the thing for those warm Mediterranean summer days, and a quantity of underwear. Nevertheless, the rationing system, in trying to be fair to all, allocated to a priest a pair of bloomers.

The one thing that Sir Edward did not mention was the shortage of fuel.

The ration system marked one big difference between Maltese practice and that in the United Kingdom at this time. In the UK, rationing worked on a points system, in Malta there was no such system simply because there was nothing on which to spend the points. The truth was that Malta had no food reserves on which to fall back by this time, and no guarantee of another convoy. When Italian air raids started, those who had lost their homes and their contents, could be sure of receiving at least some food from their neighbours, but by mid-1942, no one had any to spare. Even the bread ration would be locked away. This was also a feature of the difference between the situation in Malta and the UK; throughout the war, bread was not rationed in the UK, although after the war it was eventually rationed.

Victory Kitchens

Introduced in January 1942, the Maltese Victory Kitchens were based on the Communal Feeding kitchens. They had the advantages of helping those whose homes had been damaged or destroyed in the bombing, and relieving others of the time-consuming queuing and preparation of food after long shifts on war work. They also made the best of scarce reserves of essential food and of fuel. At first, the take up of the Victory Kitchens was relatively low, with just 269 subscribers in January. The Council of Government was told that each managed to feed 200 people, and it was believed that many more would have registered with the Victory Kitchens but for the fact that they had to surrender half of their rations when they did so. Even so, by the end of May, there were forty-two Victory Kitchens throughout Malta.

The Victory Kitchens provided one cooked meal daily, which had to be collected either at 12 noon or at 17.00. Those registered with a particular kitchen often used to leave their pots and pans outside before 09.00, in a long line which no one tampered with through the morning or even the whole day, as they went off to work. Fuel and food were both scarce by this time, and many homes were without gas or electricity for long periods.

Despite surrendering half their rations, those using the Victory Kitchens were not immune from the general shortages. At first, a family of three could expect the meal for them all, the main meal of the day, to be three thin sausages and fifteen peas, plus a small ration of bread. Twice a week, there would also be half a potato. The menu varied, but it could include the vegetable soup, *minestra*, or beans, tinned sardines or herrings, *bulbuliata*, a mixture of beaten egg powder with tomatoes and left-overs, and goat's meat. The island's goat population was by now figuring on the diet, and as a direct consequence, there was a growing shortage of milk, now reserved for the very young and invalids.

Despite this, by the end of June, the food supply situation was such that more than 7,000 people were being fed in this way, and by September, the figure had risen to 60,000! To encourage greater use as the food supply situation became more serious, by mid-July, the proviso that subscribers should lose half their ration was dropped. People on relief nevertheless lost their allowance and their ration. People registered with the Victory Kitchens for a week at a time, with meat and vegetable stews

195

costing 6d, while *minestra* dishes cost 3d. Goat's meat appeared on the menu as much as five times a week, until someone realized that most people couldn't stomach this so often.

While some of the kitchens were praised for the quality of their cooking and cleanliness, many left much to be desired, and especially since much of the labour was untrained. Sometimes people had to queue for most of the day to register. Much of this can be attributed to communal catering and the fact that many felt that this was being forced on them, while no doubt the ingredients were far from top quality given the necessity of ensuring that there could be no waste.

With a diet like this, hunger was a big problem, with one Maltese who lived throughout the siege recalling in later years that his belt could go half way around his waist again! There were health problems too, with scabies from the poor diet, and lice from the lack of adequate washing facilities.

The shortage of fuel meant that hot water was scarce. Some left a tin bath of water on the flat roof of their building in summer, so that at the end of a hot day, the water would be warm, although often rather dusty after the air raids. Fuel for hot water was obtained by scavenging through bombed buildings looking for wood. Later, as the crisis really bit hard, even this source was barred and any wood collected from bombed ruins was allocated to the Victory Kitchens.

Lighting was often no more than a bootlace or piece of string stuck in a potted meat jar containing some paraffin.

Tinned milk was reserved for young babies. Powdered milk, when it did arrive by one of the fast minelayers or by submarine, was barely a relief from the tedium, since the ration was just two tablespoonfuls for sixteen days. Locally-grown fruit was plentiful at times, but sold out quickly, especially if the vendor was spotted by thirsty soldiers. There was no beer.

Tales abound of a thriving black market, but there was little to buy, even so. Eggs could command 15 shillings (75p) for a dozen. Someone maintained that they had spent 17s 6d (87.5p) on a rabbit, but then couldn't eat it since they were convinced that it was the grocer's cat.

Clothing was soon in short supply, as was furniture. Anyone leaving would be pressed to sell as much as they could.

By summer 1942, the food situation was so desperate that around 100,000 people were registered with the Victory Kitchens, more than a third of the civilian population at the time.

Gradually, the normal life of the islands was coming to a standstill. The people were starving and waiting, for either salvation or invasion. Shops were closed since there was nothing for them to sell – even though at one stage many of the food shops had taken to selling secondhand clothes and household possessions. The bus service was little more than a rush hour only service. The Victory Kitchens were serving one hot meal, consisting of a few small pieces of goat's meat. There was very little tea and no sugar. For most meals, a single slice of bread sufficed, and for the lucky, who had hoarded their rations carefully, that might be enlivened by a thin smear of tomato sauce. As fuel reserves fell even further, water became another scarcity, with queues in the hot summer sunshine for water as there was insufficient fuel to keep all of the pumps working. Many of the water mains had in any case been fractured in the constant bombing.

Surrounded by the sea, the normal Maltese diet had always included fish. They were surrounded by plenty, but the coastal defence regulations prevented fishing at night, while German fighters strafed any fishing boat whose crew were desperate enough to venture out to sea during the day. Two-thirds of the Malta fishing fleet was sunk before the end of the war.

Saved, but for How Long?

The arrival of the famous Operation Pedestal on 13 August, 1942, covered on pages 206–211, meant that Malta had been saved from starvation, but times of plenty were still far away. One of the worst aspects was that most of the grain carried by the convoy had been in just two ships, both of which had been sunk.

This meant that the wheat situation was now the major problem. In a heart-to-heart with Bishop Gonzi, emphasizing the great secrecy of the predicament, Lord Gort was frank about the problem. It was once again clear that Gonzi harboured no resentment, for he immediately offered to find the wheat in Gozo, where the harvest was just starting. Gort provided Gonzi with the petrol necessary to visit the farmers on Gozo and ask them to supply their surplus wheat for their neighbours in Malta. The high regard in which the Bishop was held by his flock was soon reflected in the provision of enough grain for the wheat target date to match that for fuel and other necessities. This was a burden lifted off Gort, and of the Maltese, but for any wartime governor, it seemed that resolving one problem only brought another to the top of the pile – the new target date was December, but would another convoy arrive in time? Operation Pedestal would show that it could be done, but at what cost?

Nevertheless, there were other improvements, with weekly instead of fortnightly issues of kerosene. Edible oil was also to be issued every ration period, but the sugar ration could not be increased given that much of the consignment had been damaged by sea water. Coffee would also be issued every ration period.

Having got so close to the target date, and been saved at the eleventh hour at such a heavy price, rationing was maintained and the supplies were eked out. The Victory Kitchens' role was to ensure that everyone should be treated equally, providing a communal meal so that no one should starve, or, as one wag put it, 'so that everyone should starve equally'.

The new ration served by the Victory Kitchens meant that a typical meal would consist of a plate of vegetable soup, an ounce of corned beef or tinned fish. When available, 'veal loaf' was served, and this was regarded as a rare treat, but the 'veal' consisted mainly of slaughtered sheep or horse. The animals themselves had not been well fed, so the quantity of meat was limited. The rule of each person having a single meal from the communal kitchens at either midday or 17.00 continued, and meals were still collected by families in their own utensils. In addition to the communal meals, each person was allowed a meagre ration of a tin of corned beef and a small tin of fish every fortnight, a few beans, some coffee mixed with barley to eke it out, and when it was available, a small quantity of tea and sugar.

Tinned milk was reserved for small children and those who were ill. For everyone else, there would be an occasional ration of powdered milk and powdered eggs.

The complaints about the standards of the Victory Kitchens continued at this time, and rebellion nearly broke out on 1 September. Liver stew had been served and thousands found the taste unpalatable, throwing the dish away in protest and leading to what must have been an unprecedented promptness in the bureaucratic response of the Communal Feeding Department, which immediately ordered that those who had had an unsatisfactory lunch be given a portion of corned beef either immediately or later in the day. When, *balbuliata*, on this occasion minced vegetables with powdered eggs, was served for the first time, many found it to be unpalatable and badly cooked, but there were also protests over the small portions served, two tablespoonfuls with another two of peas.

On 10 September, the Council of Government decided to appoint a select committee to investigate the running of the Victory Kitchens. It reported on 7 October, finding many of the criticisms justified, with no uniformity in the taste or quality of meals, food often overcooked or burnt, or left raw, inexperienced cooks, and poor supervision. The Committee recommended closure, but with 100,000 people now subscribing, the Government rejected this recommendation. The numbers peaked at more than 175,000 by the following January, but within a month, this had dropped to 20,000.

Meanwhile, in an attempt to brighten things up, the Communal Feeding Service introduced a new menu:

Sunday	– Stewed meat with tomatoes and baked peas.
Monday	– Macaroni with cheese and tomatoes.
Tuesday	– *Balbuliata.*
Wednesday	– *Minestra.*
Thursday	– Stewed meat with tomatoes and peas.
Friday	– *Minestra.*
Saturday	– Macaroni with cheese and tomatoes.

Gort's Compromise

Deciding just how to cut rations was bad enough, but deciding how and when to ease the restrictions was also difficult. In November, the safe arrival of a convoy intact so that there were no imbalances in the food supply situation, presented Gort with a fresh problem. The Maltese were starving and had given their all, and it was too soon to relax their guard with the enemy still present in Sicily, just sixty miles away. Should he relieve the hunger of those in Malta by increasing rations to a more sustaining level, or, in case the convoy had been a fluke, maintain them at the same severe level? After all, Gort had no idea, no guarantee, of just when the next convoy might be. Gort decided to compromise. He introduced a graduated increase in rations, one that would take full effect by January 1943, but overall the effect would be still far less than what the people needed. Gort's caution was understandable, with all too recent memories of the desperate situation the previous August, but he needn't have worried, for within a month a further nine ships arrived with food and aviation spirit.

This large batch of supplies, coming so soon after the November convoy, meant that Gort was now free to make the increase in rations that he had wanted. The bread ration for working men was increased by a quarter for five days a week. The sugar, cheese and fats ration was increased in December, and a special issue of sugar, flour, beans and dried fruit was made with Christmas in mind. The Victory Kitchens once again became an option, not a necessity, not least because of the increased availability of kerosene for cooking at home.

XIV

SALVATION –
OR A FALSE DAWN?

Summer meant harvest. Even troops were released to help farmers reap the harvest. Yet, much of the farmland had itself been disturbed by bombs. Normal planting and the crop cycle had been disrupted by the war. There was little manure and no artificial fertilizers. The fate of the ship bringing seed potatoes has already been described, and the replacements from Cyprus produced a lean crop. Most of the goats on Malta, Gozo and Comino had been killed, along with any poultry and the wild rabbits.

The poor diet was taking its toll. The worst affected women and young children, Maltese and British, were evacuated by air to Cairo aboard two bombers. This was a risky venture, but the planes got through and those doctors and nurses waiting for them in Egypt were appalled at their condition.

Malta was once again dependent on the large minelaying submarines for supplies, augmented by the fast minelaying cruiser HMS *Welshman*, capable of making a 40-knot dash, carrying fuel and other urgent supplies on what became known to the Royal Navy as the 'Club Runs'. The air link with Gibraltar could carry only limited supplies, and of course the aircraft were dependent on the runways being clear. The big problem with air transport at this time was that the aircraft, converted bombers, had to bring with them the fuel for their return flight, limiting the weight of supplies that could be carried.

If the news wasn't bad enough, on 21 June, Rommel's *Afrika*

Korps took Tobruk. The airfields in North Africa could be added to those of Sicily in menacing Malta. Rommel had at a stroke captured 1,400 tons of petrol, 2,000 serviceable military vehicles and 5,000 tons of provisions, as well as large quantities of ammunition. His supply problems might not have been solved forever, but they had at least been relieved. The day after, he was promoted to Field Marshal.

The victory may have been Rommel's undoing. It seemed that nothing was impossible for him and his troops, and that the British were defeated. Instead of using the breathing space afforded by a great victory to consolidate his position, ideally by invading Malta, that thorn in his side, he decided to head for Egypt and the Suez Canal. Rommel forgot his claim a year earlier that Malta had to be occupied. He bypassed the Italian High Command, who were strictly speaking his superiors, and approached Berlin direct. Militarily weak, the Italians had to accept that Malta would have to wait, and that the objective was to be Egypt.

The summer and autumn of 1942 saw Malta surrounded by minefields that could not be swept as the Luftwaffe attacked the minesweepers. In North Africa, Rommel's advance eastwards continued, so much so that Mussolini moved to North Africa and set up his headquarters at Derna in Cyrenaica. *Il Duce* was ready and waiting to make a triumphal entry to Cairo. He even procured a white stallion and had a sword, modelled on those carried by the crusaders, specially made.

It was at Derna in June that Kesselring tried to inject a note of realism into the ambitions of Mussolini and Rommel. The fighter pilot pointed out that the enemy's position had vastly improved, while the *Afrika Korps* was being dragged further from its bases and overextending its supply lines. He also drew attention to the growing aerial superiority of the British. Kesselring advised that Rommel's advance should stop at El Alamein.

Rommel had not been present at the meeting, so Kesselring and the rest of the combined German and Italian High Command visited him shortly afterwards at his forward field headquarters at Sidi Barrani. Strangely, Rommel admitted that his troops were short of both petrol and water, 'but we cannot stop for that'. These were the two most vital commodities for desert warfare. Rommel's enthusiasm infected those at the meeting, with the exception of Kesselring.

Rommel's overstretched and under-supplied troops spent July struggling with the British Eighth Army. The results were inconclusive, but it was clear that an early victory was unlikely. Disappointed, Mussolini returned to Italy.

Gort continued his predecessor's practice of broadcasting to the Maltese people. He had addressed them on 16 June to tell them about the failure of the two convoys.

'If the enemy failed in his main purposed, he succeeded in part of it,' the Lieutenant-Governor, Sir Edward Jackson, explained in a radio broadcast on 20 June.

> He has delayed the arrival of our much needed supplies, and as His Excellency the Governor has told you, a time of further privation, greater privation than we have known hitherto, lies ahead of us ... We received about 15,000 tons of stores from the two ships which arrived. That is something and certainly a help, but it is a very small part of what we had hoped for ...
>
> I have said that in examining our position, we first calculated the time for which our bread could be made to last. That calculation gave us a certain date which I shall call the 'Target Date', the date to aim at. Our next task was to see how we could make our other vital necessities last to the Target Date.[1]

An Important Visitor

On 2 August, the Chief of the Imperial General Staff and War Cabinet Member, General Sir Alan Brooke, later Field Marshal Lord Alanbrooke, flew into Malta on his way to visit Egypt. He not only saw for himself the plight of the islanders, but also

[1] Rediffusion Broadcast.

briefed Gort on the plans for a major offensive against the Axis in North Africa. This was undoubtedly a morale booster for Gort and Jackson, since Malta would cease to be a beleaguered outpost, and would become a springboard for the assault on the enemy.

Brooke had served under Lord Gort during the Battle of France. His visit to Malta was by way of Gibraltar, where he had toured the defences. His *War Diaries* recall the trip.

> For the next hop it was essential to reach Malta before dawn, otherwise there were chances of being shot down by Italian fighters . . . I was especially anxious to visit Gort in Malta as I knew he was in a depressed state, feeling that he had been shoved away in a corner out of the real war, and in danger of his whole garrison being scuppered without much chance of giving an account of themselves. His depression had been increased by the fact that he insisted on living on the reduced standard of rations prevailing on the island, in spite of the fact that he was doing twice as much physical and mental work as any other member of the garrison. Owing to the shortage of petrol he was using a bicycle in that sweltering heat, and frequently had to carry his bicycle over demolished houses.
>
> I wanted to tell him about the plans for a new command in the Middle East with an advance westwards combined with American-British landings in West Africa moving eastwards, destined to meet eventually. I wanted him to feel that if all this came off he would find himself in an outpost of an advance instead of the backwater he considered himself in. I felt certain that to be able to look forward to something definite would do much to dispel his gloom.[2]

Brooke's flight from Gibraltar took six-and-a-half hours. Learning from experience on earlier flights, he had borrowed some ear plugs to protect against the noise of the aircraft engines,

[2] *Lord Alanbrooke's War Diaries 1939-1945.*

and was able to snatch some sleep. He woke to find that the aircraft was bumping badly, and his first reaction was to assume that they had flown into turbulence, but instead the aircraft was landing on Malta in the dark. He was taken to Gort's house where he slept. Meetings with the senior service officers on Malta followed.

' . . . After lunch we went to the docks and to Valletta,' he wrote.

> The destruction is inconceivable and reminds one of Ypres, Arras, Lens at their worst during last war. We travelled about in Admiral's barge and examined wrecks of last convoy. Finally examined new dock workshops that have been mined into the rock. Had tea with Admiral in charge of the docks. 5 air raid alarms during the day, but no serious bombing. Finally at 10.45 before we were to start a German plane came over, but did not remain.[3]

Brooke then continued on to Cairo, a seven-and-a-half hour flight. His visit to Malta had been worthwhile.

> The conditions prevailing in Malta at that time were distinctly depressing, to put it mildly! Shortage of rations, shortage of petrol, a hungry population that rubbed their tummies looking at Gort as he went by, destruction and ruin of docks, loss of convoys just as they approached the island, and the continual possibility of an attack on the island without much hope of help or reinforcements.[4]

Interesting to note what Brooke did not say in his *War Dairies*. This was a man who did not suffer fools gladly, in fact he did not suffer them at all! His criticisms of those he met were often damning. He gave praise to few, although one of these was later to be Cunningham when he took over from Pound as First Sea

[3] *Lord Alanbrooke's War Diaries 1939–1945.*
[4] IWM Sound Archive, Accession No.10462/5/2.

Lord. Gort seems to have escaped the withering criticism, and no doubt Brooke played a part in obtaining for him an appointment later as Governor of Palestine, no doubt meant as a compliment, but for Gort it was probably a case of 'out of the frying pan into the fire'.

Operation Pedestal

Malta's situation was indeed serious. Top secret plans for surrender had already been prepared, but to maintain morale, these were known to few. The target date really did mean a surrender date.

As the target date drew near, in August, 1942, a final all-out effort was made to fight supplies through to the beleagured population of Malta. This was the convoy known to the British as 'Operation Pedestal', but to the devout Maltese, it was to be the 'Santa Marija Convoy', as it was due to arrive on 13 August, just two days before the feast day of the Ascension of the Virgin Mary. The lessons of the recent past were not lost, and this convoy had naval air power in abundance, and what is more, higher performance aircraft in the shape of the Sea Hurricane and the Martlet.

The Sea Hurricane was the naval variant of the Hawker Hurricane and the first attempt to give the Fleet Air Arm the high performance aircraft it needed. That the Hurricane prototype had made its first flight in 1935 shows the lack of urgency that had been given to making good the deficiencies of the fleet! The Sea Hurricane first entered service with the Fleet Air Arm in July 1941, and the aircraft were all basic conversions from RAF standard machines fitted with arrestor hooks, without folding wings so that not every carrier could operate these aircraft because of the limitations on wingspan imposed by some carrier lifts. The lack of folding wings also severely limited the number of aircraft that could be accommodated. The Hurricane had two advantages over the faster Spitfire, of which the Seafire variant had folding wings. It had a tighter turning radius, always an important feature for a fighter, and it was easier to repair, again important with the limited number of aircraft that can be carried aboard ship.

Better still in many respects was the Grumman Martlet, as the Fleet Air Arm liked to call its Wildcats early in the war. Here at last was a purpose-designed high performance naval fighter, designed for the rough life of carrier operations. First flown in 1937, it entered FAA service in September 1940. Designed for the United States Navy, the Martlet had folding wings. Its retractable undercarriage was mounted under the fuselage, giving a narrow track, so that in rough seas the aircraft appeared to 'dance' from one undercarriage leg to the other!

Despite the substantial escort and the new aircraft, this was a large convoy of fourteen merchant vessels since heavy losses were expected, for Malta's smallscale port facilities could not cope with anything like fourteen merchantmen at one time. The escort, designated Force Z, was commanded not by the more usual commodore, but by Vice Admiral Syfret with the two powerful battleships *Nelson* and *Rodney*, sister ships nick-named 'Rodnol' because of their supposed similarity in appearance to tankers, with a superstructure well aft and all nine 16-inch guns in three turrets all forward. The large ships could not be risked in the confined waters of the Sicilian Channel, so the convoy would actually be taken into Malta by Force X, under Rear Admiral Burrough. There were no less than four aircraft carriers. The veteran *Furious*, the world's first aircraft carrier when she joined the Royal Navy in 1918, carried Supermarine Spitfire fighters to reinforce Malta's air defences. The other carriers were part of the convoy escort and included the elderly carrier *Eagle*, and the new *Victorious*, a true sister of *Illustrious*, and even newer, *Indomitable*, a modified variant of *Illustrious*. Finally, there were no less than seven cruisers, Force Z's *Sirius*, *Charybdis* and *Phoebe*, as well as *Nigeria*, which was to be Burrough's flagship, *Manchester*, *Kenya* and *Cairo*, and thirty-two destroyers, of which eight would be protecting the carrier *Furious* and her valuable cargo of fighters, as well as towing vessels. A supply force would accompany the convoy, known as Force R and consisting of two tankers and three corvettes, with a tug. Additional protection came with the creation of a submarine patrol line south of the Italian island of Pantellaria with six boats, while another two were placed off the north coast of Sicily at Cape St Vito and Cape Milazzio.

Aboard *Victorious* were sixteen Fairey Fulmar fighters as well as five Sea Hurricanes and, for anti-submarine and reconnaissance work, twelve Fairey Albacore biplanes, supposedly an improvement on the venerable Swordfish but in fact disliked because of its poor reliability. *Indomitable* had nine Grumman Martlet and twenty-two Sea Hurricane fighters. *Eagle* had twenty Sea Hurricanes. Although working as an aircraft transport, *Furious* carried four spare Albacores for *Victorious*.

The strains of war were already beginning to show, and an early indication of the poor strategic position of the Axis powers can be gathered from the fact that the Italian Navy was confined to port by fuel shortages. The Germans were keeping all of the fuel to themselves, and in the Mediterranean they had E-boats and U-boats as well as the Luftwaffe.

On 10 August, the convoy left Gibraltar with its escort, with its presence immediately reported by a Spanish airliner flying to North Africa, and the following day the Axis attack started. An attack by Junkers Ju88s at 10.00 was warded off by the carriers' fighters, while the RAF from Malta and the USAAF from the UK bombed three airfields in Sardinia, destroying twenty-two enemy aircraft. At 12.29, *Furious* launched thirty-eight Spitfire Vs towards Malta, and of these just one aircraft failed to get through. The carrier *Eagle* was hit by four torpedoes from *U-73* at 13.15 on 11 August. The old carrier, a converted battleship that should have been retired had not war intervened, immediately started to list to port. Within four minutes she had gone. Despite sinking so rapidly, just 160 of her ship's company of 953 died, but many survivors had to spend hours in the water before a destroyer could risk stopping to pick them up. The old ship would be missed by those in Malta because she had flown off 183 fighters to Malta on several ventures into the Western Mediterranean.

Later, at 20.45, thirty-six Luftwaffe aircraft from Sardinia attacked. After a peaceful night, twenty Luftwaffe aircraft attacked at 09.15, followed at noon by a combined force of seventy Luftwaffe and *Regia Aeronautica* aircraft. That afternoon, at about 16.00, a destroyer found and sank a U-boat. Three hours later, another combined strike hit the convoy, this time of a hundred aircraft, sinking a merchantman and so badly damaging *Indomitable* that those of her aircraft in the air had to be recovered onto the crowded decks and hangars of *Victorious*. The Sea Hurricane could cope easily with the Ju87 Stuka, but was a poor match for the faster Ju88.

'The speed and the height of the Ju88s made the fleet fighters' task a hopeless one,' wrote Syfret. 'It will be a happy day when the fleet is equipped with modern fighter aircraft.'

The day hadn't finished: at around 20.00, twenty Luftwaffe aircraft attacked, sinking the cruiser *Cairo* and two merchant vessels, as well as damaging the cruiser *Nigeria* and three other ships, including the fast oil tanker *Ohio*, American-owned but on this occasion British-crewed. One merchantman, the *Deucalion*, was so badly damaged that she had to make for the coast of Libya. As darkness fell, E-boats attacked, sinking five ships and so damaging the cruiser *Manchester* that she had to be sunk later.

The Italians now attempted to use their new weapon, the *Motobomba FF*, a motorized bomb dropped by parachute, which started its engine once it had contact with water, and then drove in a circle with a radius of around fifteen kilometres in an attempt to hit a ship. Fortunately, it had little effect.

At 08.00 the next day, 12 August, twelve Luftwaffe aircraft from Sicily struck at the convoy, sinking another ship and battering the *Ohio* still further. At 11.25, fifteen *Regia Aeronautica* aircraft attacked. By now, the battered *Ohio* with her highly flammable cargo was ablaze and her master gave the order to abandon ship. The ship remained stubbornly afloat, so before they could be picked up, they reboarded her.

Meanwhile that day, the destroyer *Foresight* was so badly damaged that she had to be sunk by another destroyer, *Tartar*. Later, Force Z turned back to Gibraltar, leaving the convoy with the last, and most dangerous, thirty-six hours of its passage to Malta. Later, amidst heavy air attacks, the *Empire Hope* was set on fire before being sunk by an Italian submarine, while the

209

Glenorchy was sunk by a torpedo from *E-31*. Badly damaged by a torpedo, the *Brisbane Star* was given makeshift repairs by her crew, and then headed south in search of shelter. *Clan Ferguson*, carrying ammunition, was hit by an air-dropped torpedo, and set on fire, before being sunk by another Italian submarine. Three more merchant ships were sunk that night in the E-boat attack that had also sunk the cruiser *Manchester*.

On 13 August, the main body of the convoy, just four merchant ships, finally reached Grand Harbour, but the *Ohio* had to be taken alongside a warship and helped into Grand Harbour two days late, on 15 August. She was lucky, for another straggler, the *Dorset*, was sunk by dive-bombers.

In Malta, the heavy aerial activity off the coast and the presence of patrolling Spitfires over the approaches to the Grand Harbour confirmed what the Malta rumour mill had been predicting; a convoy was close. Those waiting on the walls of the bastions strained their eyes, looking far out to sea. Then a ship was spotted, and the crowds broke into loud cheers. As she drew closer, they could see that she was a battered merchantman, the *Melbourne Star*. Then another ship appeared, the *Rochester Castle*, followed a little later by the *Port Chalmers*. The ships received a tumultuous welcome from the crowds lining the walls, and another warm welcome awaited the *Ohio* when she arrived two days later, with those present marvelling at how this blackened wreck could have remained afloat.

The cost had been considerable. Nine merchantmen were sunk or forced to withdraw, as well as an aircraft carrier, two cruisers and a destroyer. There was serious damage to the *Ohio*, two aircraft carriers and two cruisers. Yet, the five merchant ships that reached Grand Harbour were spared any further attacks, at a time when they would have been most vulnerable, despite the efforts of the defenders, waiting to unload at Malta's very limited port facilities. The *Ohio* gave up her cargo of oil, with her oil tanks being emptied and their contents replaced by sea water so that she wouldn't break her back, and then afterwards, she slipped beneath the waters of Grand Harbour. She was refloated, but the damage was so great that she eventually broke her back whilst at her moorings. She was made watertight and the two halves were used as floating stores. It was impossible to repair the ship and after the war ended, the two halves of the *Ohio* were towed out to sea to provide target practice for a destroyer's gunners. The aft portion sunk quickly, but the buoyant forward section lasted a while longer before reluctantly slipping beneath the waves.

Her master, Captain Dudley Mason had been taken to hospital after arriving in Malta, but he recovered and was later awarded the George Cross.

The convoy had come just in the nick of time. Malta had had just thirteen days of supplies left when the first ships entered Grand Harbour.

George Cross Ceremony

A month later, on Sunday 13 September, 1942, Lord Gort finally found the time and the opportunity to make the presentation of the George Cross to the people of Malta, on whose behalf the award was received by the Chief Justice, Sir George Borg, in a ceremony in Valletta. The ceremony was also attended by the Archbishop of Malta, Dom Maurus Caruana, and the Bishop of Gozo, Monsignor Michael Gonzi, later to be Caruana's successor as Archibishop of Malta, and whose anti-British sentiments had proved to be an unjustified slander. There were others there too, for amongst the crowds, representatives of all walks of Maltese life were present, representing Maltese women, dockyard workers, farmers, the military, telephone exchange workers, the rescue services and so on. Before presenting the medal, Gort read out the citation, written in George VI's own hand.

Afterwards, Gonzi asked for a repeat ceremony in Gozo, knowing that few of his flock would have been able to travel to Valletta. Gort agreed instantly, and promptly offered to do it the following Sunday.

The air raids in October 1942, reflected Malta's strength rather than that of the Axis, with fourteen bombers escorted by no less than ninety-eight fighters.

It was to be some months before the war in the Mediterranean reached the turning point, the defeat of the Italian and German armies at the Battle of El Alamein which started on 23 October with a thousand gun barrage and ended on 5 November with Rommel retreating into Tunisia. The start of the offensive caught the Germans ill-prepared, with Rommel absent, convalescing in Austria, and their difficulties were not lessened when, on the very day that Montgomery's offensive started, the Malta-based submarine *Umbra* found the supply ship *Amsterdam,* 8,670 tons, carrying tanks and motor vehicles for the *Afrika Korps* and sank it with her torpedoes. Victory at El Alamein marked a further step forward, removing German pressure on the Suez Canal, which had been threatened at one point with Rommel's forces just eighty miles from Alexandria.

When would the next convoy arrive? An answer was not long in coming the Axis forces in North Africa were not simply being rolled back in what might be yet another swing of the pendulum, they were on the road to defeat. The beginning of November showed the way the war was going, as within days, on 8 November, victory at last appeared possible with the successful Allied landings in North Africa. Vichy French resistance did not last long – it could not since their fuel and armaments position was precarious. The *Afrika Korps* risked being squeezed.

Fears that Malta might be forgotten in the excitement of the new advances were unnecessary, as the small country once again assumed a vital strategic role as the RAF in Malta saw its strength rise to 200 front line aircraft, half of them bombers. A new airfield was constructed in great haste near Qrendi, known as Safi, and opened with great ceremony on 10 November by Lord Gort, while Air Vice Marshal Keith Park landed the first aircraft on it. From that day, until 23 November, Malta-based aircraft kept up an unending series of attacks on airfields in Sicily, and on that day, with just thirteen days of supplies left, a convoy of four merchantmen sailed into Grand Harbour, the Stoneage Convoy, the first to reach the island unmolested since June 1940. The siege was lifting.

That day was also memorable for Park, who was awarded the KBE.

Nevertheless, all was not well as the New Year dawned. The food situation was much improved, but the many ailments that had arisen due to malnutrition and the absence of soap and other washing and cleaning materials, were still there. Scabies was still rife, and the usual remedy, sulphur, didn't seem to have much impact. Then in January, a new dread appeared, acute poliomyelitis, striking hardest at children so that it was popularly known as infantile paralysis, often killing, and for those spared, it usually maimed for life. Places of popular entertainment that had remained open during the worst of the blitz were now closed to prevent the dreaded infection spreading unchecked.

Nevertheless, there was more good news from North Africa, with the fall of Tripoli on 23 January.

The final air raids on Malta came on 26 February 1943, with the *Regia Aeronautica* sending one bomber that approached the coast just before daybreak, but did not cross it, followed in the evening by a few fighters attempting a quick hit and run raid. All in all, the Maltese had seen 1,597 killed in the air raids, another 1,818 seriously injured, and less serious injuries to another 1,889. Yet, the figures for the dead and wounded do not give the true picture of wartime casualties in Malta. The poor diet took its own toll over and above the official casualties, with the most seriously affected being the very young, the very old, and the infirm. To take the worst year, 1942, infant mortality was 345.15 per thousand, meaning that more than one baby in three, 2,336 babies, under the age of one year died. At the other end of the scale, elderly people died at 31.97 per thousand. Together these cruel statistics meant that the population fell for the first time on record by 1,835. This, after all, was in a devout Roman Catholic country with a high birth rate.

The worst damaged place in Malta was Senglea, which had all but ceased to exist. This dockyard town suffered eighty per cent of its buildings destroyed, and the other twenty per cent damaged so badly as to be uninhabitable, with the streets impassable because of the rubble.

No less than 547 British aircraft had been lost in the air battles over and around Malta, with another 160 lost on the ground, but the Germans and Italians had between them lost 1,252 aircraft over Malta, with another 1,051 probables.

The British started to increase their air power in Malta, but other units were rotated out of Malta to join the Eighth Army in North Africa. Rations had been increased following the arrival of the August 1942 convoy, Operation Pedestal, but the Devonshires for one found the going tough, as after some leave in Egypt, they started training as a commando battalion, ready for the assault on Sicily.

'I think that we ate more than the stomach could reasonably accept in those days,' Norman Travett remembers of his arrival in Egypt.[5]

Now the Maltese had to rebuild their country, and also welcome the many visitors who wanted to see for themselves how they had fared. Their old friend Admiral Andrew Cunningham was among the first, as was Admiral Harwood, and then Air Marshal Lord Trenchard, the father of the RAF, and from further afield, Archbishop Spellman of New York. Then, on 20 June came King George VI, Colonel-in-Chief of the Royal Malta Artillery. On a warm sunny day, so much like that June day three years earlier when war had broken out, the cruiser *Aurora* steamed slowly into Grand Harbour with His Majesty on the bridge wearing the tropical No.1 uniform of an Admiral of the Fleet. At a signal from the bell of Fort St Angelo, a general salute was fired not by the guns of the Royal Malta Artillery, but by the church bells of Valletta, Cospicua, Senglea and Vittoriosa, determined to show that they were still standing. Loud cheers followed from those on the bastions and on the harbour front, and from those in the many brightly coloured *dghajsas*.

After inspecting a guard of honour provided by the Royal Malta Artillery, the King proceeded to the Governor's Palace where he presented a Field Marshal's Baton to Lord Gort, while Gort in turn presented Monsignor Gonzi to the King, explaining his role in saving Malta from starvation.

A new understanding of Gonzi meant that British objections

---

[5] IWM Sound Archive, Accession No.10462/5/1.

to his becoming Archbishop of Malta in succession to Caruana were lifted, and not only did he become Archbishop on the death of Caruana, he was also awarded the honorary rank of a major general in the British Army.

The King then embarked on the expected round of inspections of the various service units on Malta, and, just as he had done so often in London, he also saw the effects of the blitz and met those who had suffered so much. He saw the tunnels, many of them with names such as Petticoat Lane or Lambeth Walk, he saw the shrines and chapels underground, and he saw just why Malta had so deserved the George Cross.

Malta the Springboard

Now Malta went beyond simply taking the offensive to the enemy, and became a base for the first invasion of enemy-occupied Europe. The RAF's combat strength in Malta trebled to 600 aircraft, the ships entering Grand Harbour brought not just fuel and provisions for the Maltese and for British units based on the island, but also the tanks and artillery needed for an invasion, and for this there were the landing craft, so much more efficient and effective than the barges that the Germans and Italians would have used for an invasion of Malta.

Now, it was not Malta that would be invaded, but a much larger island. The invasion was not long in coming, in July 1943, after which Malta was no longer in the front line. This time, however, in contrast to the situation after the Battle of Lepanto in 1571, Malta was not to become a backwater. Not only did British ships, and especially the aircraft carriers, bound for the British Pacific Fleet use Malta to work up as they passed through the Mediterranean on their way to take the war to Japan, but the post-war world brought a massive realignment in strategy with the onset of the Cold War. For most of those years, until the end of the British presence in the late 1970s, Malta was on the front-line of the Cold War with a NATO headquarters just outside Valletta at Floriana.

On 9 July 1943, the invasion convoys for Operation Husky, the

215

Allied invasion of Sicily gathered to the east and to the west of the island. The Eastern British Task Force had 795 vessels with 715 landing craft under the command of Vice Admiral Sir Bertram Ramsay, while to the West lay the Western Naval Task Force under the US Vice Admiral H. Kent Hewitt, with 580 vessels and 1,124 landing craft, as well as three convoys with the 45th, 1st and 2nd Infantry Divisions, the 2nd Armoured Division and the 1st Canadian Division. The degree to which the Allies had aerial and naval supremacy in the Mediterranean, can be gathered by the fact that, out of all these ships, just four ships and two LSTs, landing ships tank, were lost to submarine attack. A far worse opponent was the weather, with a storm developing during 10 July, but nevertheless, it was decided to press ahead in the belief that the Italians would not expect an attack in such conditions. The date was exactly a year after the date set by the Germans for the invasion of Malta.

General Kurt Student, who would have led the invasion of Malta, wanted to counter-attack with his two paratroop divisions, but this was refused. Eventually, his 1st Parachute Division was dropped in Sicily to defend a bridge leading into the Plain of Catania – one of the first British units they faced was the 231 Brigade from Malta, one of the units that had expected to repel an Axis invasion!

On 3 September that year, Allied forces crossed from Sicily into mainland Italy, and Air Vice Marshal Sir Keith Park formally marked the end of Malta's place in the front line by presenting *Faith*, the sole survivor of the three Gloster Gladiators, to the people of Malta, choosing once again the Palace Square in Valletta where a year earlier the George Cross had been presented, and once again the recipient on behalf of the Maltese people was Sir George Borg, the Chief Justice.

There was more to come. On 8 September, people flocked to Senglea for the popular feast of Our Lady of Victories, which had signified the defeat of the Turks in 1565 and which was, by coincidence, the titular feast of Senglea. The atmosphere was charged with optimism, and the usual procession with the statue of the Lady of Victories passed the usual church, now in ruins, and headed for the church of St Philip, taking the place of the parish church. The crowds followed the statue into the church, with many having to stay outside. The joyful babble of the crowd faded away into a respectful silence, when suddenly there was a disturbance, and the parish priest in his vestments was seen running to the pulpit. All eyes turned to him, and he seemed to find it impossible to speak at first, but he struggled and then out came the message and there was never a more welcome pronouncement from that pulpit: 'My brethren, rejoice,' he shouted. 'I have just had the news, Italy has surrendered.'

There was a stunned silence for the briefest of moments, then the people inside the church exploded in a roar of shouting that spread like wildfire through the crowds outside, then the bells started to ring, first in Senglea and then throughout Malta, giving the ultimate all clear!

Two days later, the crowds who so quickly assembled on the bastions to see ships enter port, saw twenty-eight warships approach the Grand Harbour, but this was no convoy, but the van of the Italian Navy, anchored outside. During the week that followed, the number of ships increased to sixty-five. Cunningham signalled the Admiralty:

> Pleased to inform their Lordships that the Italian battle fleet now lies at anchor under the guns of the fortress of Malta.

Cunningham would not be with the Mediterranean Fleet for much longer. The following year he would become General Eisenhower's naval deputy, but in October 1943, still higher demands were placed on him, as he became First Sea Lord, taking over from the ailing Dudley Pound. By that time, Allied naval supremacy in the Mediterranean had been re-established.

XV

THE TIDE TURNS

Operation Pedestal was not the end of Malta's travails, but it was the beginning of the end. For those on the island, this was hard to grasp at the time. The convoy had brought them from the brink of starvation, but afterwards, the enemy seemed to close in more closely than before.

While Gort had taken a gamble with the bread ration, increasing this after the arrival of the Santa Marija convoy, the action soon seemed premature. True, *Welshman* continued to make her 'club runs', joined now by her sister ship *Manxman*, but grain hardly ever seemed to figure in the supplies carried. Most foodstuffs would last until December, but Gort knew that grain would run out well before then.

Yet, all was not well with the enemy. The loss of so many ships during Operation Pedestal couldn't disguise the fact that five had got through, and that this had been a victory for the Allies and a defeat for the Axis. Kesselring described his men being in a state of nerves which he described as 'Malta Fever'.

The day of the convoy's arrival, 13 August, also marked another change with the arrival of General Montgomery and Field Marshal Lord Alexander in Egypt, to relieve Lord Auchinleck and Corbett. Brooke had been unimpressed with Corbett and believed that Montgomery would not work well under Auchinleck. These changes were essential to get the Eighth Army ready for the offensive for which Churchill was pressing.

Malta had once again become an offensive base. Rommel's men were falling prey to many of the diseases caused by malnutrition.

That autumn Kesselring once again ordered *Fliegerkorps II*, now only the remnants of what had been a powerful force, into the air battle over Malta, appreciating that it could only be a matter of time before Rommel came under attack, and knowing that the 'Desert Fox' was short of fuel and water. The air raids started again on the night of Saturday 10–Sunday 11 October. This time, the new AOC, Air Vice Marshal Sir Keith Park, tried different tactics, sending Spitfires out to intercept the raiders before they reached Maltese air space. It worked the first time, with a third of the bombers turning back without flying over Malta, but the Germans were made of sterner stuff, and the raids increased in their intensity, with the airfields once again the main targets. The Luftwaffe began attacking from all directions, hoping to confuse the defenders. Even so, on the first day of the new air assault, the Luftwaffe lost fifteen aircraft, with thirty more so badly damaged as to have been unlikely to have made it home. The second day saw twenty-four shot down, and forty-one seriously damaged. The RAF lost three Spitfires. The RAF continued to attempt to disrupt the bomber formations while they were still over the sea, and continued to enjoy considerable success, while air/sea rescue launches patrolled the waters offshore so that any pilot able to bale out was likely to be quickly rescued.

On 13 October, the 1,000th enemy plane to be shot down over Malta was reached. This milestone has been credited to an American pilot flying a Spitfire, Squadron Leader J. J. Lynch from California, but officially the Air Ministry credited this crucial kill to a Canadian, Pilot Officer George Frederick 'Screwball' Beurling, only twenty-one years old, and already the holder of both the Distinguished Flying Cross and the Distinguished Flying Medal, the latter indicating that he had started his career as an NCO pilot.

There was another discrepancy. Kesselring maintained in his diaries that heavy losses forced him to terminate this last fling air campaign after just three days, but British and Maltese sources maintain that it continued until 19 October. On this last day, fighters were sent to intercept an enemy formation as dusk approached, but it seemed that this was a decoy of fighter-bombers while a larger bomber formation was hoping to sneak in from the west while the Spitfires were heavily engaged and attack under cover of darkness, but another squadron of Spitfires was scrambled to meet the new threat. Most of the bombers dropped their bombs in the sea and fled back to their bases, while yet a third formation of bombers came in from the east, and were met by the Spitfires racing across the island. Then a formation of bombers came in from the north, and met a squadron of night fighters. Out of the four Luftwaffe formations, just a tenth of the aircraft managed to cross the coast; the AA gunners were waiting.

In North Africa, the great Battle of El Alamein had started on 23 October. At last the British Army had the tanks it needed, while many of those fielded by the Germans and the Italians were obsolescent. A thousand gun bombardment took place during the night of 23–24 October, and although the initial attacks by British infantry and armour were unsuccessful, by 5 November, Rommel's forces were in retreat. At first, Montgomery feared that Rommel was setting a trap for him, but when the Anglo-American landings in North Africa, Operation Torch, occurred on 8 November, Montgomery was able to chase Rommel's forces into Tunisia.

At last, the territory to the south of Malta was free of Axis forces. The aerial assault on Malta had been conducted from Sicily, but German and Italian occupation of North Africa had been a major factor in the aerial attacks against the convoys.

The Stoneage convoy mentioned earlier was, of course, further confirmation if any was needed that Malta's agony was drawing to a close when it arrived on 26 November, with four ships in the Grand Harbour.

Sadly, the fast minelayer *Welshman* that had done so much to relieve the distress of Malta, was sunk off Tobruk on 1 February 1943, with just half her ship's company rescued.

The Mediterranean Reopens

On 26 May 1943, for the first time in almost three years, a convoy arrived in Gibraltar from Alexandria without losing a single ship. Italy had surrendered. The Mediterranean was no longer '*Mare Nostrum*', 'Our Sea', to the Italians. The effort to make it so had cost Germany and Italy almost a million dead and wounded, as well as 8,000 aircraft, 1,500 of them shot down over Malta, 6,000 guns, 2,500 tanks and 70,000 motor vehicles, in addition to 2,400,000 tons of shipping. By contrast, the Allies had lost just two per cent of the ships sent into the Mediterranean, with 70,000 men dead and wounded.

This state of affairs was obviously of great benefit to Malta, but it had far wider implications. The passage from the UK to the Middle East was reduced from 13,000 miles to just 3,000 miles, saving an average of forty-five days per convoy passed through, the equivalent of providing the Allies with more than a million tons of shipping.

The Stoneage convoy arrived when there was just thirteen days' of siege ration food left on Malta. They were followed by other ships, but it was not until Christmas that the food situation began to ease. Four ships alone could not change the picture overnight, especially when the cupboard was almost bare.

'We stopped being hungry in March,' recalled Mabel Strickland, editor of *The Times of Malta*, meaning March 1944. Even so, there were few luxuries at first, with no jam or even oatmeal.'[1]

---

[1] IWM Sound Archive, Accession No.1173.

XVI

WHAT MIGHT HAVE BEEN

With just sufficient supplies for another thirteen days, the arrival of the convoy Operation Pedestal was a close run thing, and all the closer if one remembers that almost two-thirds of the merchant ships were lost, and that the fate of the tanker *Ohio* with her vital cargo hung so precariously in the balance. The cost of Pedestal also has to be borne in mind, for this was the most heavily escorted convoy ever, yet one aircraft carrier was lost and another two badly damaged, while two cruisers were also lost.

Nor should we forget the cost to those ashore. The sum total of deaths and injuries in Malta are one thing, and while the official death toll might not seem unduly high compared with the other great sieges of the Second World War, and especially that at Stalingrad, it is surely only right to take into account the high mortality rate amongst infants and the increased death rate amongst the elderly, the two most vulnerable age groups in any society. No doubt the polio outbreak after the siege had ended had its origins in the hardships of the siege and the breakdown of the utilities.

The Maltese never doubted the British resolve, but the trouble was that the resolve came far too late. As with Singapore, we had these strong fortresses but sadly lacked the means of defending them.

The policy of successive British governments between the two world wars was one of neglect of the armed forces. Some suggest that this was largely because of the effect of the Great Depression, although it is strange that the country was supposed to work its way out of the Depression years by the application of Keynesian economics, which should at least have meant that the armed forces received their share of public expenditure! The real culprit was the 'Ten Year Rule', that stipulated that the country would have ten years between a threat emerging and war breaking out. Looked at in hindsight, we can see how Hitler achieved absolute power in 1933, and war broke out in 1939. Had Britain started to rearm in 1933, it would have been less costly and far more successful than waiting until it was almost too late.

Another culprit was the defeatist attitude of 'the bomber will always get through'. Bombers often did get through, but usually only when there were insufficient fighters and anti-aircraft defences.

This brings us to the crux of the matter. Britain's neglect of her defences between the wars meant that there were no fighters assigned to Malta because they were all desperately needed else-where. The way in which naval aviation had been handed over to the newly-formed Royal Air Force in April 1918, had also meant that no one had bothered to equip the Royal Navy with fighter aircraft capable of holding their own against the enemy. Had the Mediterranean Fleet had Sea Hurricanes or, even better, Seafires in 1940, rather than Fairey Fulmars, the initial balance of power would not have been so overwhelmingly in favour of the Italians. It would have been better still if there had been two modern aircraft carriers in the Eastern Mediterranean rather than just one plus the ailing HMS *Eagle*. The Maltese appreciated the dispatch of twelve Hurricanes in August 1940, at a time when the RAF was under great pressure at home, but there should have been levels of expenditure during the 1930s that would have guaranteed adequate fighters in Malta in June 1940.

The absence of barrage balloons around the Grand Harbour was another omission.

Procurement also comes into this. Why did the Fleet Air Arm have to work with the Fairey Swordfish when the Germans, Japanese and the United States all had far better aircraft for tactical strike operations? Why did we build Gloster Gladiators and Sea Gladiators, biplane fighters, when for a decade earlier, the monoplane had shown that it was the way forward? Hurricanes would have entered service in greater numbers if the decision had been taken to concentrate on these aircraft while the Spitfire was awaited. Why, again, was the Mosquito ignored when it first flew, losing a year at least in its introduction to service?

Given the high cliffs running from the south-west of Malta to the north-west, why didn't proposals to cut a submarine base into these cliffs go ahead? Ta'Qali was well placed to have an aircraft hangar cut under the rock on which the twin cities of Mdina and Rabat stand – the Germans were convinced that this must have been done, and indeed a start was made, but why didn't the work go ahead? For both these projects, skilled local labour was available, at a reasonably low rate by British standards. No doubt, this was due to the defeatist attitude that Malta couldn't be defended. In this case, they were nearly right, but not because Malta couldn't be defended, but because many in London had decided that it wouldn't be defended! It was thanks to the Royal Navy that Malta survived at all. Yet, no hidden submarine base, and no attempt to get hold of the *Surcouf* to augment the submarine supply shuttle.

Nevertheless, there were also some poor decisions at the local level in Malta, for which the pre-war Governor must take some of the blame. Lord Strickland urged a programme of building public air raid shelters, but this wasn't done. Smokescreens for the Grand Harbour, and perhaps also for the submarine base and the dockyard, should have been introduced much earlier, but these were left to Lord Gort. Given the lack of substantial public shelters, other than the famous railway tunnel, at first, one wonders just how much of the precious supplies were lost in air raids. Goods already in the shops were inevitably lost when these were bombed, but what else was lost? Photographs show supplies being unloaded in the open, in the countryside away from the main target areas, but the Axis airmen didn't confine all of their attacks to the convoys, the Grand Harbour, the main towns, the dockyard and the airfields – those in the countryside were not immune to aerial attack.

It also became clear that holding a stock of supplies for seven months was insufficient to prevent starvation, or to allow the defenders free use of their weapons, let alone mount offensive raids against the enemy. Indeed, the shortage of fuel also threatened the survival of those on Malta as fuel was needed to pump water, despite the high number of wind-powered pumps on the farms. The lack of fuel also made it difficult to transport workers to where they were needed.

For the authorities to take over the import of supplies was understandable, since these needed to be pooled. It would have been wrong for one importer to have lost his goods in a convoy while another found that his got through, and more difficult for the authorities to have a clear picture of the supply position at a critical time. Yet, why was rationing introduced so late, and in such a piecemeal manner?

Without Malta, the Second World War would have taken much longer, certainly in Europe. Indeed, so much longer that it would have strengthened the argument of those in the United States who believed that they should finish Japan off first, and then turn their attention to Europe. Without the disruption of the Axis supply lines to North Africa inflicted by forces based in Malta, the Axis armies would almost certainly have had all of the material necessary to sweep eastwards to the Suez Canal. Without the defeat suffered by the Axis forces in North Africa, squeezed between the advancing Eighth Army and the Torch landings further west, with their supplies hindered by Malta-based forces, the invasion of Sicily would have been immeasurably more difficult, and possibly the landings on mainland Italy and then in the South of France might not have taken place, leaving the soft underbelly of Axis power untouched and meaning that everything would have depended on the Normandy landings. Without German preoccupation with the situation in Italy, and the loss of so much in North Africa, resistance in Normandy could have been much stronger. If Germany had gained the Suez Canal, the way would have been open to the oilfields of the Middle East, and especially those of Persia. It has been argued, rightly in my view, that the RAF and USAAF bombing campaign was the second front that Stalin constantly demanded, but without British and American armies engaged with the Germans in North Africa and then in Italy, would Stalin have been so inclined to mount his own campaigns against Germany, and perhaps instead have looked to some sort of armistice? This threat, after all, was the justification in providing so much material for the Soviet Union at such great cost in the Arctic convoys, material that could have been used by the RAF in the Far East, where the Japanese assault on Malaya was faced by obsolete aircraft while more modern equipment was shipped to Russia.

Yet, given all of this, it is incredible to think that there were those who would not have bothered to defend Malta. The consequences of defending Malta were grim indeed, and costly, but the consequences of not defending Malta would have been far worse.

While there were those Maltese who favoured Italy, although more usually it was Italian culture and language, most were resistant. Had Italy taken over Malta, the likelihood is that it would have been seen as a poor colony, strategically important in that it was denied to the enemy, but economically unimportant, especially given the limited agricultural output and the fact that Italy already had a great naval base not far away at Taranto. It is certainly hard to believe that the Italians would have held the Maltese in the same high regard and affection accorded them by the British.

CHRONOLOGY

1935

Italy invades Abyssinia, provoking crisis. AA defences of Grand Harbour strengthened, and plans laid for Fleet Air Arm attack on Italian fleet at Taranto.

1938

29 September, Munich Agreement allows German demands for Czechoslovak territory.

1939

16 March, German troops enter Prague completing annexation of Czechoslovakia.

7 April, Italian troops enter Albania.

20 April, British merchant shipping banned from Mediterranean.

July, Governor of Malta's Advisory Council creates Central Committee.

September, District Committees start to be formed on a parish basis throughout Malta. First two battalions of Territorial King's Own Malta Regiment ready by end of month.

3 September, United Kingdom and France declare war on Germany following invasion of Poland.

1940

2–3 May, Blackout practice between 22.00 and dawn.

11 May, Air raid warning practice.

20 May, Newspapers carry appeal for volunteers for what was to become the Malta Volunteer Defence Force.

27 May, Curfew introduced between 23.00 and 05.00. Emergency hospitals established.

10 June, Italy declares war at midnight if Malta is not surrendered.

11 June, First Italian air raid at 07.00.

15 June, Governor announces protection officers to work with district committees.

17 June, French seek armistice. In Malta, seven 'Economical Kitchens' are already operating to help feed refugees from the towns.

22 June, Armistice signed by France and Germany.

25 June, Italy signs armistice, which now takes effect, leaving Britain standing alone. French troops in Egypt outnumber those of Britain.

26 June, Bomb hits a bus crowded with passengers at Marsa, killing twenty-eight people.

30 June, First offensive operation from Malta: 830 Naval Air Squadron's Fairey Swordfish attacking the port of Augusta.

10 July, Convoy MA-5 evacuates British civilians and dependents to Alexandria. All eight ships arrive safely.

13 July, From midnight, private cars and hire cars other than taxis banned.

19 July, 830 Squadron sinks a U-boat.

12 August, Twelve Hawker Hurricane fighters flown to Malta from HMS *Argus*.

15 August, Last day on which sales of ice cream permitted.

1 September, First convoy arrives. All three ships in MF-2 reach Malta safely from Alexandria.

5 September, First appearance of Junkers Ju87 Stuka dive-bombers in Italian markings.

13 September, Italian forces invade Egypt.

21 September – 21 October, Police crackdown on overcharging in food shops.

11 October, Convoy MF-3 arrives from Alexandria with all four ships.

13 October, Taxis banned and hours of bus operation curtailed.

9 November, Convoy MW-3 arrives safely from Alexandria with all five ships.

11–12 November, Successful Fleet Air Arm attack on Taranto using aircraft from HMS *Illustrious* and *Eagle* flown off the former ship, crippling half of Italy's battleships.

17 November, Fourteen Hurricanes flown off *Argus*, but only four manage to reach Hal Far as the others run out of fuel.

26 November, Convoy MW-4 arrives safely with all four ships from Alexandria.

29 November, Convoy code-named Operation Collar from Gibraltar arrives safely with two ships.

20 December, Convoy MW-5 arrives safely from Alexandria with eight ships. Cunningham aboard HMS *Warspite* enters Grand Harbour on first visit since May, to a warm welcome.

December, Government ensures abundant supplies of kerosene to allow householders to lay down reserves.

December–January, Luftwaffe moves *Fliegerkorps X* from Poland to Sicily.

1941

10 January, Convoy operation Excess nears Malta from Gibraltar with one ship for Malta and several for Alexandria, with another two ships in MW-5 ½ from Alexandria. In heavy aerial attacks by the Luftwaffe and *Regia Aeronautica*, HMS *Illustrious* is crippled and limps into Grand Harbour.

13 January, Start of the *Illustrious* blitz.

16 January, Heaviest air raid to-date, fifty-three Maltese civilians killed, 300 houses destroyed in Senglea.

23 January, *Illustrious* leaves Grand Harbour after nightfall.

February, Rationing announced. Conscription introduced. U-class submarines deployed to Malta for the first time, as well as four J-class destroyers.

6 February, Rommel ordered to take command in North Africa with two crack German divisions; he urges that Malta be invaded.

March, Air raid precautions eased to allow work to continue

away from target area, while during previous four months, Axis shipping losses exceeded 100,000 tons.

28 March, Mediterranean Fleet sinks three Italian cruisers and two destroyers in the Battle of Cape Matapan.

April, Lieutenant Commander Wanklyn in *Upholder* starts a year of successful attacks against Axis convoys.

3 April, Axis forces in North Africa take Benghazi.

7 April, Rationing introduced.

11 April, Good Friday, but church bells are rung for the first time ever in Malta on this day to sound the 'all clear' after Luftwaffe air raids.

12 April, Twenty Hurricanes flown off *Ark Royal*, boosting strength of 261 Squadron.

15–16 April, In a successful night action, Malta-based destroyers wipe out Italian convoy of five ships and sink one of the three escorts, but HMS *Mohawk* is sunk.

20–21 April, A single ship, the armed-tanker *Breconshire*, arrives from Alexandria protected by naval forces.

21 April, Mediterranean Fleet bombards Tripoli just before daybreak following air raids by Malta-based RAF and Fleet Air Arm aircraft.

27 April, Germans enter Athens.

28 April, Dockyard Defence Battery disbanded, and its role taken over by the Royal Malta Artillery.

May, Rationing extended to kerosene. Coffee, tea, sugar, lard, margarine, rice and matches all rationed by this time.

9 May, Convoy MW-7 arrives from Alexandria with seven ships, although two badly damaged, one by a torpedo and the other by a mine.

20 May, German airborne invasion of Crete begins.

1 June, Last troops evacuated from Crete.

9 June, Buses withdrawn in middle of day except at weekends.

July, No further supplies of fresh imported meat.

21 July, RAF Blenheims attack convoy of five ships, destroying two of them.

24 July, Convoy Operation Substance arrives from Gibraltar with six ships, with one having turned back. The previous day,

seven ships from the previous convoy trapped in Grand Harbour sailed.

26 July, Just before dawn, Italians attempt attack on Grand Harbour using explosive-filled motorboats, or *barchini*, and two-man torpedoes.

28 September, Convoy Operation Halberd from Gibraltar reaches Malta with eight out of the nine ships, one having been sunk.

October, Axis losing more than sixty per cent of supplies sent to North Africa. Two light cruisers and two destroyers based at Malta as Force K.

November, Axis losses reach seventy-seven per cent.

9 November, Force K attacks Italian convoy, sinking all seven merchantmen and two destroyers.

13 November, *Ark Royal* torpedoed, and sinks the following day.

24 November, HMS *Barham* torpedoed and blows up.

5 December, Single ship slips out to Alexandria.

18 December, Italian human torpedo attack on Mediterranean Fleet at Alexandria cripples two battleships. A single ship arrives from Alexandria.

26 December, Convoy ME-8 takes four merchant ships to Alexandria.

1942

January, Victory Kitchens introduced.

1 January, twenty-six killed and fourteen injured in first air raid of the year.

2–3 January, Malta's airfields suffer a full thirty-six hours of aerial bombardment.

6 January, Single ship sails for Alexandria.

8 January, Single ship arrives from Alexandria.

19 January, Convoy MW-8 arrives, having had one of the four ships sunk.

25 January, Convoy ME-9 takes two ships to Alexandria.

27 January, A single ship arrives from Alexandria.

February, Baking of cakes and pastries banned. Axis convoy losses fall below thirty per cent in this month. Kesselring revives plans to invade Malta.

12 February, Convoy of three ships from Alexandria fails to get through, with two ships sunk and one turned back.

13 February, Convoy of four ships leaves, including tanker *Breconshire*, with one of the ships taking Maltese with Italian sympathies to internment in East Africa.

23 February, Weekend buses withdrawn and all routes stopped short of 'country' terminus, with many smaller villages losing services completely.

17 March, Red flags introduced for areas targeted in air raids, allowing those elsewhere to continue with work.

20 March, Heavy air raid on Ta'Qali, with Jabo projectiles used to blast hillside in belief that it included underground aircraft hangars.

23 March, Convoy MW-10 from Alexandria arrives having lost one of the four ships. Tanker *Breconshire* is towed into Marsaxlokk badly damaged, the other two ships are attacked repeatedly over the next six days until both sink with most of their cargo. Convoy from Gibraltar wiped out.

April, One in seventy of the population has been either killed or wounded. Kesselring obtains Hitler's approval for invasion. Almost 7,000 tons of bombs dropped on Malta's airfields during the month.

7 April, Opera House destroyed in air raid. King George VI becomes Colonel-in-Chief of the Royal Malta Artillery.

8 April, HMS *Penelope* escapes to get repairs.

9 April, 2,000kg (4,400lbs) bomb crashes through dome of packed church in Mosta, but fails to explode.

15 April, King George VI awards George Cross to the people of Malta.

20 April, USS *Wasp* flies off forty-eight Spitfires to Malta, of which forty-seven arrive, but twenty destroyed and twelve badly damaged within twenty minutes of landing.

28 April, Electricity supplies cut for several days.

May, By end of month, forty-two Victory Kitchens opened.

5 May, Bread rationing introduced.

7 May, General Lord Gort arrives and takes over as Governor from Sir William Dobbie.

9 May, HMS *Eagle* and USS *Wasp* fly off sixty-four Spitfires to Malta; sixty-one reach the island.

10 May, Smoke canisters used to protect shipping in Grand Harbour for the first time. Kesselring forced to transfer Luftwaffe units to Eastern Front.

19 May, By this time, the British have asked if they could pass hospital ships through to Malta; the Italian Navy agrees, but the Germans and Mussolini object.

20 May, Further reductions in rations.

15 June, Second rehearsal of exercise to expedite distribution of supplies after first rehearsal was sabotaged by people fearing that lights would be seen by enemy bombers.

16 June, Two convoys sent to Malta, Operation Harpoon from Gibraltar and Operation Vigorous from Alexandria. The former has just two out of six ships arrive, while Vigorous loses two ships and the other nine are forced to turn back because of poor air cover.

20 June, Tobruk falls to Rommel's *Afrika Korps*. In Malta, Lieutenant Governor explains that situation is critical and makes first announcement of the 'target date', the date on which Malta could no longer continue and would have to surrender.

1 July, Householders ordered to declare stocks of essential commodities.

13 August, First ships arrive of Convoy Operation Pedestal, with tanker *Ohio* arriving on 15th. Just five merchantmen out of fourteen reach Malta, while an aircraft carrier and two cruisers are lost, and another two carriers severely damaged. In Egypt, Field Marshal Lord Alexander and General Montgomery relieve Lord Auchinleck and General Corbett.

13 September, Lord Gort presents George Cross to Sir George Borg, the Chief Justice, who receives it on behalf of the people.

10–11 October, German air raids start again, but being confronted by Spitfires while still over the sea.

19 October, Although Kesselring maintained that the new air offensive lasted just three days because of heavy losses, British and Maltese sources record this as the last day.

233

23 October, Battle of El Alamein starts.

5 November, Rommel's force in retreat.

8 November, Operation Torch, the Allied landings in North Africa.

10 November, New airfield opened at Safi, between Luqa and Hal Far.

23 November, Convoy Operation Stoneage reaches Malta with four ships, the first to reach the island unmolested.

1943

January, Victory Kitchens are feeding 175,000, but as rations are increased, numbers fall away rapidly over the month.

23 January, Tripoli falls to British Eighth Army.

1 February, Fast minelaying cruiser *Welshman* lost off Tobruk, with just half her ship's company rescued.

26 February, Final air raids.

26 May, First convoy for three years to arrive in Gibraltar from Alexandria without the loss of a single ship.

20 June, King George VI visits Malta.

10 July, Operation Husky, Allied landings in Sicily.

3 September, Allies cross into mainland Italy.

8 September, Feast of Our Lady of Victories in Senglea; Italian surrender announced.

10 September, First units of the Italian fleet arrive off Malta to surrender.

BIBLIOGRAPHY

Alanbrooke, Field Marshal Lord, *War Diaries, 1939-1945*, Weidenfeld & Nicolson, London, 2001

Attard, Joseph, *Battle of Malta*, William Kimber, London, 1980

Bradford, Ernle, *Siege:Malta 1940-1943*, Hamish Hamilton, London, 1985

Cunningham, Admiral of the Fleet Lord, *A Sailor's Odyssey*, Hutchinson, London, 1951

Hay, Ian, *The Unconquered Isle*, Hodder & Stoughton, London, 1943

Kemp, Paul, *Submarine Action*, Sutton, Stroud, 1999

Micallef, Joseph, *When Malta Stood Alone*, privately published, Valletta, 1981

Norman, Kathleen, *For Gallantry: Malta's Story by a Navy Wife*, Arthur Stockwell, Ilfracombe, 1956

Oliver, R. Leslie, *Malta at Bay*, Hutchinson, London, 1942 *Malta Besieged*, Hutchinson, London, 1943

Perowne, Stuart, *The Siege Within the Walls*, Hodder & Stoughton, London, 1970

Thomas, D. A., *Malta Convoys 1940-1942: The Struggle at Sea*, Pen & Sword, London, 1999

Tonna, Emanuel, *Aspects of War in Floriana*, privately published, Valletta

Wragg, David, *The Fleet Air Arm Handbook, 1939-1945*, Sutton, Stroud, 2001

Night of Judgement, The Illustrious Attack on Taranto, Weidenfeld & Nicolson, London, 2003

INDEX

Anti-Aircraft defence, 51, 60–2, 72, 74, 76–9, 95, 121, 125–7, 135, 140, 150–1, 157–160, 162–3, 169–170, 184–5

Abyssinia, 2, 6–8, 10–12, 28–9, 31, 34–5, 42, 61

Admiralty, 7, 26, 35, 65, 91–2, 117, 217

Afrika Korps, 79, 87, 115, 146, 154, 201–2, 212

Agnew, Captain W.G., 147

Air raid precautions/wardens, ARP/ARW, 13–16, 51–2, 80, 94

Alanbrooke , Field Marshal Lord, see Brooke, General Alan.

Alexandria, 21, 43–4, 47, 50, 64, 69, 73, 88, 90, 92–3, 99, 113, 116, 125, 137, 139, 142, 145–6, 159–160, 164, 180, 212

Amato-Gauci, Lieutenant Gerald, 157

Archbishop of Malta, 151, 211, 215

Auchinleck, General Sir Claude, 177

Axis Powers/Treaty, 6, 35, 47, 57, 59, 67, 75, 78, 87, 92, 94, 98, 106, 121, 138–142, 144, 154–5, 159, 173, 178, 204, 211, 216, 218, 225–6

Axisa, Joseph E., 155

Barla, Sergeant Luigi, 96, 98

Beak, General, 171

Belgium, 9–10, 18–19, 107

Benghazi, 90, 122–3, 146, 178

Beurling, Pilot Officer George Frederick, 219

Birgu, 1, 23, 25

Bir-id-Deheb, 174

Birkikara, 20, 54, 60

Birzebbugia, 20, 78, 151, 174

Bishop of Gozo, 151, 211

Bonello, Major Walter, 153

Bonham-Carter, Sir Charles, 13, 16

Bonham-Carter, Lady, 16

Borg, Dr George, 174–6

Borg, Sir George, 211, 216

Borghese, Valerio, 96

Boyd, Captain (later Admiral) Denis, 71–3

Brewster Buffalo, 119

Bristol Beaufighter, 119–20, 125
    Beaufort, 132–3
    Blenheim, 37, 65, 89, 118, 121–3

Britain, Battle of, 10, 119, 130, 177

British Army, 7, 28, 40–2, 46, 56, 67, 77, 93, 152

British Expeditionary Force, 118, 179

Brooke, General Sir Alan, later Field Marshal Lord Alanbrooke, 203–6, 218

Broom Air Marshal Sir Ivor, 122–5

Brueys, Admiral, 26

Burrough, Rear Admiral, 207

Cairo, 123, 202, 205

Camilleri, Constable Carmel, 62

Camilleri, Emanuel, 155

Campioni, Admiral Inigo, 45

Cantieri Cant Z506, 78

Cape Matapan, Battle of, 88, 178

Cape of Good Hope, 69, 88, 91, 94, 113

Cape Milazzio, 208

Cape St Vito, 208

Caruana, Archbishop Dom Maurus, 54, 211, 215

Casino Maltese, 160

Cassar, Gerolamo, 25
Castel Vetrano, 159
casualties, civilian, 157, 159, 161,
    168–9, 177
Cavagnari, Admiral Domenico, 42
Cavallero, Francesco, 131
Cavallero, General, 110–11
Caylet, Lieutenant Commander C.D.,
    140
Cheshire Regiment, 97, 121
Churchill, Winston, 90, 128–9, 179
Ciano, Count Galeazzo, 6–7, 98–9,
    110–11, 178
Collins, William, 117–18
Comino, 3, 14, 19, 201
Communal Feeding Service, 54–5, 79,
    194, 199
conscription, 79–80
Convoy GM2, 101–3
MW10, 164–8
 Stoneage, 212, 220
convoys, 21, 44–5, 60, 68–70, 79, 87–8,
    90–2, 94, 101–3, 121–2,
    139–141,144–9, 155, 164–8, 171,
    182–4, 197–8, 206–12, 221
Copperwheat, Lieutenant D.A., 167
Cospicua, 16, 20, 51 53, 214
Costa, Lieutenant Francesco, 96, 98
Council of Government, 186, 199
Crete, 94, 120, 135, 154, 182
Crete, invasion and evacuation, 89,
    91–2, 107–9, 161
Cunningham, Admiral Sir Andrew
    Browne, 33–4, 39, 43–5, 47, 64,
    70, 73–4, 90, 92–5, 117, 145–7,
    154, 156, 178, 205, 215, 217
curfew, 15, 59, 80
Curtiss, Admiral, 182
Curtiss P–40, 119
Cyprus, 35, 50, 201

Decima Flottiglia Mas, 96, 155
Deichman, Air Marshal, 161, 163, 166
de Havilland Mosquito, 125, 224
Derna, 115, 202
Devonshire Regiment, 40, 113, 185,
    214
de la Penne, Luigi, 99–100
de Wolf, Colonel, 41
Dingli, 3, 36–7, 52

District Committees/Commissioners,
    13–14, 54, 57
Dobbie, Lieutenant General Sir William
    15, 48–50, 87, 108, 133–4, 143,
    152–3, 176, 179–180
Dockyard, Malta, 1–2, 51, 53, 74–9, 86
Dornier Do17, 158
Dorsetshire Regiment, 1st Battalion,
    40, 113
Drummond, Lieutenant Commander,
    117

E-boats, 31, 58, 208–10
Eastern British Task Force, 216
Egypt, 31, 35, 47, 91, 113, 115, 119,
    202–3, 214, 218
Eighth Army, 138, 203, 218
Eisenhower, General Dwight, 217
El Alamein, 115, 138, 202, 212, 220
Eritrea, 11, 34, 42, 64
Ethiopia, 2, 11, 29

Fairey Albacore, 127, 132, 136–7, 208
    Fulmar, 45, 61–3, 69–71, 73, 77–8,
        82, 90, 146, 223
    Swordfish, 43, 62, 71, 89, 98, 102,
        116–17, 122, 127, 132, 137, 140,
        145, 223
Faith, 41, 52, 117, 177, 208, 216
Farrugia, Very Reverend Canon Paul,
    57
Fiat Br20M Cicogna, 32
    CR42, 32, 75
    CR50, 32
Fighter defences, 32, 41, 52, 60–1, 65,
    125–137
Filfla, 19
First Coast Regiment, 50
Fleet Air Arm, 21, 42, 60, 63–4, 89,
    102, 116–17, 125, 132, 136, 138,
    145, 151, 158, 206–7, 223
Fliegerkorps II, 135, 161, 170, 219
Fliegerkorps X, 67, 70, 79, 87, 100, 108
Flint, Capt Anthony, 62
Floriana, 3, 15–16, 20, 52–3, 56–7,
    134, 160–61, 215
Focke-Wulf Fw190, 130
    Fw200 Condor, 70
Food and Commerce Control Officer,
    186–87, 189
Food Distribution Office, 188–89

238

Force B, 160
Force H, 43, 63, 69, 89–90, 94, 101, 154
Force K, 147, 154
Force N, 164–8
Force R, 207
Force T, 182
Force X, 207
Force Z, 207
Ford, Vice Admiral Sir Wilbraham, 16, 64, 79, 90, 155–6
Fougier, 111
4 Searchlight Regiment, 162
France, 5, 9–10, 17–18, 26–7, 29, 35, 41–2, 47–8, 66, 107, 116
France, Battle of, 116, 130–31
Franco, General, 8, 179
French Creek, 74–5, 156

Geissler, General, 67–8
George Cross, 151, 167, 176–7, 211, 215–16
Germans/Germany, 5–7, 9–10, 31, 64, 66–7, 69, 77, 82, 90, 92, 107, 126, 131, 136, 138, 178
Gibraltar, 21, 30, 35, 43–4, 64, 67–9, 90, 94, 101, 117, 122, 125, 128–130, 139, 142, 144, 147, 164, 170, 179–80, 182–3, 201, 204, 209
gliders, 92, 104–6
Gloster Gladiator/Sea Gladiator, 41, 43, 45, 52, 61, 82, 117–18, 216, 223
Goering, Herman, 135
Gonzi, Bishop, later Archbishop, 197–8, 211, 214–15
Gort, Lord, 143, 151, 177, 179–81, 183–4, 198, 200, 203-6, 211–12, 215
Gozo, 3, 5, 14, 19, 81, 105, 151, 160, 168, 179, 198, 201
Graziani, Marshal, 42
Greece, invasion of, 34, 66, 81, 90–91, 108
Grumman, Martlet/Wildcat, 206-8
Gudja, 174

Hal Far, 21, 30, 37, 42, 62, 73, 77–8, 117, 120–21, 129,151, 161, 166, 177

Hampshire Regiment, 1st Battalion, 113, 121
Harwood, Admiral, 214
Hastings, Second Lieutenant, later Colonel, Martin, 40–2, 105, 108, 152, 164, 171–2, 185
Hamrun, 15, 20
Hawker Hurricane, 32, 60–1, 65, 69, 76, 78–9, 82, 88–9, 93, 95, 97, 118–21, 125–6, 158, 165–6, 177, 206, 223
   Sea Hurricane, 206–9
Heinkel He111, 68, 165
Hewett, Vice Admiral H. Kent, 216
Hitler, Adolf, 6, 11–12, 17–18, 35, 66–7, 81, 87, 99–100, 107–10, 115, 161,164, 178, 223
'HMS Pepperpot' 147, 170
Home Defence Force, 15, 190
Home Fleet, 8, 30
Howie, Lieutenant Commander F.D., 117
Hozzel. Lieutenant Colonel Paul-Werner, 78
human torpedoes, 96–100, 155
Hyeres de la Palyvestre, 116

Iachino, Admiral, 101–2, 164–5
Imtarfa, 16, 114
invasion, fears, plans, 18, 65, 67, 79, 86, 88, 104–15, 161–74, 202
Italian Army, 42, 64, 90, 107

Jackson, Paymaster Lieutenant Robert, RAN, 16
Jackson, Sir Edward, 152–3, 192, 194, 203–4
Junkers Ju52, 104
   Ju87 Stuka, 62, 68, 71, 73, 75, 158, 166, 174, 176, 183, 209
   Ju88, 75, 90, 129, 135, 146, 158, 163, 165, 176, 209
   Ju290, 70

Kalafrana, 22, 30, 42, 52, 62, 120, 180
Kalkara, 51
karozzin, 60
Keighley-Peach, Commander C. L., 43, 45
Kerkenah Bank, 121, 140

Kesselring, Field Marshal, 99, 109–11,
    115, 135, 158, 161, 164, 168,
    178, 202–3, 218–9
King George VI, 153, 169, 176, 211,
    214–5
King's Own Malta Regiment, 21, 40, 56
Kingsway, 28–9, 60, 160
Knights of St John, 23–6

Laferla, Dr A.V., 155
Laparelli, Francesco, 24–5
Lascaris, 58–9, 70
La Spezzia, 34
Lavington, Second Lieutenant Richard,
    62
Lazaretto Creek, 96, 140
League of Nations, 6, 12, 28, 35
Leatham, Vice Admiral Sir Ralph, 155
Lee, Queenie, 1, 53, 76, 82–4, 127, 150
Lepanto, Battle of, 25, 34
Libya, 8–9, 11, 32, 42, 47, 99, 110, 117,
    209
Lieutenant Governor, 152–3, 180, 192,
    194, 203
Light Division, 5th, 87
Lija, 54, 187
Lloyd, Air Vice Marshal Hugh, 89, 123,
    129, 155, 160
Lorzer, General, 111
Lucas, 'Laddie', 127–33
Luftwaffe, 2, 17, 46, 67, 74–9, 84, 91,
    95, 100, 104, 107–8, 137–8, 146,
    154, 157–8, 165–6, 168, 170,
    177–8, 202, 208–9, 219–20
Luqa, 22, 89, 105, 118, 120–1, 124,
    133–4, 159, 161, 177
Lynch, Squadron Leader J.J., 219
Lyster, Captain, later Rear Admiral,
    Lumley, 8–9

Macchi C200, 3, 32, 75, 97, 102, 119
Maiale, 96
Malaya, 30, 35
Malta Chronicle, 2
Malta Artisan Section, RAOC, 40
Malta Auxiliary Corps, 40
Malta Night Fighter Unit, 125
Malta Relief Fund, 55
Malta Volunteer Defence Force, 15
Manchester Regiment, 40, 121
Manoel Island, 19, 140

Marceglia, 100
Marfa, 81
Marine Nationale, 31
Marsa, 52, 174
Marsamxett Harbour, 23–4, 84, 88, 96,
    98, 140
Marsaxlokk, 84, 105–6, 124, 155, 161,
    166, 174
Marsa Scirocco Bay, 105, 113
Martellotta, 99
Martin, Lieutenant Commander
    'Pincher', 77
Martin Baltimore, 61, 65, 119–20, 144
Mason, Captain Dudley, 211
Mater Boni Consilii School, 15
Maynard, Air Vice Marshal, 89
Mdina, 19–20, 22, 24, 56, 86, 89, 174,
    224
Mediterranean Fleet, 4, 8, 12, 28, 30,
    33, 43–4, 48, 61, 63, 68–73,
    89–92, 94–5, 100, 104, 106–7,
    116, 119, 146, 154–5, 217
Mellieha/Mellieha Bay, 20, 52–3,
    105–6
Merchant vessels:
    Breconshire, 145, 160, 164
    Brisbane Star, 210
    Capo Vita, 141
    City of Calcutta, 182
    Clan Campbell, 165
    Clan Chatten, 160
    Clan Ferguson, 210
    Deucalion, 209
    Elizabeth Bakki, 182
    Empire Hope, 209
    Essex, 69, 73, 75
    Fenicia, 141
    Galilea, 141
    Glenorchy, 210
    Heraklia, 141
    Imperial Star, 102–3
    Kentucky, 182
    Leinster, 94
    Melbourne Star, 210
    Ohio, 137, 209–11, 222
    Oronsay, 44
    Pampas, 166–7
    Picchiatelli, 62
    Port Chalmers, 210
    Rochester Castle, 210
    Ruhr, 141

Sagona, 99
Sydney Star, 95
Talabot, 166–7
Mercieca, Sir Arturo, 54, 152–3
Messerschmitt Bf109, 68, 76, 88, 130,
    132, 135–6, 158,163, 165–6
    Bf110, 75, 158, 165
    Me323, 114
Mgarr, 81
mines/minesweeping, 84–5, 90–1, 156,
    202
Mizzi, Fortunato, 4
Moccagatta, Commander, 96
Montgomery, General, later Field
    Marshal, 212, 218, 220
Mosta, 20, 54, 105, 134, 153, 170
Motorbomba FF, 209
Msida, 20

Naples, 65–6, 69, 101–2
Naval Air Squadron Malta, 137
Naxxar, 153
Nicholl, Captain, 170
Norman, Lieutenant E.D., 140
Norman, Mrs Kathleen, 16–7, 48–9, 77
North Africa, 42, 44, 47, 58, 64, 66, 81,
    87–8, 98, 100–1, 108–9, 121, 123,
    138, 146–7, 154, 160, 171, 176,
    179, 182, 202, 204, 212–4, 220

Operations:
    Barbarossa, 95, 109, 135, 179
    Excess, 68–74
    Harpoon, 182
    Hercules, 114–5
    Husky, 215
    Pedestal, 147, 197–8, 206–11, 214,
        218, 222
    Substance, 94
    Tiger, 91, 93
    Torch, 220
    Vigorous, 182
Operazione C3: Malta, 106
Oran, 47, 50

Pagliano, Franco, 111
Pantellaria, 70, 149, 208
Panzer Division, 15th, 87
Paola, 14, 15, 20, 113, 174
paratroops, 91–3, 104–6, 109–11, 114

Park, Air Vice Marshal Sir Keith, 212,
    216, 219
Parlatorio Wharf, 74–5
Pedretti, Chief Diver, 96
Petain, Marshal, 6
Pieta/ Pieta Creek, 4, 20
Pisani, Carmelo Borg, 114
Police, 54, 62, 104, 167
Pound, Admiral Sir Dudley, 8, 39, 63,
    68, 205, 217
price controls, 187, 192
Pridham-Whippell, Vice Admiral, 146
Pro-Italian Maltese, 54, 152–3
Protection Officers, 54, 187
Public Works Department, 15

Qormi, 54
Qrendi, 14, 212
Queen's Own Royal West Kent
    Regiment, 40

Rabat, 3, 16, 20, 22, 54, 105, 134,
    173–4, 224
radar, 32, 34, 36–8, 85–6, 96–7, 120,
    122, 131, 134, 140, 164
Raeder, Grand Admiral, 67, 157
Royal Air Force, 3, 7, 10, 21–2, 30, 32,
    35–8, 46, 61, 64, 67, 85–6, 89,
    93–5, 98, 109, 117, 119, 121,
    125–6, 132, 137, 144–5, 158,
    168–9, 173, 206, 212, 215, 219,
    223
RAF Observer Corps, 179
Ramsay, Vice Admiral Sir Bertram, 216
Refugee Central Office, 54
Regia Aeronautica, 31–2, 42, 45, 63,
    67–8, 75, 78, 101–2, 104, 111,
    126, 137–8, 213
Regia Navale, 32–4, 66, 69, 87, 104,
    111, 178
relationships, British and Maltese,
    150–3
Republic Street, 25, 29
Ricasoli, Fort, 95
Riccardi, Admiral, 33, 157
Roger the Norman, 23
Roman Catholic Church, 28, 49, 54,
    152, 213

Rommel, General (later Field Marshal) Erwin, 79, 87, 100, 108–10, 114–15, 121, 123, 135, 138, 144, 146, 161, 178–9, 201–3, 212, 218–20
Roosevelt, President, 128–9
Royal Army Ordnance Corps, 40
Royal Artillery, 40, 51, 104, 162
Royal Engineers, 49, 121
Royal Malta Artillery, 21, 40, 51, 62, 86, 104, 157, 162, 169, 214
Royal Naval Dockyard School, 76, 127
Royal Navy, 4, 28, 30, 44–8, 74, 77, 87, 89, 93, 97–8, 107, 109, 148, 154, 170, 178, 201, 207, 223
Royal Opera House, 169
Royal West Kent Regiment, 40, 62, 121

Safi, 54, 121, 212
St Angelo, Fort, 214
St Elmo, Fort, 23–4, 50, 61, 95–6
St George's barracks, 49
St George's Bay, 98
St Juliens, 15
St Paul's Bay/St Paul's Island, 19, 105–6
St Peter Battery, 157
Santa Marija Convoy, 206–11, 218
Sarbelloni, Gabrio, 24
Sardinia, 102, 208
Saumarez, Captain, 26
Savoia-Marchetti SM79, 3, 31–2, 69
Sceberras, Monte/Peninsula, 23–5
Schembri, Fredu, 190
Scobell, Major General S.J., 155
Selmunett, 19
Senglea, 20, 51, 75–6, 213–4, 216
shelters, 57–8, 80, 82–3
shipping losses, Axis, 98–9, 148
Short Sunderland, 130
Sicily, 8–9, 21, 58, 66–7, 69–71, 93, 98, 100, 102, 117, 122–23, 125, 131, 133, 135, 159, 161, 164, 166, 170, 202, 207–8, 212
Sicily, Kingdom of, 7, 13
Sidi Barani, 115, 202
siege rations, 180
Siggiewi, 52
Siluro a Lenta Corsa, 96
Sirte, Second Battle of, 165
Skerki Channel, 95, 102

Sliema/Sliema Creek, 19–20, 23, 53, 84, 88, 114, 140
Smith, Petty Officer Francis, 126–7, 136–7, 151
smokescreen, 167, 183, 224
Somalia, 11, 34
Somerville, Vice Admiral Sir James, 43, 102
Soviet Union, 67. 95, 100, 109, 135, 178
Special Constabulary, 6, 54, 56
Spellman, Archbishop, 214
Spooner, A.J., 120
Squadrons:
Fleet Air Arm:
Nos: 767, 116–7
   806, 70
   812, 8
   823, 8
   825, 8
   828, 126, 136–7
   830, 60–1, 65, 98, 117, 127, 137
RAF:
Nos: 21, 123
   26, 89
   37, 120
   82, 89
   105, 123
   107, 123
   126, 177
   185, 89, 177
   217, 132
   249, 89, 131, 177
   261, 89, 120–1
   601, 177
   603, 177
Starkey, Sir Oliver, 24
Storace, J., 51
Strever, Ted, 132–3
Strickland, Hon Mabel, 169, 193, 221
Strickland, Lord, 13, 17, 224
Student, General Kurt, 91, 110, 114, 216
submarines, 139, 159, 208–10
submarine base, 87–8, 224
Suez Canal, 11–12, 19, 25, 27, 31, 34, 47, 67–8, 88, 90–1, 113
Supermarina, 63, 178
Supermarine Seafire, 206, 223
   Spitfire, 32, 126–8, 130–1, 134–6, 138, 156, 160, 162–3, 165–6,

176–7, 179, 206, 207, 209, 219–20, 224
Syfret, Vice Admiral, 207, 209

Ta'Qali, RAF, 22, 86, 89, 120–1, 127, 129, 134, 161, 163, 173, 224
Taranto, 8, 34, 62–3, 65–6, 81, 133, 147, 159, 168
Tarxien, 14, 19, 113
Ten Year Rule, 12, 28, 35, 223
Tesei, Major Teseo, 96–7
Three Cities, 20, 23, 75
Times of Malta, 2, 13, 169, 193, 221
Tobruk, 111, 115, 182, 220
Tonna, Emmanuel, 57, 160
Townson, Reginald, 36–8, 85
Travett, Norman, 112–3, 185, 214
Tripoli, 23–4, 66, 110, 122–3, 141, 145–6, 154, 182, 213
Tunis, 50, 118
Turkey, 11, 23–24, 32
Turner, Squadron Leader, later Group Captain, Stanley, 130–1

U-boats, 31, 117, 141–2, 208–9
United States Army Air Force, 67, 208

Valletta, 3–4, 15, 20, 24–5, 28–9, 41, 51, 53, 56–8, 60, 75–6, 84, 86–8, 114, 133, 140, 159–61, 168, 205, 211, 214–16
Vian, Rear Admiral, 99, 160, 164–6, 182
Vickers Wellington, 62, 65, 69, 88, 102, 120, 145, 159
Victory Kitchens, 192–200
Victoria Lines, 105
Vittoriosa, 20, 23, 51, 76, 168, 190, 214

Wanklyn, Lieutenant Commander Malcolm, 141
Warburton, Wing Commander A., 119–20
Warships:
  British:
    HMS *Ajax*, 147
    Aphis, 4
    Arathusa, 182
    Argus, 60, 89, 116, 119–20, 135, 165, 179, 182

Ark Royal, 43, 63, 89, 94, 102, 117, 121, 135
Aurora, 147, 155, 214
Avondale, 167
Barham, 145, 154
Birmingham, 182
Cachelot, 142–3
Cairo, 128, 182, 207, 209
Calcutta, 61
Carlisle, 160, 164, 166
Charybdis, 128, 182, 207
Cleopatra, 182
Clyde, 142–3, 155
Coventry, 61, 182
Dido, 182
Eagle, 39, 43, 61–2, 128, 134–5, 165, 179, 182, 207–8, 224
Euryalus, 182
Fiji, 93
Foresight, 209
Formidable, 88, 90, 92–3, 145–6, 154, 183
Furious, 135, 207–8
Galatea, 155
Gloucester, 45, 69, 113, 145–6
Grampus, 43
Glorious, 8, 39
Hermione, 164, 182
Illustrious, 61–3, 67–81, 88, 166, 181, 207
Indomitable, 207–9
Janus, 139, 145
Jervis, 99, 139, 145
Kenya, 182, 207
Ladybird, 4
Lance, 147
Lively, 147
Liverpool, 182
Malaya, 39, 62, 164, 182
Manchester, 207, 209–10
Manxman, 136, 218
Maori, 126, 159
Mohawk, 139, 145
Naiad, 93
Nelson, 94, 102, 207
Neptune, 155
Nigeria, 207–9
Nubian, 139, 145
Odin, 43
Olympus, 155
Orpheus, 43

243

Warships: British: *(continued)*
   Pandora, 163
   Penelope, 147, 155, 160, 166–7,
      170
   Perth, 77
   Phoebe, 145, 207
   Porpoise, 144, 155
   Prince of Wales, 34
   Queen Elizabeth, 93, 100, 155
   Renown, 69, 128
   Rodney, 207
   Rorqual, 142–3
   Royal Sovereign, 39
   Safari, 148–9
   Saracen, 148
   Sealion, 148
   Sirius, 207
   Southampton, 69
   Southwold, 166
   Talisman, 143
   Tartar, 209
   Terror, 4
   Truant, 145
   Umbra, 212
   Unbending, 149
   Unbroken, 149
   Undaunted, 139
   Unique, 139–41
   United, 149
   Upholder, 139, 141
   Upright, 139–40, 142
   Urge, 139, 165
   Ursula, 139, 141
   Usk, 139
   Utmost, 139–41, 149
   Valiant, 61, 99–100, 145–6, 155
   Victorious, 207–8
   Warspite, 39, 61, 64, 145
   Welshman, 136, 181–3, 201, 218,
      220
   Westgate, 61

French:
   Surcouf, 142–3, 224
Italian:
   Armando Diaz, 140
   Caio Duilio, 33
   Conte di Cavour, 33, 182
   Diana, 96–8
   Duca degli Abruzzi, 101
   Giovanni delle Bande Nerre, 165
   Gorizia, 101
   Guilio Cesare, 33
   Littorio, 101, 164–5, 182
   MAS451, 96
   MAS462, 96
   Tarigo, 145
   Trento, 101
   Trieste, 101
   Vittorio Veneto, 101
German:
   Hipper, 69
   E-31, 210
   U-73, 208
   U-81, 154
   U-331, 154
Polish:
   Sokol, 163
United States:
   USS Wasp, 128–9, 135
Washington Naval Treaty, 32–3, 63,
   164
Wavell, General, 64, 66, 90
Wembley Ice Cream Factory, 55
Wilson, Woodrow, 12
Woodhall, Woody, 131

Young, Lieutenant, later Captain,
   Edward, 148
Yugoslavia, 34, 66, 81, 86

Zabbar, 51
Zebbug, 54
Zejtun, 54, 174